THE COMPLETE GUIDE TO
DIGITAL AUDIO

A comprehensive introduction
to digital sound and music-making

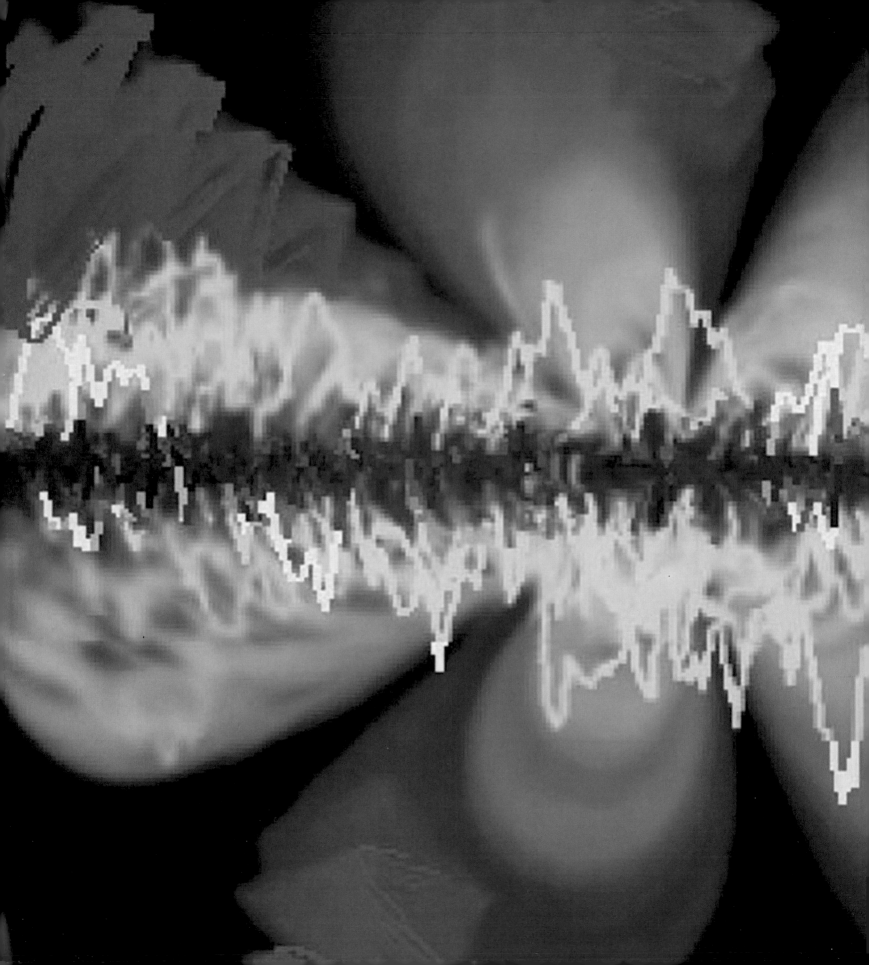

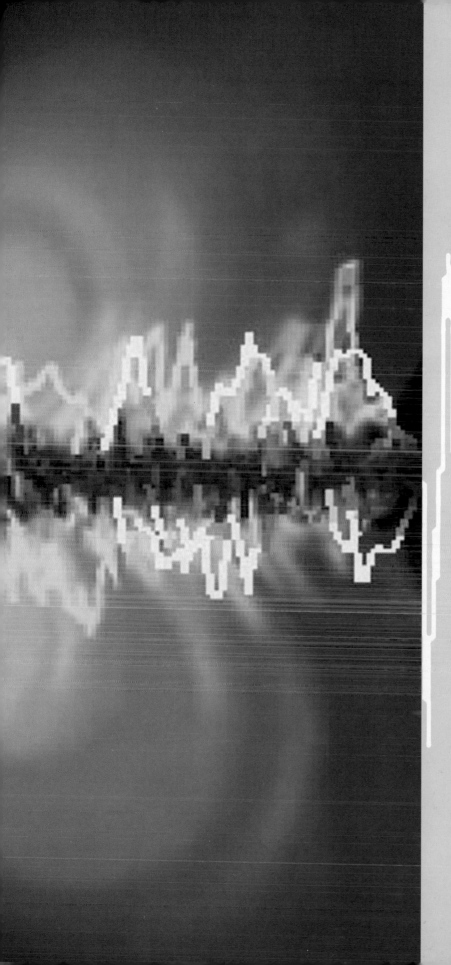

THE COMPLETE GUIDE TO
DIGITAL
AUDIO

A comprehensive introduction
to digital sound and music-making

Chris Middleton
Consultant Editor Allen Zuk

MUSKA&LIPMAN
Publishing

For Muska & Lipman Publishing:
Publisher: Stacy L. Hiquet
Senior Marketing Manager:
Sarah O'Donnell
Marketing Manager: Heather Hurley
Associate Marketing Manager:
Kristin Eisenzopf
Senior Aquisitions Editor: Kevin Harreld
Manager of Editorial Services:
Heather Talbot
Senior Editor: Mark Garvey
Retail Market Coordinator: Sarah Dubois

ISBN 1-59200-102-5

5 4 3 2 1

Library of Congress Control Number:
2003108312

Educational facilities, companies, and organizations interested in multiple copies or licensing of this book should contact the publisher for quantity discount information. Training manuals, CD-ROMs, and portions of this book are also available individually or can be tailored for specific needs.

Muska & Lipman Publishing,
a Division of Course Technology
25 Thomson Place
Boston, MA 02210
www.muskalipman.com
publisher@muskalipman.com

This book was conceived, designed, and produced by
THE ILEX PRESS LIMITED
The Barn, College Farm
1 West End, Whittlesford
Cambridge CB2 4LX
England

Sales Office:
The Old Candlemakers
West Street
Lewes
East Sussex BN7 2NZ
England

Publisher: Alastair Campbell
Executive Publisher: Sophie Collins
Creative Director: Peter Bridgewater
Editorial Director: Steve Luck
Senior Project Editor: Rebecca Saraceno
Design Manager: Tony Seddon
Designer: Jonathan Raimes
Cover Art: Jonathan Raimes
Picture Researcher: Vanessa Fletcher
Photographer: Calvey Taylor-Haw
Photographer: Rob Turner

Printed in China

00

01

CONTENTS

This is a book about sound and music-making for creative beginners. Audiophiles have a distorted sense of history, and music-makers want to "go create." This book is for both camps, and also for those other creative people who want to learn about sound, record audio, write music, add audio content to websites, videos, and games—or simply share it with their peers.

Digital audio and music have driven the uptake of new technology and new possibilities since their inception. Who would have thought even ten years ago that your laptop could be a virtual recording studio to rival the greats?

This book sweeps aside the technobabble and puts today's leading-edge technology back into the hands of people who just want to be creative. More than that, it discusses the history of audio and music-recording from the 19th century to the future, tunes into the basics of sound and acoustics, and shares production tips and creative strategies from some of the biggest names in the business.

Just like the technology it discusses, this book samples audio in depth to build up a more accurate picture of what digital technologies really mean for audio and music recording today. It sets out the options—it might even make you think.

No book can ever be a guide to all the software packages, and all the latest features—publishing moves far too slowly for that. But in a world of speed, disposability, and yesterday's news, the basic principles of sound and digital technology stay rooted to the spot.

This book doesn't attempt to be a magazine or a website. Instead, it offers an introduction to first principles and best practice, for today, and for the foreseeable tomorrow. Where you take your creativity next is up to you. Wherever you go, enjoy it.

You have the right to remain silent. But if you do, this is not the book for you.

Chris Middleton
Brighton U.K., 2003

FEATURED IN THIS BOOK:

■ History of audio recording ■ Peter Gabriel's OD2 venture explained
■ Production tips and secrets from some of the U.K.'s top engineers ■ Tips on how
to make it in audio ■ Jargon busters on all the digital audio terms you need to know
■ Q&A from ADULT. and DAT Politics ■ Insider views on audio in computer games
■ A tour of the major software packages and tools ■ Future views on audio in the
online world ■ Vector audio unveiled by one of its designers.

HOW TO USE THIS BOOK

The Complete Guide to Digital Audio is divided into four
parts. Channel One deals with audio history, the theory
of sound, and the simple facts about analog and digital
recording, then offers a personal view of the digital world.
The Channel Two looks at the basic technologies, the
hardware, and the software, and matches your needs to
equipment choices. You'll find a software guide in the
middle. Channel Three discusses recording strategies and
techniques. And Channel Four looks ahead to emerging
technologies, innovations, and distribution channels, and
throws a variety of other voices into the mix.

**So, what are your chances of getting a foot through the door
of the music industry? Find out how some of the U.K.'s top
engineers got there and formulate your plan of action. Turn to
page 176 for insider views.**

SOFTWARE FEATURED IN THIS BOOK

Logic Audio and Platinum
Cubase SX/SL and 5 VST
Reason
Ableton Live
ACID-PRO
Pro Tools and LE
Cool Edit Pro
BIAS Peak and BIAS Deck
Steinberg Nuendo
Native Instruments FM7, Kontakt,
Reaktor, and Absynth

THE BOXOUTS

In February 2003, *The Complete Guide* was invited to spend a day at Peter Gabriel's Real World studios in Box, near Bath in England, while the man himself was taking a break between the U.S. and European legs of a tour.

We spoke to engineers, technical managers, and studio assistants about everything from analog versus digital, software, and mikes, to the importance of collaboration and getting a life.

In particular, we cornered technical manager Geoff Pryce (CP), chief sound engineer Marco Migliari (MM), and studio manager Owen Leech (OL). You will also find quotes from Peter Gabriel on digital rights and the direction of music technology.

The Complete Guide also opened channels to Abbey Road engineer Chris Clark; Tim Cole, one of the inventors of generative music and vector audio; digital giants ADULT. and DAT Politics; and games audio guru Mark Knight.

You'll also find strategies and insider views from a host of other big noises.

" Music should reflect the excitement of the process that made it. **Brian Eno** "

CHANNEL ONE

TUNE IN...

IN THIS SECTION:

COMING UP:

01.01

In an interview in 2002, singer, composer, and Real World impressario Peter Gabriel said, "Music used to be about what you could achieve for yourself independently. Now it's about what you can conceive."

    Gabriel was talking about digital audio and music technology opening up path after path of possibilities. Each one leads to other paths of technology choices, recording methods, and strategies for turning what we hear in our heads into a finished piece of audio. Or at least, into content that is frozen for an instant in time before passing on somewhere else. So many forking paths!

Today, everyone's a music-maker, and everyone's an audio buff—from the hardcore instrumentalist who sets aside the cash for a new piece of gear, through digital video makers, animators, and Web designers, to desktop DJs, remixers, and MP3 fans. Millions of people use their computers to sample, loop, program, and record digital music and audio. Many of them do it legally.

    The choice of technologies is astonishing, and so are the opportunities. Do you want to use your laptop to jam in real time with other musicians? Find out how on page 114.

    The problem with all this choice, though, is how do you choose? Gabriel is not immune from the problem. His 2002 album *Up* includes the line "What's left out and what's left in?", a plea perhaps, from a man who took ten years to record it, and emerged from his Real World studios saying, "I could have done with a little more time." This book is about matching technology choices to content to create stunning digital audio—before time runs away with your ideas.

PART 01. TUNE IN

CHAPTER ONE

BE CAREFUL, MR. BEETHOVEN, THAT WAS YOUR NINTH!

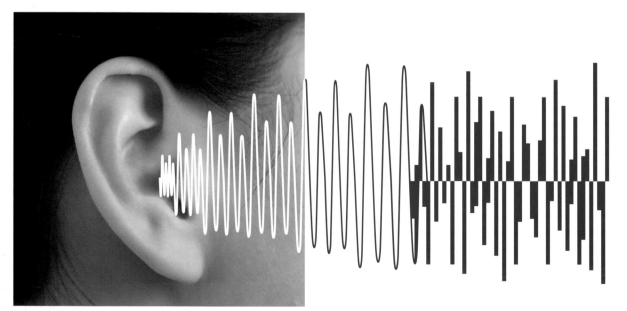

Left: **While it is often said that digital audio can only imitate analog audio, what we eventually hear through speakers or headphones is always analog.**

Right: **This Pro Tools studio is a complete digital audio production facility. See pages 118 and 148 for more on this technology.**

> "Music used to be about what you could achieve for yourself independently. Now it's about what you can conceive. **Peter Gabriel**"

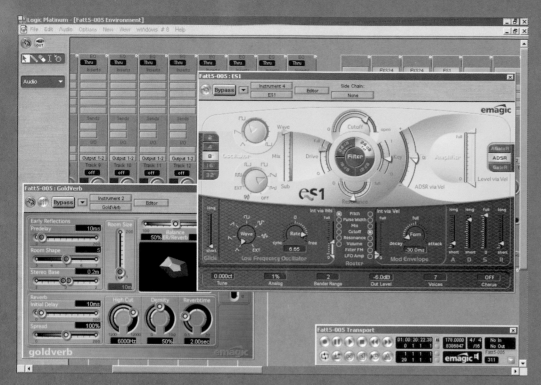

Before audio and music became part of the digital datastream in the early 1980s—before the birth of the sampler, and of cut-and-paste, GUI-based software—recording was solely about capturing a performance. If multitracking were stripped away in the 1970s, recording would still be about immortalizing a one-off event, then consigning it to a format, such as a spool of magnetic tape, a vinyl disk, or an audio track on a strip of celluloid. Today, much of that has changed, and there are risks to both audio and music because of it. We'll examine the problems as we sweep aside the buzzwords and jargon.

Glance at our timeline of audio history, and you will see enough patterns and trends to challenge a belief that today's technology landscape is "new." Did you know that tape recording was invented in the 19th century? Or that surround sound, click-tracks, and optical recording had their heyday in the 1940s? Get informed; it's the only way to put yourself in the stereo picture, and surround yourself with sound.

Audio has always been about escaping the boundaries that technology imposes on it. It's about making sounds that are "too big for the boxes that contain them," according to producer and artist Brian Eno (quoted from his book, *A Year with Swollen Appendices*). Whenever there is an obstruction—technical, or sometimes legal—technology routes around it and moves faster to compensate.

Most digital commentators predict that we will soon hit a "singularity," where the speed, intelligence, and capacity of the network far exceed our own. What happens then is up to you. The consensus is that it will happen in around 2035.

Above right and above left: **Just as CD and DVD formats have, in the consumer market at least, replaced larger, heavier vinyl records, software-based VST filters are now able to reproduce effects that were once the exclusive domain of bulky and expensive hardware units.**

When that happens, we will also become nostalgic about the past. In time, the errors and artefacts of all recording technologies—their limitations and defining characteristics—become desirable ends in themselves.

This has already happened with analog processes. Distortion, compression, phasing, and tape delay (originally an accident in a two-machine recording process) all helped define not just the technology of the time, but also much contemporary music in the 20th century. But you might be surprised to know that their influence is just as strong and vital today. As sound engineer Marco Migliari says, "In the end, everything's analog. We couldn't hear it otherwise."

Today, thousands of people are using VST (virtual studio technology) instruments and analog-style filters to emulate the sound of the past. But the successful ones are those that understand what the original technologies were doing in the first place. However, this same contingency of content and technology is creating new sounds and possibilities in the digital age, and uncovering new uses to which audio can be put.

Nearly a hundred years ago, it took nine shellac disks to store Beethoven's Ninth Symphony. Today, a single DVD could hold his entire works, and you could watch the orchestra playing them—and follow the score.

Content, then, is losing the constraints of the technology that's available to make it—and store it. The limits are, as Gabriel says, solely within your imagination.

So what is new about digital technology? One thing above all else. The digital realm is putting professional, broadcast quality audio and video within everyone's grasp.

The $1,500 that might buy you a day in one of the world's skrinking handful of top recording studios could also buy you a computer, audio production software, a DVD recorder, and a gateway to a worldwide audience of file-sharing communities and Internet radio fans.

But don't get ahead of yourself too quickly. They push the peak higher, but digital technologies also make your mistakes more obvious. It's an unforgiving medium that promises much, but leaves novices exposed. Music software throws open the door to play, fun, and experimentation, but it can leave you empty when you compare your work to a truly professional CD. The highest peak can always be seen from farthest away, so be sure to listen to our experts' voices to maximize your gain.

This book is about being positive—but also realistic. We are no longer just consumers. Anyone with a computer can create broadcast-quality content. "Go create," as Sony says. But in an age of technology convergence, this means that content is evolving into new forms, and merging with others.

Historically, content has always been dictated by format—just look at how "talkies" transformed not only the experience of cinema, but also the type of movies that were made. We'll look at how digital content is changing in Channel Four, along with audio for games. In that section, we'll also look at new forms of audio that could not exist outside the digital realm. As our timeline suggests, it's inevitable that technology will take us this way.

But this same technology is also moving faster than many people's ability to assimilate it. Indeed, many of our conceptions about what content is—or could be—are lagging behind. This book will get you up to speed, and it also includes a look at what lies ahead—at new ways of making and consuming audio—as well as at the new forms that audio content will take.

So, this is a good time to learn the first and most important lesson about sound: "digital" audio is a misnomer. As soon as sound arrives at a loudspeaker then enters your ears, it has made several journeys through the analog domain. To get sound into a digital format, it must also pass through analog stages.

Digital and analog technologies offer unique ways of creating, storing, and interacting with sound. Analog recording can exist without digital; but digital audio *cannot exist* without the analog dimension, except as a stream of data. That's why it is essential to understand what sound is, and how it behaves, before we look at the technologies to deal with it and play with it.

So where are we now? Well, the simplest way to answer that question is to look at where we've come from.

Below: The most obvious benefit of choosing a digital setup over, for example, hi fi coparates is the conservation of space. Most basic notebook computers are now capable of saving and cataloging a massive library of songs. Also, most MP3 players can now store more than enough music to get you through a long commute or an average plane journey.

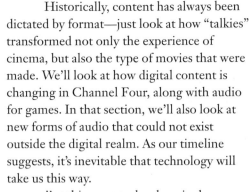

TUNE INTO HISTORY: THE FIRST 50 YEARS OF AUDIO HISTORY

The analog century begins with a nursery rhyme...

1887

The familiar Gramophone is introduced by Emile Berliner. Vulcanite disks are engraved laterally (the needle moves from side to side) in a spiral groove toward the center. Like the Phonograph, its capacity is limited to two minutes of recorded sound, at a hand-cranked 30 revolutions per minute (rpm). Soon the search will be on for new content to fit the limitations of the format, heralding a later boom in the writing and recording of two- and three-minute songs.

1877

In December 1877, Thomas Edison makes the first undisputed audio recording: his recitation of "Mary had a little lamb" on the Edison Phonograph, patented two months later for use as a dictation machine. The recording is etched into a hand-cranked cylinder covered with tinfoil. A horn gathers the sound of his voice, causing a diaphragm to vibrate and an attached needle to etch a track onto the cylinder as it turns. The characteristic soundwaves of his voice forming the words literally "write the sound" onto the foil. Reversing the process plays the recording back—the founding principle of audio recording. "Phono" comes from the Greek *phoné*, meaning sound, and "-graph" from *graphein*, to write. So "Phonograph" means "written of sound," a principle obeyed literally by Edison's patented machines. (Also "Phonogram," "Gramophone," and so on. The format wars had begun!)

Above left: **Thomas Edison with his Phonograph machine, a very early example of audio technology.**

Above right: **Emile Berliner takes the concept a step farther with the Gramophone.**

1888

Berliner establishes the principle of pressing copies from a master disk after years of research at an independent lab in Washington, D.C. This principle continues through shellac and vinyl to glass-master CDs a century later. The latter will employ the photoelectric effect to etch data optically into foil with a laser; a distant echo of Edison's first experiments. In Berliner's analog process, a reverse mold is taken of the recording, coated in nickel, and pressed into vulcanite blanks. The era of mass production begins with seven-inch disks: a classic format arrives before its time. But Edison's cylinder is still going strong in the new world of nickel—and dimes.

THE CALL OF THE NEW

Prior to Edison's "Mary had a little lamb" recording in 1877, some historians believe he may have recorded the word "hallo" onto a paper-based prototype of the Phonograph, earlier in the same year. If made, this first ever audio recording was soon lost.

Edison's machines were based on the same technology as the telegraph ("written from afar"), the device that had linked America from city to city, and coast to coast, helping to define new frontiers and emergent businesses that we still have today. Its impact was greater than that of the Internet.

"Hallo" was originally a hunting call that carried well over long distances. But with the rise of the telegraph and the telephone, it was soon adopted as a polite way of signaling when a conversation had begun over the new network (the first example of netiquette). It was an electronic whisper over much greater distances—both geographically, and of the mind. Fittingly, its use filtered down into everyday conversation as our personal horizons expanded with the network.

The electronic conversation had certainly begun. Arguably, the rise of audio over the Internet has simply returned audio recording to its roots in telephony—a technology for "sound from afar."

Above and right: **The telegraph, important as a means of communication over long distances, influenced Edison's machines and arguably predicted the shape of the digital future.**

Right: Valdemar Poulsen's Telegraphone was an early ancestor of the tape recorder, recording audio using magnetic flux on a spool of wire.

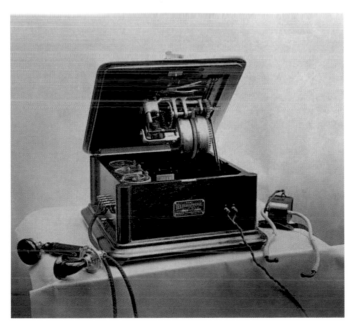

1889

Edward Easton founds the Columbia Phonograph Company in the US, later to become Columbia Records. Like today's multinationals, it finds selling content more profitable than making hardware. But the technology is poor at recording music.

1890–1897

A teenager, Guglielmo Marconi, begins the experiments that will lead to the invention of radio. Record companies proliferate, and both hardware and recorded music sales begin the upward swing that lasts until the present day. Combined with sheet music sales and multiple versions of songs, the philosophy of "pile 'em high, sell 'em again and again" is firmly established.

1898

Valdemar Poulsen invents the Telegraphone, the ancestor of the magnetic tape recorder. It records soundwaves as magnetic flux onto a steel wire, from changes in voltage (see What is sound?, page 28). Later technologies will replace wire with metal oxide tapes—the wider and faster, the greater the bandwidth. The era of editing and re-recording is born. It's called the 20th century.

1901

The recording industry's first bankruptcy: the Indestructible Phonograph Record Company fails to live up to its billing—in any sense of the word.

1902

Popular ten-inch disks of opera star Enrico Caruso spearhead the global rise of inferior, mass-produced disks over expensive cylinders. An unstoppable revolution begins for format, content, artists, and publishers. In fact, there are now 78 revolutions per minute. Regal Zonophone introduces double-sided disks, halving the number of disks needed to store the same quantity of information. This process, equivalent to Moore's Law (and Moore's Wall) of computer processor power is discussed on page 65.

Above: **The not-so-humble phonograph record, while no longer the most popular format, endures over generations. Ironically, the Internet has now facilitated a global trade in 78rpm records (such as the one above).**

Left: **An early version of the nightclub sound system, perhaps? Note the price, and imagine trying to DJ a party with one of these!**

1904

The sensible walls of the short-play format are breached when the U.K.'s His Master's Voice (later HMV) records an entire opera over 40 disks, which weighed nearly as much as Mr Caruso himself. In 1909, these "books" of records will become known as albums. Meanwhile, HMV's famous logo depicts a faithful dog listening to his master's voice on a Gramophone. Edison and Berliner live on in spirit, perhaps?

1908

The U.S. establishes the first national audio archive of folk songs and local singers. This is the recording tradition of preserving a "folk" performance that continues right up to Sam Phillips' recordings of local boy Elvis Presley in 1953, at Sun Studios in Memphis. The use of the studio as a creative tool will begin in earnest with multitrack recording in the 1940s—creating performances that would not be possible as "audio

1909

The word "album" is applied for the first time to a packaged multi-disk recording, Tchaikovsky's *Nutcracker* ballet suite. The "album" as we know it will be popularized after World War II by artists such as Frank Sinatra and Ella Fitzgerald with their songbook-style collections on a single disk. This concept is being lost in the Internet age, as content escapes format.

1913

Edison abandons cylinders, and pioneers superior plastic disks played by a diamond stylus. (Vinyl records employing a similar playback process, microgrooves, and slower revolutions of 33.3 rpm and 45 rpm will appear in 1948–1949.) But prime-mover Edison's cylinder technology will live on in dictation machines, its original purpose, as far as the late 1960s. In the 1990s, of course, digital dictation machines will allow voice recordings to be translated directly into editable text—the logical conclusion of Edison's vision. From 1913 onward, however, the development of audio technology is driven by music, radio, and the movies, and not by "office" tasks.

Above: The development of audio technology is driven by music, radio, and the movies.

Left: Musical styles and recording technologies have been influencing each other for almost a century; a recorded version of *Livery Stable Blues* spawned the beginning of the Jazz Age in 1917.

1916

Case Research begins experimenting with adding soundtracks to celluloid film—a technology a decade or so younger than audio. The first step on audio and video's long, shared journey is taken.

1914–1918

World War I builds the momentum of popular music sales. Audio, video (in the form of film) and stills photography all become mobile within a few years of each other. The Jazz Age begins in 1917 with the first "Dixieland" recordings. From here on, musical styles and recording technologies will become contingent on each other, encouraging each other's development. A new front has indeed opened.

1919

Lateral-cut disks (records) are declared a public-domain technology, as postwar economic imperatives and competition force audio technology out of proprietary strongholds. The era of cross-licensing begins: technologies that fail to license themselves usually face dwindling market shares, as Apple is to discover to its cost in the 1990s.

1920

Record sales dip as the public discovers it can listen to music for free (does this sound familiar?), thanks to the emerging phenomenon of commercial radio throughout the U.S. Soon, however, the technology begins driving music sales to new heights by introducing popular songs to a mass audience. 21st-century intellectual property lawyers please take note.

1925

Commercial electric sound recordings, pioneered by research at Bell (Telephone) Labs, finally replace Edison-style acoustic recordings. Again, the telephone ("sound from afar") concept is the impetus behind audio technology. Microphones, such as Neumann's first condenser model (1928—see also microphones, page 154), turn soundwaves into electrical pulses that can be transmitted along wires. Amplified, these pulses are turned back into vibrations that we can hear. This takes place in another electrical innovation: moving-coil loudspeakers. The improved dynamic range of these technologies, especially in

PRODUCTION TIPS

Audio is a way of reaching someone, especially if your ideas come from far away.

Always expose the primitive roots of your work.

"Equipment has a tendency to blow up or malfunction. Fortunately I like the excitement of things going wrong. It's my only chance in a highly technological situation, to improvise." (from *Laurie Anderson*, by RoseLee Goldberg)

"Artists have always enjoyed being ahead of their times. But there's a hysteria not to get left behind. I think amazingly dangerous and beautiful art can be made with a pencil. And it's the dangerous part that matters." **Laurie Anderson**

"There's no such thing as digital silence, because silence triggers the 'disconnect' button." **Laurie Anderson**

Left: **Postwar economic realities force the recording industry to let lateral-cut disk technology enter the public domain in 1919.**

Below: Condenser microphones, coupled with moving-coil loudspeaker technology, improve the quality of recorded audio. Their "proximity effect" influences new singing styles across a range of popular musical genres.

improved dynamic range of these technologies, especially in the mid- (transient) range, brings true audio reproduction closer to reality. Meanwhile, the "proximity effect" (see page 155) of condenser microphones encourages a new style of singing, "crooning," popularized by Bing Crosby and others. Elvis Presley's singing style in the 1950s is also influenced by the proximity effect, and by Sun Studio's innovation of "slap-back" tape echo. Audio technology begins dictating form, style, and content, as it will from here on in.

1926

The motion picture *Don Juan* uses Bell Telephone Labs' Vitaphone system of multiple 33.3 rpm disks to generate a musical soundtrack. *The Jazz Singer*, starring Al Jolson, then becomes the first "talkie" motion picture with recorded dialog. Soundtracks transform the style of acting, and of film-making, almost overnight. Later, film-makers such as Orson Welles, Carol Reed, Walt Disney, Powell and Pressburger, Francis Ford Coppola, Martin Scorsese, and George Lucas, will expand the creative use of sound to create a whole new dimension of cinematic experience. In the 21st century, it becomes available in the home.

1928

Walt Disney's *Steamboat Willie* becomes the first motion picture to create a soundtrack of dialog, music, and spot-effects entirely in post production. In this sense, it is the first truly modern movie. Meanwhile, John Logie Baird, Vladimir Zworykin, and Manfred von Ardenne separately begin the experiments that will eventually create television—and, something that is often forgotten—Baird records vision onto disk.

Fifty years after the invention of the Phonograph, Edison halts production of his cylinders and disks. Audio's infancy is over. The analog century comes of age.

AUDIO HISTORY: DECADE BY DECADE

THE ANALOG CENTURY CONTINUES
THE ELECTRIC AGE: ENERGIZING SOUND
↓

AMI Electric jukeboxes appear
Choice, sales, and royalties boom.

1929
↓

Affordable Recording studios
"End of pier" booths are common.

First amplified guitars
Slow to catch on due to major difference in sound from acoustic guitars, but would cause new styles to emerge about ten years later; eventually distortion would become an end in itself.

↓

First TV broadcasts, cathode ray tubes
Sound and vision in the home.

First magnetic tape recorders
Audio goes rewritable.

BASF/AEG develop plastic tape
20 minutes of audio per reel.

EMI Abbey Road Studios opens
Biggest studio in the world, in the U.K.

Bell Labs' stereo experiment
Transmits orchestra over multiple phone lines to live audience.

Blumlein's "Binaural" sound
UK's EMI patents stereo technology.

↓

RKO's *King Kong*
Multilayered sound effects (using varying tape speeds).

The Muzak Company founded
Domestic audio streams on demand.

Conclusion: the populist era begins in the Depression

1937
↓

First vinyl disks
33.3 rpm fails to catch on.

Acetate disk recordings
These reach new professional standards.

↓

Welles' *War of the Worlds* broadcast
The "listener's task of reconstruction" frightens America, proving audio is a powerful means of evoking reality.

"Academy curve" monitoring (film)
Movie studios and cinemas agree first sound-monitoring EQ standard.

Disney's *Fantasia*
The mouse that roared. Stowkowski *et al* invent modern multitracking, overdubbing, panning, panpots, click-tracks, etc via eight optical recorders and two projectors.

↓

Crosby's *White Christmas* debuts
36 million sales over decades.

Overdubbing
Courtesy of guitar maestro, Les Paul.

Tape becomes mastering format
Fast, efficient, high bandwidth.

Citizen Kane, Magnificent Ambersons
Sound enhances narrative conventions in film.

1947
↓

33.3 rpm vinyl finally takes off
More durable format, 25 mins a side (before high compression needed).

Frank Sinatra, Ella Fitzgerald, *et al*
Modern concept of "the album."

45 rpm vinyl and EPs
Pave way for singles, pop charts.

The Leo Fender and Les Paul guitars
Solid body reduces feedback.

First uprising of independents
Teenage buyers spurn major labels.

Top 40 appears in U.S.
First barometer of popular taste.

Bill Haley's *Rock Around the Clock*
Names new 4/4 music movement.

Open-reel stereo tape recorders
Faster machines; better, wider tapes.

Improvements in amplification
More powerful, lower distortion.

"Cinerama" surround sound
Seven-track 3D sound in cinemas.

Transistors become commonplace
Miniaturization arrives.

Portable radio, tape players
Cheap, mobile, disposable audio.

The Goon Show
Surrealism in sound.

Fender Stratocaster
The single-coil pick-me-up.

Conclusion: Era of lifestyle audio begins

1957

Two-track stereo standardized
Mono age ends, stereophonic begins.

Stereo headphones appear
Replace dual mono.

Speakers become smaller, better
Miniaturization trend continues.

Integrated circuitry
Smaller, and so much better.

First lasers
Another building block in place.

First 16-bit audio recorder
40 years ahead of schedule.

Mellotron tape-driven keyboard
Sampling's ancestor; recording medium becomes sound-generator.

Stockhausen's influence spreads

Helical-scan video-to-reel tapes appear
Television no longer ephemeral.

Audio taping creates new effects
Echo, phasing, via two mono machines.

Elvis Aaron Presley debut recording
Merges folk, blues—and tape effects.

IBM 7030 computer 8-bit computing arrives.

Debut of prerecorded cassettes
Home taping/compilation trend alarms.

Four- then eight-track studio recording
This offers separation, overdubbing: audio no longer about "performance."

Phil Spector's "wall of sound"
Multilayered, expansive, distorted.

Digital tape experiments at MIT
Forerunner of DAT, and so on.

Loops, quadrophonic sound, electronics: composition goes 3D.

Dolby A noise reduction
Quiet is the new loud.

IMAX prototype exhibited
One projector, one big image.

Conclusion: 3D era begins in earnest

IBM personal computers
The end, but not the means.

The Sony Walkman is born
"Personal" mobile audio begins.

Portable camcorders
Content creation, not consumption.

1967

Beatles' *Tomorrow Never Knows*
Tape loops enter music mainstream.

Video disks in TV studios
Era of instant replay arrives.

Monophonic synthesizers
One step at a time…

↓

Primitive sequencers
Complex arpeggios, machine-style.

Digital effects units
Thanks to medical research!

Polyphonic synthesizers
An orchestra in the home?

Video cassettes appear
Home taping resuscitates TV.

IBM's first hard drives
Sealed with a disk.

VHS trumps Betamax
Cheaper format wins against quality.

↓

Laser video disks debut
Herald digital age and CDs.

Dolby X-Curve replaces "Academy"
Roll off those decibels!

Dolby stereo movie sound
A Star is Born (1976): in every sense.

↓

Apple I, then Apple II
Take a byte.

Nintendo games cartridge
Say goodbye to the outside world.

Conclusion: The second *son et lumière* **era begins**

1977

↓

First optical fiber transmissions
AT&T returns to the fray.

PCM consumer audio recording
14-bit, 80dB dynamic range.

CD format finalized
16-bit, 44.1 kHz sampling.

16, 24, 48 tracks, and beyond
Sound separation = divorce from reality?

Star Wars, Close Encounters
Low-frequency effects channels create unease in audiences.

↓

Super-VHS, Hi-8 formats
Video improves, audio lags behind.

Digital Audio Tape (DAT)
Portable, master-quality audio.

Apocalypse Now surround sound
Anticipates Dolby 5.1 (left, center, right, left surround, right surround, plus low-frequency effects channel)

NOW AN INCREDIBLE EXPERIENCE IN SOUND CREATION...

Lucasfilm THX sound
Unequalized, and unequaled, frequency response.

MIDI arrives
Audio/music devices learn to talk.

Apple Macintosh appears
Lifestyle desktop GUIs take over.

Microsoft Windows
Let proprietary battle commence!

CDs enter mainstream
Audio merges with personal computing.

First digital recordings hit charts
Analog community goes "hiss."

Mirror in the Bathroom
U.K.'s first digitally recorded single, by The Beat.

CD-ROMs debut
Video, data, audio streams unite on PC.

Digital and optical phone networks
Global computer, or global village?

Sampling experiments
Inputs examined 44,100 times a second.

RAM replaces tape
Soundbytes are born.

Fairlight CMI, Emulator, *et al*
Eight-bit digital sampling, then beyond.

SMPTE time code
Even the drummer plays in time.

Akai S612 12-bit sampling
12 seconds at 40 kHz.

16-bit sampling
CD-quality audio.

Akai S900/S1000, Ensoniq Mirage
Two ends of the sampler market.

Sample-driven audio/music
Remake, remix, re-edit, remodel.

Dolby SR in movie production
Full signal processing, not just noise reduction.

Intellectual property laws debated
A winter of dis(k)content?

Conclusion: Era of "re-" begins

1987

Internet and World Wide Web
The network lives; the rest is academic.

Desktop publishing
A design for life.

Digital radio experiments begin
Audio is focus, but data will be key.

QuickTime, *et al*
Players, plug-ins, proprietary problems.

Flash
Timeline interfaces get moving.

QuickTime™

CDs take over from vinyl
Arguments rage over frequency range.

Multinationals dominate
As 1940s, before teen explosion.

ADAT debuts
Multitrack audio... onto Super VHS.

Rewritable Minidisk
Small but perfectly formed audio.

Digital TV research
Hard technologies, soft datastream.

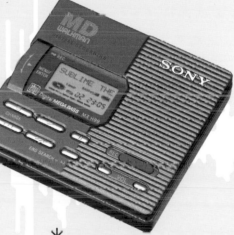

CD-I, enhanced CDs
Hear the music—then watch the video.

Flash memory
No flash in the pan.

Cinema Digital Sound (surround)
Pixel-array 5.1, with no analog backup.

Sequencing software
Cut-and-paste audio arrives.

THE GENERATIVE AGE: AUDIO AND VIDEO COME ALIVE
↓

↓

DVDs take a bow
The format with everything—for now at least.

Sampling rates double
Everybody hertz.

Digital multitrackers
Home studios become viable again.

Bit depths multiply
Pieces of eight: it must mean piracy!

↓

Gaming platforms
Immersive entertainment, audio, video.

Sony Dynamic Digital Sound (film)
7.1 arrives: adds mid-left, mid-right channels.

CD-Rs affordable
Intellectual property = theft?

Conclusion: Broadcast era ends; "pull" era begins

↓

1997

Internet popular explosion
Network becomes computer, and vice versa.

The "new economy"
Soon "e-" equals "I.O.U."

Portals and communities
Nations of shared interests unite.

Personalization
"One to one" replaces "one to many."

Mobile phone explosion
Europe, Japan talk in earnest.

Virtual instruments and samplers
Plug in an orchestra to your PC.

↓

Virtual studios
Your PC eats Abbey Road.

Digital dictaphones
Voice recognition? *Hello?*

Generative music software
Grow your own audio in your PC.

Generative Flash movies
Audio generates realtime animations.

ISDN, ADSL, broadband
And the bandwidth plays on...

↓

MP3 players, iPod
From gig to Gigabytes: your
personal space gets much, much
bigger.

DVD-R, SACD *et al*
New formats, new possibilities.

Vector audio
It's all in the maths.

Conclusion: the era of "Me-"
begins

↓

MPEG standards, MP3
Audio escapes hard formats.

Napster, *et al*
Bill of rights? Or rights to bill?

Digital rights management
Lock up your audio!

**Games overtake music, video,
movies**
Virtual environmental activists.

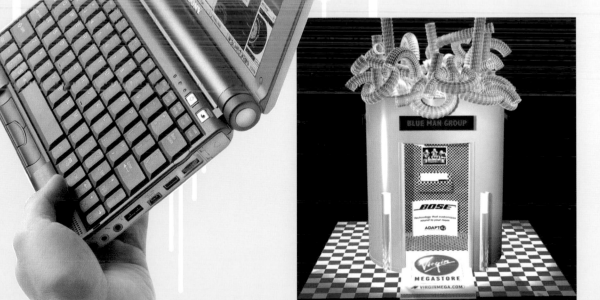

2007
↓

See "Future views," pages
176–179 for this, and much, much
more. But in reality, The future is
up to you.

So, that's where we've come from. But what are the underlying principles beneath all that historical innovation? Once you strip away all the logarithmic calculations, equations, and baffling acronyms that fill textbooks about sound engineering, the underlying principles of sound, recording, and today's digital technologies are simple.

Indeed, once we've grasped some of the basics, we can logically infer many of the rest. So, now it's time for the really big questions. Afterward, we'll take a personal view of the digital age, then move onto hardware and software choices. We'll also be taking the pulse of the heart of digital audio: MIDI.

WHAT IS SOUND?

Sound raises a classic philosophical question: does it exist if you lack the means to hear it? It is known that profoundly deaf people are sensitive to vibrations, and there are famous examples of deaf musicians, such as the percussionist Evelyn Glennie. So, given that sound can be meaningful to people with no auditory faculty, this gives us a clue as to what sound really is.

When something "makes a sound," it vibrates and emits pressure waves—periodic variations in atmospheric pressure—that are received in the human ear. The brain interprets these as sound, but the body can sense many of them, and absorb all of them. (A soundcheck in an empty hall has to compensate for the different acoustic signature of the space when it is full of thousands of people.)

If someone stands in a field and screams, the unique vibrations of their vocal chords force air molecules together and propel the molecules away from their mouth at high speed. This creates what is known as a compression wave, an area of higher than normal atmospheric pressure (but one that's too small to be measured by a barometer).

PART 01. TUNE IN

CHAPTER TWO

BASIC THEORY

Right: **A sudden noise—such as a person's scream in the middle of a field—propels molecules at high speed creating a compression wave, a ripple of higher than normal atmospheric pressure that travels away from the source of the sound. Volume can thus be defined as SPL: sound pressure level.**

Obviously, sound pressure waves cannot be created where there is no atmosphere, because there are no molecules for the source to vibrate against. That's why, to borrow the tagline from the movie Alien:
"In space, no-one can hear you scream."

GOOD VIBRATIONS

Different types of sounds, such as a scream, are characterized by different waveforms, or complexes of waveforms. In the case of the human voice, soundwaves emitted from the vocal chords are modulated by movements of the mouth. We'll talk about waveforms in more depth shortly.

Our profoundly deaf person feels some of these vibrations, and learns to distinguish between waves of a higher or lower frequency and amplitude. Meanwhile, a hearing person's ears translate the sound pressure waves into something that the brain can recognize, understand—and locate spatially—in other words, hear. When we discuss volume, we are really talking about SPL (sound pressure level).

But what do we mean by waveforms, frequencies, amplitude, and so on? You already know part of the answer to this question. In fact, frequency is just one characteristic of all types of waves...

LOOKING THROUGH THE WAVE
The most common illustration of simple wave behavior is dropping a stone into calm water, then watching the ripples (small waves) fan out from the point of origin. This is misleading when it comes to sound, so let's use a similar, but more accurate example.

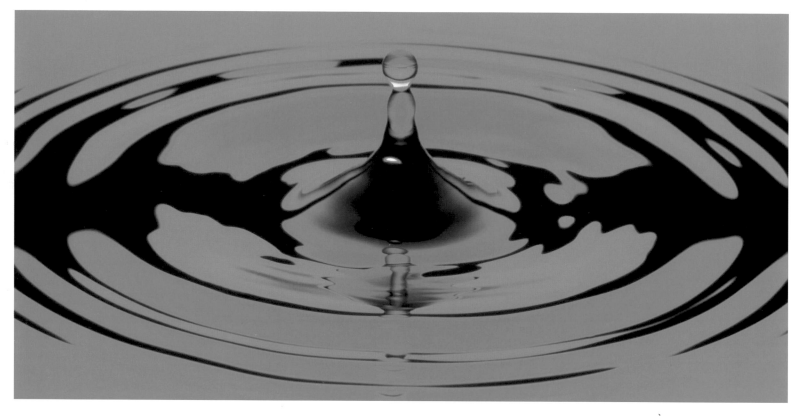

Above: **Sound waves can be imagined as the 3D equivalent of the ripples we see in water, but in a spherical form moving outward through space.**

Picture a glass bowl full of water. Looking down from above, imagine a vibrating object—an electric toothbrush, perhaps—being lowered into the center of the water. You know from experience that ripples will spread out from the object toward the edge of the bowl, and that they will increase in frequency (there will be more of them, their production cycle will increase) if we speed up the vibration.

Next, imagine for a moment that our circular bowl is now a rectangular glass tank, and that the ripples are moving in a single direction—let's say from left to right. Picture yourself looking through the side of the tank, with your eyes at water level as the ripples pass before you. You are now seeing the repeating pattern of the waves created by the object vibrating in the water. This is a simple waveform.

Finally, keep the same view, but imagine that the ripples are once again moving in all directions, and that you are looking through the side of the circular bowl. The ripples will be moving toward you, as well as to all other points of the circle.

MOVING AT THE SPEED OF SOUND

This is how soundwaves behave in the atmosphere, except that they move more slowly through air—at 344 meters/376 yards per second, and in three dimensions. In effect, sound describes a sphere. So, let's get back to our screaming person in a field. You can now imagine the pressure waves and their unique waveforms moving invisibly through the air—at the speed of sound, of course—from the person's mouth to your ears.

In reality, most sounds are more or less directional. While a thunderclap might be heard equally at all compass points from the point of origin, human voices and loudspeakers are designed to project sound pressure waves in a specific direction. And we can choose to listen to them, or merely to hear them.

Below: Although sound naturally travels in all directions, musical instruments, loudspeakers, and other devices propel it in a specific direction. Plus, many microphones capture sound from a general direction rather than from all angles.

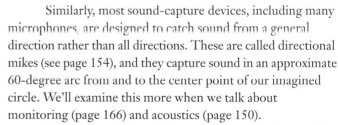

Similarly, most sound-capture devices, including many microphones, are designed to catch sound from a general direction rather than all directions. These are called directional mikes (see page 154), and they capture sound in an approximate 60-degree arc from and to the center point of our imagined circle. We'll examine this more when we talk about monitoring (page 166) and acoustics (page 150).

The horn on Edison's Phonograph captured as much sound as possible from the wide, open end, and funneled it toward a narrow end containing the diaphragm and recording needle. Such a diaphragm is similar in principle to that found in the human ear. Together, the diaphragm and needle formed a primitive transducer. When the process was reversed, the horn amplified the soundwaves—it made them bigger.

WHAT IS ANALOG RECORDING?

Analog recording is a process of transduction, and transducers are nothing less than the keys to all sound recording and listening. A microphone, a loudspeaker, and your ears are all types of transducer. The word comes from the Latin preposition *trans*, (a)cross, and the verb *ducere*, to lead.

Literally, a transducer is a device that leads energy from one realm into a different, but corresponding, energy realm—in other words, it is a way of changing one type of energy into another. In all recording techniques, energy is changed in such a way that it can be changed back again when the recording is played. And the clever part that makes it work is usually our brightest spark: electricity.

All acoustic musical instruments, such as flutes, saxophones, classical guitars, snare drums, and so on, are primitive transducers as well, but most need electrical amplification or sympathetic acoustics to be heard over any distance.

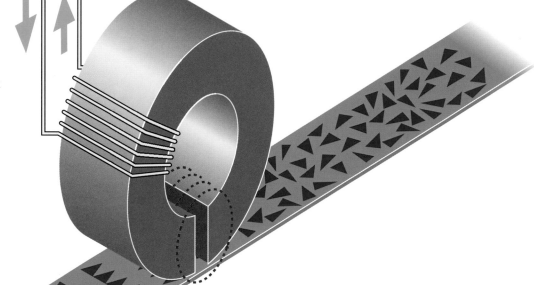

Above: **Magnetic tape converts electrical signals to a magnetic flux which is applied to the oxide on the tape. This is one process of transduction that will cause a small amount of degradation each time it is repeated on the same analog audio signal.**

THE FLAW OF ANALOG

Here is an example of the "chain" of induction involved in an average analog recording. A microphone leads soundwaves from the atmospheric into the electrical realm by turning them into electrical signals (or radio signals, in the case of radio mikes).

Via an amplifier, magnetic tape recorders convert these signals into magnetic flux and store it, then reverse the process at the playback head. At this point the energy might be transduced again, this time by being stored in grooves cut into a piece of vinyl. Either way, the signal is amplified electrically at the playback stage.

Loudspeakers change the electrical signal back into a close approximation of the original soundwaves, by a process called magnetic induction. This causes the speaker cones to vibrate according to the voltage levels in the signal. And your ears turn the soundwaves back into electricity again, this time in the form of nerve impulses in the brain. Simple, isn't it?

Right: **Even the best loudspeakers subject analog audio to degradation, in the process of converting an electrical signal into an approximation of the original soundwaves.**

The flaw in the analog process is plain to see. It is not that it is somehow unable to reproduce the same range of frequencies, the same dynamic range, as digital technology (quite the reverse), but that there are so many stages at which the energy is transduced, stored, then transduced again.

At any one of these, the process is subject to degradation, or to the inherent frailties of the transducer, the storage medium, the amplifier, or the loudspeaker. This degradation is passed on from stage to stage and accumulates in effect. Professional studios are on top of the problem, but you are not.

"Hi fidelity," or "hi fi" as we know it today, is merely a vague guarantee that the chain of transduction processes will introduce only minor departures from the integrity of the signal. A good hi-fi, then, will reveal deficiencies in a bad recording, rather than compensate for them.

All of this brings us to the exciting part for creative people. Once sound has been turned into electrical energy, you discover that you can change the sound in as many ways as you can effect a change in the energy. But things get even better once we move into the digital realm. When energy is stored digitally, you can affect the sound in as many ways as you can rewrite the information. You can change "the story" in the retelling.

So, is your creative energy up to the challenge?

PRODUCTION TIPS

REAL WORLD TECHNICAL MANAGER, GEOFF PRYCE

There is so much choice of digital technology. You can go into any computer shop, pay a little money, and pick up the means to multitrack onto hard disk. But when I started, I just had an old TEAC tape recorder, a microphone, and an effects pedal. Audio recording is all about maximizing the performance of what you have. Just look at what [late 1950s and early 60s producer] Joe Meek achieved with ancient equipment in a bedsit—or what George Martin did on a four-track recorder with The Beatles.

We said earlier that you can logically infer many of the building blocks of audio once you've grasped some of the basics. So, let's test that theory.

In analog recording, we've examined how sound is emitted as waves of pressure, and is captured as changes in voltage, for example, or as physical displacement in a medium such as vinyl. It follows, then, that sound can be expressed, described, and measured as changes in atmospheric pressure, or as changes in voltage. Congratulations: you've arrived at the decibel (dB).

The decibel is a logarithmic measurement of amplitude, where sound pressure is compared to a reference pressure. This probably seems complicated; but all you need to remember is that 0 dB is the Holy Grail of the recording process; all professional mixes are done with reference to it.

In digital recording, boosting decibel levels beyond the reference level produces destructive distortion; in analog recording, it may introduce an attractive fuzziness that you can live with.

Just think of the decibel as a measure of loudness (more accurately, of relative intensity) and remember to use zero as your reference decibel level whenever you are mixing signals, particularly when adjusting the Gain on input. "Decibel," incidentally, means "one-tenth of a bel." And yes, that refers to Alexander Graham Bell—another reminder of audio technology's lasting debt to the telephone, and also the telegraph.

We've also learned that any reproduction method is a reversal of the recording process; Edison's Phonograph defined this principle. A microphone turns soundwaves into electrical impulses; a loudspeaker turns electrical impulses back into soundwaves. (If you plug a pair of stereo headphones into a microphone jack socket and shout into one of the earpieces, it will act as a microphone, albeit a poor one.)

PART 01. TUNE IN

CHAPTER THREE

RING THOSE DECIBELS!

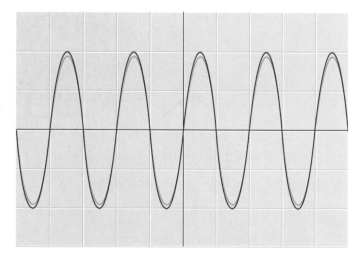 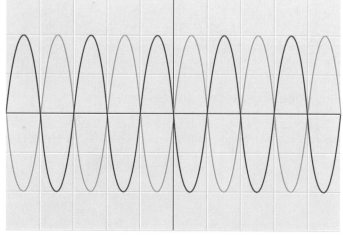

Above: **When two waveforms are in phase, such as when your left and right speakers are playing the same tone, the resulting sound will double in amplitude. If the two waveforms are completely (180 degrees) out of phase—which** **would happen if you were to reverse the polarity of one speaker, for example—the resulting tones will subtract from each other, canceling each other out and producing a weak sound.**

part 01. tune in

So where does this leave us? Well, in possession of some valuable facts, if we test the principle in other ways. If any sound produces a characteristic waveform, or complex of waveforms, then generating those waveforms by other means should produce the same specific sound.

Congratulations again: you've uncovered the principle of synthesis. We'll discuss this further when we talk about keyboards, VST instruments, virtual synths, and samplers.

But while we are on the subject, let's quickly look at waveforms, then examine their relationship to digital recording. As you will see, it's a crucial one. (And just what is "digital" audio anyway? The answer's on page 46.)

Left: Many virtual synthesizers or audio editing programs offer a detailed graphical representation of the waveform, along with the ability to modify it globally with filters, or to edit very specific portions of it by zooming in and manipulating points along the curve.

Key and volume range of sample

Navigate through preset sound patches

Modify samples

SURFING THE SOUNDWAVES
Waveforms are graphical representations of different types of signal. Some are simple, pure-tone waves, such as a sine wave; but most sounds are made up of complex interactions of different waveforms. (Synthesizers enable you to play with these building blocks of sound, and construct complex sounds from simple components.)

As every sound consists of "signature" waveforms, it follows that what distinguishes one type of sound from another one—let's say a snare drum from a human voice—is represented by characteristic differences in the components of each waveform. A good way of remembering what the components of waveforms are is to memorize the following acronym: WAVE PFH. This stands for Wavelength, Amplitude, Velocity, Envelope, Phasing, Harmonics, and Frequency.

But what does each of these mean?

WHAT IS WAVELENGTH?
The physical distance through a medium, such as the atmosphere, that a soundwave travels to complete one cycle. The term is usually applied, therefore, to continuous, predictable waves whose cycles are uniform and easily measurable.

WHAT IS AMPLITUDE?
A complicated way of referring to the level of a signal—its peak, in other words. All waveforms have both a positive and a negative peak. Have a look at a signal in a sample-editing package such as BIAS Peak (below) to see what we mean,

or in the Edit View Screen of a multitrack recording package such as Cool Edit Pro (PC).

When represented graphically, waveforms rise above and fall below an imaginary center line. In many packages, such as Cool Edit Pro, you will see two distinct waveform lines, one for each stereo channel.

A signal's amplitude, then, is the distance between the positive or negative peak and this center line. The greater this distance is, the higher the signal's amplitude is said to be.

The "cycle" we mentioned previously refers to the complete run-through of a waveform's characteristic pattern: from the center line through its positive peak, its negative peak, then back again to the center line. A continuous tone is one whose cycle endlessly repeats until the tone is switched off.

Below: The positive and negative peak of a waveform"its peak amplitude" can clearly be seen and even manipulated in sample editing software such as BIAS Peak. Note that stereo sounds are represented by two separate waveforms, one for the left channel and one for the right.

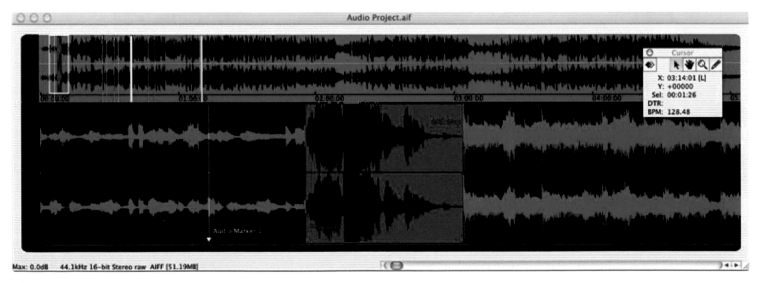

part 01. tune in

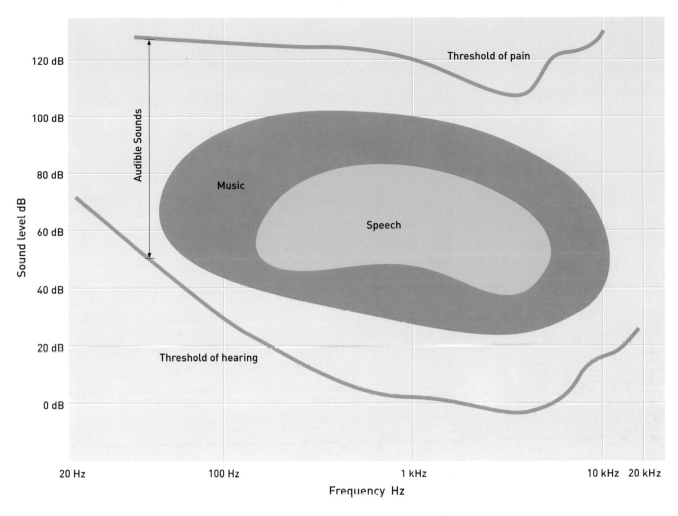

Right: This diagram is a basic graphical approximation of the range of decibels and frequency taken up by various types of sound, such as speech and music, and where our ability to perceive it begins. Note that while the human voice has a multitude of variations, it generally occupies only a relatively small place at the center of our range of hearing.

WHAT IS VELOCITY?

Speed through the atmosphere. In this case, 344 meters/376 yards per second, although the speed of sound does increase measurably in warm, moist air, and decrease in cold, dry air. (This has implications for mixing sound in large, outdoor arenas.)

In normal atmospheric conditions, all sound moves at this speed. Sounds of higher amplitude might carry farther, because they create more intense changes in atmospheric pressure, but they do not travel faster!

ENVELOPE

This usually refers to waveforms that are generated by musical instruments. Indeed, your synthesizer or sampler (see pages xx to xx) has controls that change specific parameters within this envelope. These are normally the sound's Attack (how swiftly it hits peak amplitude); its Sustain (how long it is "held" for); and its Decay (how long it takes to fade to silence from peak amplitude). They may also include its Delay (any silence inserted before the Attack); its Hold (how long the peak portion of the envelope is held); and/or its Release (the point at which the note is switched off).

PRODUCTION TIPS
■ Simple information is best expressed with clarity; complex ideas with purity
■ Noise is the absence of information. Could this be a good thing?
■ Distortion is the result of too much information. Could this be a good thing?
■ "Honor thy error as a hidden intention." (Brian Eno)

To this, most workstation keyboards add extra parameters, such as the relative volumes of the instrument's oscillators (sound generators); their relative tuning; whether the signal is "wet" (has an effect applied to it) or "dry;" and the position of sound components in the stereo image. But we will talk about all this in due course.

Illustrated above is the Malström synthesizer, in the virtual studio package, Reason. When Malström sounds are triggered via your MIDI keyboard, you can change waveform shapes, relative oscillator levels, and a variety of other factors with your mouse.

Now let's look at some examples of waveform envelopes, regardless of what device you are using.

Most drumbeats are characterized by swift attack, short sustain, and rapid decay—this is the normal signature of percussive sounds. A plucked guitar string is identified by its swift attack, long sustain, and slow decay; and a bowed violin string by its slow attack, long sustain, and fast decay. All of these sounds are also characterized by complex interactions of waveforms, and by variations in each waveform's component parts.

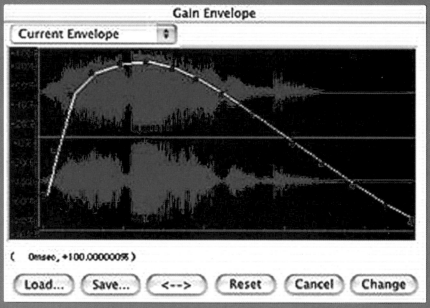

Above: **Most software with sampling and synthesis abilities allows fine-tuning of Envelope parameters. However, this is a very general means of editing a waveform, and it cannot bring up frequencies that are not already there—extreme settings will render the sound much less naturally.**

Top: **Reason's Malström synth offers a very powerful "graintable" synthesis, a combination of granular and wavetable synthesis. At first glance, the amount of options present on any virtual instrument can be overwhelming!**

A WORD ON SYNTHESIS
On a synthesizer or a sampler, then, changing the normal acoustic envelope of an instrument—whether it be a sound patch or a triggered sample—will make the sound seem less "natural," less like the real thing.

This is both the creative pleasure and the attraction of synthesis. For example, you could apply the acoustic envelope of bowed strings—a seductive fade-in and an expressive sustain—to a more aggressive, percussive sound. In Malström, for example, you can also add the characteristic modulation of a human voice, so your instrument appears to "talk."

Synthesis invariably presents you with an axis between simulation and pure artifice. It's up to you how you satisfy, challenge, or confound your listener's expectations, or evoke emotional responses through the creative use of signature waveforms.

WHAT IS PHASING?
Essentially, the relationship between simple waveforms in a complex waveform. You may be familiar with the expression "out of phase," or perhaps with the effects unit or stomp-box known as a phaser, or phase-shifter. If you're into retro sounds, you might also come across a process called tape phasing. The principle is the same.

The best way to define it is to describe how it works. In a complex sound, the amplitudes of component waveforms will almost certainly vary from each other; they will be "out of phase." If two identical waveforms are triggered at the same time, their positive and negative peaks will correspond; they will be "in phase." The effect will be to double the amplitude of the signal. **Mixing tip: record each signal to a separate track, then widen the stereo image by panning one to nine o'clock, and the other to three o'clock.**

Below: **Native Instruments'** Absynth offers a flexible waveform editor for shaping sounds; you can even draw in lines and hear the results immediately.

However, if one of the identical waves is started infinitesimally later than the other, they will clash, as the cycles will not be synchronous; again, they will be out of phase—or as sound engineers say, the phase will have shifted. And if one wave is so out of phase with the other that its positive peak coincides with the other's negative, then the two sounds will cancel each other out.

In many musical instruments, and in many other types of sound-generating device, the complex waveforms they create will often move into and out of phase with each other, generating shifting harmonic and amplitudinal relationships. The unique ways in which they do this help characterize the sound of all musical instruments.

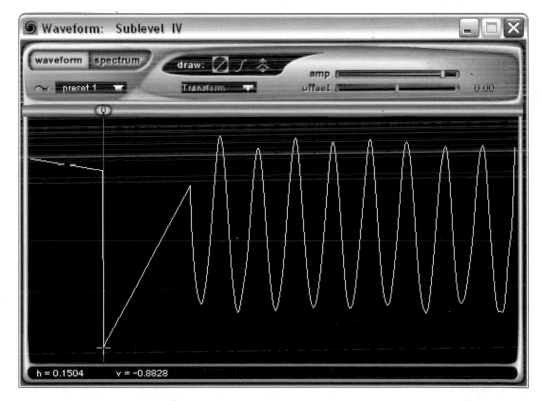

In a digital recording process, triggering two identical waves simultaneously theoretically means that they never shift out of phase with each other—they will simply "double up." But analog media such as tape are speed-dependant and reliant on mechanical movement.

Let's explore why this is important. Say that two identical soundwaves are stored on separate reels of tape. If each reel of tape is set up on a different tape recorder and the machines are started simultaneously, fluctuations in tape speed mean that the sounds will move gradually into and out of phase with each other.

This produces the sonic effect known as tape phasing, which can be heard on 1960s songs such as "Itchicoo Park" by the Small Faces. (To create this effect, the engineer made a duplicate of the two-track mixed master of the song, fading in the signal from the second tape at key moments of the song.)

In the digital realm, there are countless signal processors and VST effects plug-ins that mimic the effects of tape phasing, and of related effects such as ADT (automatic double-tracking), flanging, delay, and doppler, by creating an echo of the input signal, and delaying it by differing amounts.

WHAT IS FREQUENCY?

The rate at which a signal completes a cycle. The signal's frequency, therefore, is stated as the number of complete cycles in a second. If a wave completes 60 cycles a second, then each cycle lasts one sixtieth of a second. The units of frequency measurement are hertz (Hz), so the frequency of such a signal would be 60 Hz.

In music, bass notes are signals that have lower numbers of cycles per second and longer wavelengths, while very high notes tend to be measured in blocks of one thousand hertz—known as kilohertz (kHz)—and have shorter wavelengths.

Frequency, then, provides the time (duration) dimension in the audio realm. You know how it is: you wait ages at your input bus for a signal to arrive, then three turn up at once.

■ For more information, see also "doppler effect" in the glossary, page 184.

Left: This Moog Voyager is a newer synthesizer based on the classic sounds of the Moog synths from the 1970s. While you can theoretically get similar sounds out of a much less expensive virtual synth, some musicians swear by analog instruments.

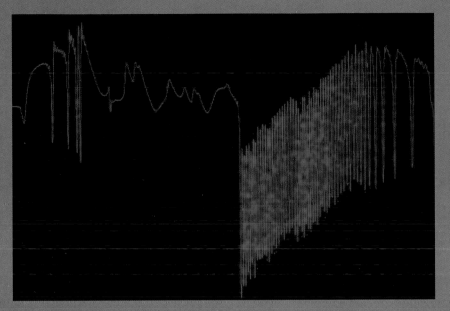

HOW THE MATH WORKS: DECIBELS, BIT DEPTH, AND DYNAMIC RANGE

You're probably not interested in mathematics, but if you're a musician as well as an audio buff, then you deal with mulitples of four every day. So, here's an easy way of calculating the dynamic ranges of 8-, 16-, and 24-bit systems. (The dynamic range is the full range of achievable volume within a system, measured in decibels—see Jargon buster, page 67.)

When you double the amplitude of an audio signal, you add +6 dB of level to it. If you think about it, this means that all you have to do is multiply the bit depth of your chosen system by six to calculate its dynamic range. Thus, 16 (bits) x 6 (dB) = 96 dB dynamic range. Similarly, 24 (bits) x 6 (db) = 144 dB.

This, however, is only the theoretically attainable figure, due to minor flaws in any recording process.

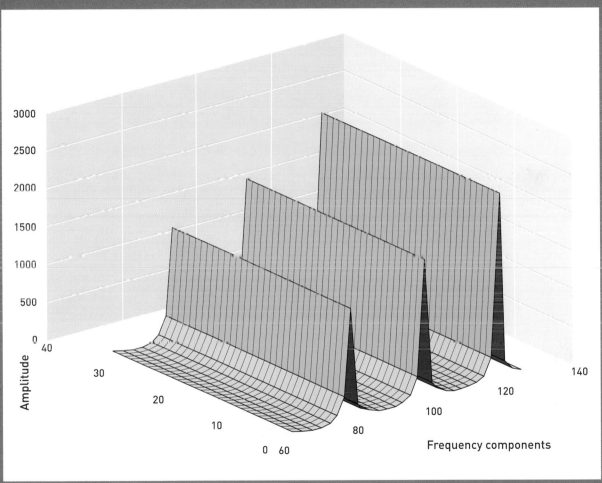

Left and above left: **While audio waveforms are often illustrated as being very simple and orderly for the sake of discussion, you will find that most waveforms you produce working with audio or music are anything but simple. An audio spectrum analyzer, such as one used to test the output of stereo speakers, can generate a graphical waveform, based on the sound you hear, that is much more true to life. You will find that all speakers will alter your sounds to some extent.**

WHAT ARE HARMONICS? "Harmony" and "harmonic" are terms of which people feel they have an instinctive understanding, but in many cases the theory is alien to them. If all musical instruments produced identical waveforms, then concert pitch (440 Hz, or middle A, the reference pitch to which orchestras tune) would sound identical on a piano, a violin, a viola, a trumpet, and a tuba.

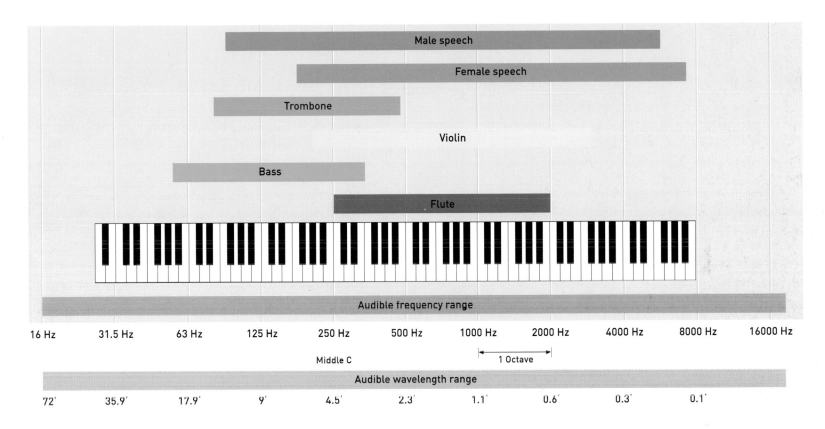

Above: The frequency range of various instruments differs, and this enables waveforms from various instruments to be combined in a way that is pleasing to the ear. This also comes into play when mixing down various instruments in a multitrack recording.

The fact that the "voice" of a note is so different from one instrument to another is mainly due to the presence of frequencies other than the fundamental pitch. These are known as "partials."

When the frequency of a partial is a complete multiple of the original pitch (for example, 440 Hz x 2 = 880 Hz), we call it a harmonic. The tones will sound related. Incidentally, the term "overtone" denotes a harmonic higher than the fundamental pitch. That's all there is to it.

We've already explored how most instruments produce waveforms that have complex phasing and amplitudinal relationships. But most also generate partials and harmonics in addition to fundamental pitch.

In some instruments, these partials have no harmonic relationship to the note whatsoever, which is what gives them their unique sound. This is often the case with metal and percussion instruments—an instrument's construction and the way it is played contribute equally to its "voice."

At this point you may be asking: why do I need to know all this? That's simple: it's about equalization (see over).

A WORD ABOUT MIXING

Sooner or later, you are going to boot up your virtual audio mixer in a package such as Reason, or Logic, or get to grips with the integral mixer in your digital audio workstation. Whether your mixer is real or virtual, analog or digital, the underlying principles of mixing remain the same.

As well as enabling you to move audio objects in stereo space, or in surround sound when the package is Pro Tools LE, Cubase SX, or BIAS Deck, mixing is essentially about equalization (EQ). This is the process of changing a signal's amplitude within specific frequency bands relative to other signals in the mix.

Equalization either amplifies a signal (makes it louder), or attenuates it (makes it quieter) within these bands. It also offers a route of compensation for the numerous changes in a signal's peak level that are introduced in an analog process.

So, the different sweepable parametric bands of an audio mixer enable you to focus in on a signal's complex harmonic structure, and

Below: Mixing can be complicated, but it shouldn't be more complicated than it needs to be. Don't be afraid to trim or add where it is needed, and to experiment. But remember that at some point you will have to call it finished! If it helps, walk away and come back later.

play with the elements that contribute to its "voice." Many of these frequencies are far higher than the highest note on any musical instrument, which is why mixers (real or virtual) allow you to sweep into and out of very high frequency bands.

Mixing—or rather, equalization—is also a way of separating sounds that have similar tonal characteristics, phasing, and frequency levels. This prevents your mix from becoming a meaningless wash of midrange sounds.

Mixing tip: a mix full of transients will make your listener move on somewhere else.

Once you've done a few mixes, you'll discover that if a particular sound or instrument adds nothing meaningful to your work, it's usually best to leave it out entirely rather than try to fix it with EQ.

The creative audio- and music-maker should always remember that the mix is a performance; the mix is about arranging features in a landscape or portrait in sound coherently and appropriately; the mix is about bringing audio to life and pulling your listener into the experience; and the mix is also about "telling a story" (so find your main character). To do any of this, you have to understand the tools of your trade before you can use them to satisfy or confound your audience's expectations.

Theory is also important for two other reasons. One, "deep" knowledge is often lost in a technology environment where speed and disposability reign. Your software designers understand this, so why shouldn't you? And two, audio is unique in that you will rarely work in a digital-only space. There will always be inputs from the real world.

Mixing tip: don't be precious; the most ruthless mix is often the one that works.

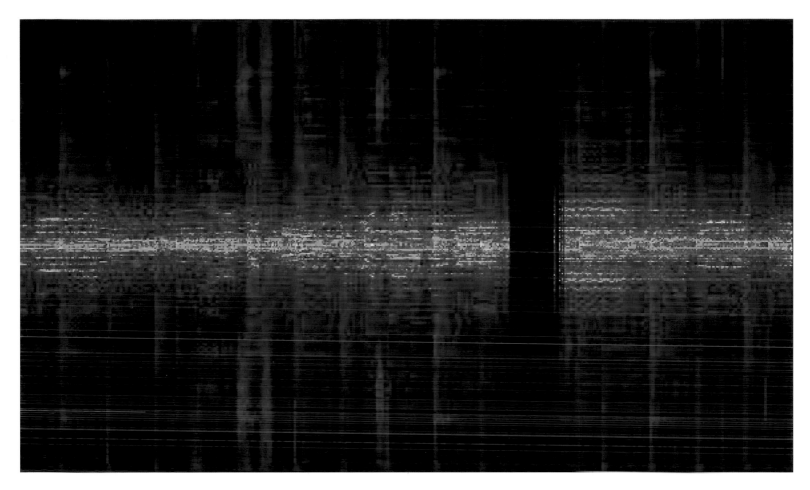

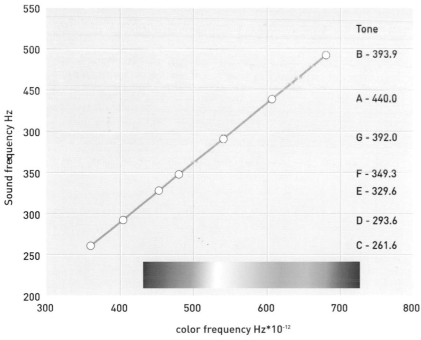

Sound frequency Hz (y-axis)
color frequency Hz*10⁻¹² (x-axis)

	Tone
	B - 393.9
	A - 440.0
	G - 392.0
	F - 349.3
	E - 329.6
	D - 293.6
	C - 261.6

DID YOU KNOW THAT...?
SOUND HAS COLOR...

...which is why we refer to a frequency "spectrum," and use spectrum analyzers to explore the relationships between audio signals, and examine their "spectral frequencies."

■ White noise: equal proportions of all frequencies are present. It sounds like a hiss more than a roar, as human ears are more sensitive to high frequencies. It has all colors, or no color, depending on how you define it.

■ Pink noise: the middle-frequency range found in the natural world in sounds like waves on a seashore, babbling brooks, and so on. If you zoom in on a tiny portion of the waveform, it will look the same as the larger waveform (like natural forms in the real world, it is fractal in design).

■ Brown noise: noise with a larger proportion of lower-end frequencies, such as, thunder and engine noise. It is noise whose waveform exhibits Brownian motion.

So, we've covered audio history, transduction, and analog recording; the birth of digital technology; the underlying principles of sound, waveforms, and synthesis; the unbroken mutual partnership of technology and creativity; and the ways in which mixing must be the culmination of all this theorizing. So what is digital recording?

Audio becomes "digital audio" when it passes from an analog source, such as a mike or the audio out of a keyboard, into your PC, Mac, or digital multitracker. It's all about ons and offs, ones and zeros, signal and silence. In other words, it's about binary (base 2) code and those bits (binary digits) that make the technophobic fall to pieces.

We know from day-to-day experience that the many languages we speak are complex, idiomatic, local, and subject to interpretation. In contrast, the one language that computers speak is simple, universal, and deals with basic truths. The only question a computer needs to ask is: what precisely is happening at this precise point? (And your audio production software bolts an attractive graphic interface onto its deliberations so that you can interact with the data.)

Binary code is a numeric system for storing the answers to these questions as strings of ons (1s) and offs (0s). In the audio realm, these translate as "signal" (voltage), and "no signal" (no voltage). Confusingly, these strings of ones and zeros are called binary "words."

In human languages a long word is no better than a short one (a dog is a dog), but in binary the longer the word is, the more accurate the description will be. (It's rather like building a picture of a dog by examining every part of it microscopically.)

Obviously a simple "on" or "off" is no adequate description of a complex waveform, so it follows that there must be a digital equivalent of amplitude (level) and frequency (duration) to describe a signal in greater detail.

PART 0I. TUNE IN

CHAPTER FOUR

WHAT IS DIGITAL RECORDING?

Left: When an audio signal is made digital by recording it onto your desktop or notebook computer, the waveform that you might see in a software program does not actually tell you how the sound is represented on your hard disk—in a series of ones and zeros. To make the editing process easier, the graphical representation is generated by the software.

Right: Software packages such as Reason, while complex in appearance, actually simplify the process of working with even the most complex digital files by acting as a sampler, sequencer, mixer, and just about everything else. But if your sounds or samples are of low quality to begin with, your final product will suffer.

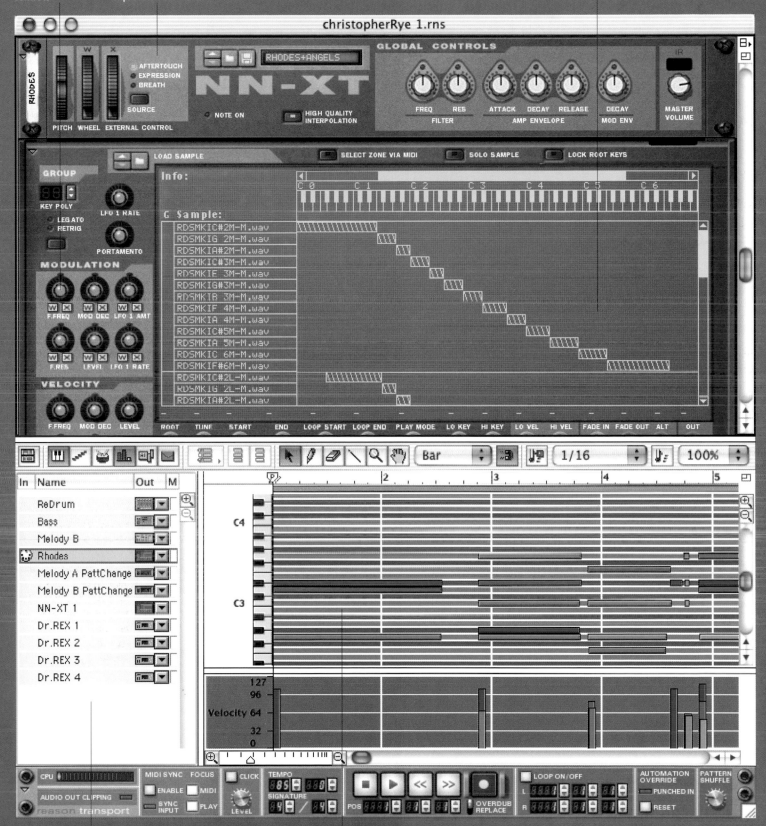

Signal modifying controls

MIDI keyboard-operated expression controls

Key range of multisamples

Instrument list

Sequencer arrange window, showing recorded performance

SAMPLING IN DIGITAL AUDIO It works like this. In digital recording, the unique shape of a signal is analyzed in minute depth over time: we call this process "sampling." The number of times that our signal is sampled in a second is measured in kilohertz—just like high-frequency signals are. This gives us the figure known as the "sampling rate." Consumer, CD-quality recordings are sampled using a process called pulse code modulation (PCM).

It follows that higher sampling rates describe a waveform more accurately, because much more data has been collected about it over the same length of time.

CD-quality recordings are "16-bit," a description of bit depth, not sampling rate—we'll look at this in a moment. Sixteen-bit recordings normally have a sampling rate of 44.1 kHz (CDs and minidisks), or 48 kHz (in the case of DAT). This means that the signal has been analyzed 44,100 or 48,000 times a second. The sampling rates 96 and 192 kHz are common in 24-bit recordings. At 96 kHz, therefore, each sample has a duration of one-96,000th of a second. This is called the "sampling time."

The 20 Hz–20kHz frequency range of 16-bit recordings is a decent enough cross-section of the range of human hearing, which is approximately 15.5 Hz–20.1 kHz. But before analog fans rub their hands at that missing bottom end, they should remember that bass frequencies are usually "rolled off" at the mastering stage for vinyl, to prevent the cutting needle from making wild, lateral swings—and to cram more information onto the record.

Cubase 5 VST and Cubase SX (see page 100 onward) boast a feature called 32-bit TrueTape mode, which emulates the tape saturation effect that analog fans know and love. As always, people will pay good money to turn back time.

Indeed, the "Grungelizer" VST plug-in in Cubase 5 VST allows you to switch between the present day and the year 1900, swamping your recording in enough hiss and crackle to make Mr Edison blush with pride.

Right: **Even though crisp recordings and mixes are made easy with digital audio, sometimes you'll want a rougher sound. Overdriving your soundcard inputs or setting levels higher than 0dB will only cause clipping in the digital world, but enough plug-ins and filters exist to simulate most types of overdrive, distortion, and other retro effects.**

But let's get back to the future. You can see from the box on page 54 that SACD (Super Audio CD) offers a quantum leap in sampling rates to 2.8 megahertz (MHz). That's 2.8 million samples per second, via a slightly different technology. Sound recording and reproduction are finally moving towards the millions of instructions per second (MIPS) environment that microprocessors operate in.

Is it a bird? Is it a plane? With SACD, the answer's "yes" to both, as it's reproduction quality exceeds the range of human hearing— just like the real world does. It's the nearest we have to "audio vérité."

Right: **Realistic drums—as opposed to electronic drums of the type normally used in house music—can be very difficult for the amateur digital producer to sample properly, but fortunately many realistic, high-quality samples exist on the Web or on CD. It is common practice to build up songs using drum loops.**

PCM AND THE VOLUME PROBLEM

From the Audio Engineers Society:

"In linear PCM, the word length in bits directly gives the dynamic range, calculated at roughly six decibels per bit. The current standard for linear PCM, 16-bit, thus gives us approaching a 96-dB dynamic range.

"As the ratio of the number of multitrack channels to output loudspeaker channels grows, so does the requirement on word length in a rational system. A fair amount of complex production is done today with two interlocked 24-track digital source machines, intended to mix down to two output channels. A 24:1 reduction in the number of channels is not unknown.

"16-bit linear PCM is seen by some in the industry as limiting to expression due to its dynamic range. But if consumer media were to jump to 24-bit audio, as some have suggested, then consumer media would support a roughly 144-dB dynamic range. This level approaches that of instantaneous hearing damage in as little as one exposure."
© AES. www.aes.org

MUSICAL ONES AND ZEROS Far from being a gray, colorless concept from the world of computers, math, processors, and geek-speak, digital recording is a concept that's surprisingly close to the basics of musical notation. Digital technology and music were made for each other—and they are certainly singing from the same songbook of twos, fours, eights, 16s, 24s, and 32s that musicians flick through every day. Indeed, "binary notation" means "two beats to the bar"—and in music a note is either on, or off.

But what do we mean by eight-, 16-, 20-, 24-, and 32-bit (the greatest bit-depth currently available in desktop audio recording software)? And why are we recording at higher quality than a CD player can reproduce? It's all to do with redundant detail and a certain Mr Nyquist (see opposite).

Think of bit-depth as being analagous to resolution in a digital image. All those samples per second gather the data for building up a picture of our elusive waveform, but it's in the binary word that all such data is stored.

It's a simple concept, and an efficient storage medium. A long binary word can hold a much higher number of possible on/off combinations than a short one. For example, in an eight-bit binary word (a word of eight binary digits, such as 01101110), there are 256 possible combinations of ones and zeros—01101111, 00001100, and so on. But in a 24-bit word (100011100110111000110101), there are a staggering 16.8 million possible combinations. It's the same principle that allows 24-bit images to reproduce 16.8 million colors.

But given that a unique binary word is assigned to every sample in the sampling process, and a waveform might be sampled 96,000 times a second, you can see why audio files are always multi-megabyte in size. Every audio track you record in Cubase, Logic 6, Cool Edit, and other packages, generates a separate audio file.

You are going to need a fast, powerful computer to process and store all this stuff. We'll look at system requirements on page 130.

A WORD ABOUT SOUNDCARDS

If you have a PC or Mac with an integral 16-bit soundcard, you may need to invest in a dedicated, higher-resolution soundcard to get the best results from your software, even though you will still be mastering to 16-bit for the foreseeable future. As we've established, it's all about redundant detail; if you can cram in more information at greater bit-depths early on, you will get superior results when you lose redundant information later in the transfer to 16-bit. For more on soundcards, turn to page 136.

A WORD ABOUT CHANGING BIT-DEPTH

Once an image has been taken in digital photography, you will not increase the amount of information in it by increasing the resolution. The same applies to audio. If you have produced a finished track in 16-bit at 48 kHz, then saved it as a WAV, you will not increase the quality of the sound by changing the resolution to 24-bit at 96 kHz.

THE SOUND QUALITY / FILE SIZE TRADE-OFF

Sample rate	Word length	Approx file size per minute
44.1 kHz	16-bit stereo*	10 MB *
48 kHz	16-bit stereo	11 MB
48 kHz	24-bit stereo	17 MB
96 kHz	24-bit stereo	37 MB

* File size will be halved for mono (one-channel, monaural) sound

Indeed, if you take a WAV (see page 120) recorded at 48 kHz to 16-bit in, for example, Reason 2, then import it into a program such as BIAS Peak or Cubase SX for further work, increasing the resolution to 24-bit at 96 kHz will have the effect of slowing the track down to half the tempo. The frequency of each audio element in the track will be halved—lowering the pitch of any musical instrument by an octave. This is an example of the Nyquist Theorem in practice.

Huge audio file sizes are one reason for the importance of MIDI to digital audio, even though MIDI is not strictly audio at all. Turn to page 122 for an introduction to MIDI.

MIDI sends directions to a soundcard and to other MIDI devices, and tells them in real time what to do at any given point. MIDI data is not stored as audio information. MIDI data says "play this note now," rather than, "here is a recording of a note."

Right: If you plan to do high quality audio work, ensure that the soundcard you buy is capable of recording 24-bit audio. While you may want to work with 16-bit for the time being—it is the standard for CD audio after all—new formats such as SACD will begin to demand better quality in the near future.

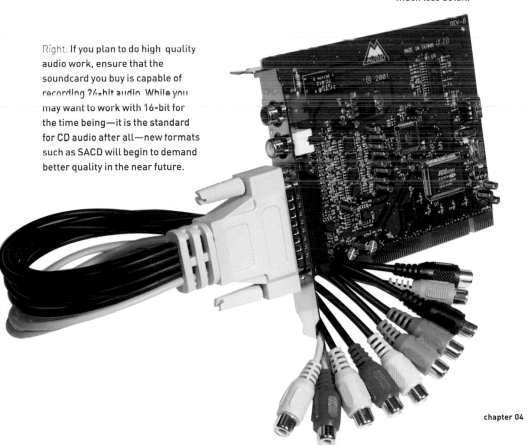

PRODUCTION TIPS
REAL WORLD TECHNICAL MANAGER, GEOFF PRYCE

PRODUCTION TIPS
REAL WORLD TECHNICAL MANAGER, GEOFF PRYCE

Analog is a more forgiving medium than digital—you can push things into the red and still get a good sound. Accuracy and subjectivity are very different things! When you start recording it can be very tempting to bust your faders and turn everything as loud as it can go. But with digital you have to be very careful with overall levels. If you push it, hard clipping [distortion from an over-loud signal] sounds awful.

Above: The simple diagrams above demonstrate how a sample rate that is too low (represented by the points) produces a noisy, aliased waveform, or at least one with much less detail.

THE NYQUIST THEOREM

Q: If CDs have a frequency range of 20 Hz–20 kHz, why do I need a sampling rate of more than twice that to capture any sound accurately?

A: The Nyquist Theorem states that the sampling rate must be at least double the number of hertz of the highest frequency being recorded. So, for CDs, the sampling rate has to be at least 40 kHz. The extra 4.1 kHz "headroom" in CDs' standard sampling rate of 44.1 kHz is there to allow for stray frequencies that exceed the 20 kHz range during the recording process. The "Nyquist Frequency" is one-half of the sampling rate, so we know that a 40 kHz sampling rate will allow us to record a signal of up to 20 kHz at best.

DID YOU KNOW THAT...?

Jazz label owner Tom Jung pioneered 20-bit digital recording to make better use of the 16-bit CD standard, reducing noise at lower amplitudes and giving his stable of musicians the confidence to let rip on their digital-only label.

WHAT ARE SAMPLERS?
We've established that digital recording and sampling are one and the same thing. So what is a sampler? In music production, a sampler is a dedicated recording device that is designed to play back digitally recorded sounds (samples) across the harmonic scale. In other words, it is a means of gathering short pieces of audio for use as the raw material for new sounds.

Arguably, the first "sampler" was the Mellotron, a 1961 mechanical keyboard that became synonymous with The Beatles' *Strawberry Fields Forever*, and with the progressive rock bands of the late 1960s and 1970s.

In fact, the Mellotron was really a "sample player," containing tape loops of choirs, strings, flutes, and other orchestral instruments. When a note or chord was played on the keyboard, the corresponding tape loops were played by the machine's internal tape heads.

Probably, the makers were hoping that it would sound exactly like a real orchestra or choir; it didn't, as the characteristic acoustic envelopes of the original sounds were changed by the recording and playback process. But it did sound unique: a warm, dramatic, saturated sound that is still sought after today. Indeed, WAVs of original Mellotron loops are freely available for loading onto today's virtual keyboards and samplers.

Above: **The Korg Electribe sampler is a popular choice for the dance musician. Like most modern hardware or software samplers, it offers a plethora of editing and sequencing tools, as well as many other features.**

But the sampler as we know it appeared with the Fairlight CMI (computer musical instrument) in 1978. The first Fairlights were 8-bit machines, consisting of a brain (a bulky hard drive), a "piano" keyboard, and a green-screen computer monitor and stylus. Retailing at tens of thousands of dollars, the Fairlights were the preserve of wealthy rock stars, and were primitive by today's standards—despite their complex operating systems.

However, like the Mellotron, the Fairlights had characteristic advantages over the later, cheaper samplers that defined digital music-making in the late 1980s and early 1990s. The most obvious of these was the stylus, which allowed users to draw and interact with waveforms on the monitor screen, freeing them up to design and edit sounds that had never been heard before.

The Fairlight was swiftly followed by the Emulator, an integrated keyboard and sampler; the Synclavier, an early music workstation; and by later devices such as the Ensoniq Mirage, and the first Yamaha and Akai machines. All of these shared the ability to manipulate sampled sounds by time-stretching, reversing, editing, and finally looping.

As if further proof were needed that technology limitations and content go hand in hand, early sample-driven pieces of music, such as Paul Hardcastle's 1985 hit *19*, s-s-s-sounded the way they did because the memory capacities of samplers at the time were limited to a second or less of recorded sound—enough for a vocal or musical "hit," or short s-s-s-stab of sound.

As processing power increased exponentially and mass storage became affordable, sampling times lengthened until complete bars of another composer's music could be sampled, stored, looped, and manipulated, spawning dozens of new musical styles—and at least as many lawsuits.

Almost immediately, digital music became as much about the selection of raw material from music's journey through time, subcultures, and continents as it was about ear for melody or skill with a musical instrument. But this did have the advantage of putting many musicians back in touch with their musical heritage, and encouraging them to experiment with untried combinations of sounds and musics.

Today, samplers are mainly software- and PC/Mac-based—a recognition that what a sampler does is pretty much what a computer does. That said, sample manipulation remains one of the building blocks of many 21st-century synthesizers and workstation keyboards, such as the successful Korg Triton range.

DIGITAL STORAGE FORMATS: PRESENT AND FUTURE

Normal frequency range of human hearing: approx 15.5 Hz–20.1 kHz

CD, CD-R, CD-RW
Offers: Mass production at low cost; widely used; standard in most PCs and Macs; only CD-RWs are re-recordable; vulnerable to dirt and damage
Sampling rate: 16-bit, at 44.1 kHz, no compression
Frequency range: 20 Hz–20 kHz
Dynamic range: 96 dB +
Capacity: 700 MB (approx 78 minutes of stereo audio)

DVD, DVD-R, DVD-RW, DVD-A (AUDIO)
Offers: DVD-A offers 400 minutes of stereo at CD resolution (44.1 kHz/16-bit); 74 minutes of 5.1 surround sound at 96 kHz/24-bit resolution; or 74 minutes of stereo at 192 kHz/24-bit resolution. All DVD formats are vulnerable to damage and dirt, but recordable options are now affordable, either standalone or as part of a standard PC or Mac package. Dedicated DVD-A players are needed to get the full dynamic range from DVD-A disks
Sampling rate: 44.1 kHz–192 kHz
Frequency range: 16 Hz–20 kHz
Dynamic range: 144 dB
Capacity: 4.5 GB approx

SACD (SUPER AUDIO CD)
Offers: a staggering frequency range above and below the normal range of human hearing, and ultra-high ("1-bit" direct stream) sampling. Special players are needed, and digital amplification is essential for the best results
Sampling rate: 2.8 MHz (2.8 million samples a second)
Frequency range: 2 Hz–100 kHz
Dynamic range: 105 dB
Capacity: 4.2 GB

MINIDISK (MD)
Offers: Easy re-recording; ATRAC 1:5 audio compression; personalisable; can be temperamental in MD-based portable integrated studios
Sampling rate: 44.1 kHz
Frequency range: 20 Hz–20 kHz
Dynamic range: 92 dB +
Storage capacity: 140 MB

MP3 (FILE FORMAT)
Stands for: Motion Picture Experts Groups level three
Offers: 1:10 audio compression ratio; easily shared via Internet, and downloadable onto portable players, such as Apple's iPod; a standard file option on audio production software packages
Sampling rate: 16-bit, 44.1 kHz
Frequency range: 20 Hz–20 kHz
Capacity: n/a, but Apple's iPod player can currently contain up to 12 GB of data and rising, holding perhaps 4,000 songs

MULTIMEDIA CARDS (MMC), SECURE DIGITAL (SD) CARDS, AND OTHERS
Offers: Portability; fast transfer speeds. Many audio players accept MMC and newer SD cards; they are used to store MP3 files for playback. Some other Flash RAM cards, including SmartMedia, Memory Sticks, and CompactFlash, are compatible with certain audio devices as well.
Sampling rate: 16-bit, 44.1 kHz (uses MP3 or sometimes WAV files)
Frequency range: 20 Hz–20 kHz
Capacity: Usually from 16 MB–512 MB

Below: Pioneer's Digital Media Player (the DMP-555) can mix, synchronize, and play CDs and Secure Digital (SD) cards. The device can be connected to PC via a USB cable so as to facilitate MP3 management and transfer.

WHY ARE MY COPY CDS NOISY?

In a purely digital recording process that has no analog input from the outside world, and in a largely digital reproduction and amplification process (with digital inputs and outputs), the only time the energy in a recording might be transduced is when it leaves the DAC (digital to analog convertor) and hits your loudspeakers.

And because the energy resides in binary code, it can be sent to any compatible device anywhere in the world with no loss of quality, as long as the code remains intact. That's the digital advantage.

So, why do some of your digital recordings degrade if you copy them from one machine to another? As you can probably guess, this happens whenever you introduce analog transduction stages into the process, such as when you copy a CD via an audio output to the analog input of a digital device, perhaps via an amplifier.

A digital connection between digital devices allows machines to exchange code; it lets them talk the same language. Transduction means something is always lost in translation, in the move from one language to another. And just like the game of Telephone, the magnitude of the change in the message increases the more devices there are in the chain.

But you're not pirating someone else's music, are you? (Go directly to page 141 if you are.)

DIGITAL AUDIO TAPE (DAT)
Offers: higher sampling rate than CD; no data compression, capacities up to 124 minutes; still standard in many professional studios, but hardware and tapes are usually only available from specialist studio suppliers
Sampling rate: 48 kHz
Frequency range: 20 Hz–20 kHz
Dynamic range: 105 dB
Capacity: n/a, but up to two hours of uncompressed audio is available, depending on the length of tape. (Forty-six-minute tapes are available if you wish to minimise waste on one-off projects)

Above: While CD, DVD, and related media do not differ much in appearance, it is the techniques used to write the data onto the disks that distinguishes one from the other in terms of quality.

BUBBLING UNDER: FUTURE FORMATS
BLUE LASER/BLU-RAY DISKS
Nine of the world's electronics giants, including Sanyo and Toshiba, are uniting behind a new optical disk system called Blu-Ray. The DVD-sized rewritable disks are encoded by a blue laser, rather than a red one. Blue light has a shorter wavelength than red, which means that blue lasers can focus on smaller areas of disk and write more data into the same space. Current estimates put the capacity of Blu-Ray disks at between 12 GB and 27 GB, depending on whether they are single- or double-sided.

BROADCAST WAVE/B-WAVE/BWF
The European Broadcasting Union (EBU) has introduced "a file format that contains the minimum information that is considered necessary for all broadcast applications." Broadcast Wave (B-Wave, or BWF) is a "higher level descriptor [that can] reference other files containing more complex sets of information." To you and me, that's an audio file format that lets all other audio file formats exist within it. In about five years' time, this will be in full swing.

01.05

In a technology landscape of PDAs, peer-to-peer computing, digital audio band, polyphonic mobile phones, Internet radio, and online games consoles, it's easy to stray off the once-simple path of technology choices into a forest of acronyms, buzzwords, and fast-moving lifestyle accessories. For "B2C" read "Me Too, See?"

For beginners and other creative people, the landscape of today's digital audio and music technologies is bewildering, and hard to map. It's become a talking point in that on/off conversation in the media about our relationship with the past, present, and future.

That said, people in the digital arts quickly acquire knowledge about new tools of their trade. This book will show you how to do just that.

If you're a photographer or video-maker (you may be both of these things), the choice is relatively simple. Which digital camera? Which editing program and plug-ins? And which computer platform? Often, the choice is made for you by sheer force of numbers, taste, and sometimes prejudice.

But if you're a musician or an audio buff, the choice can be terrifying. Which recorder? Which keyboard? Which sampler? Virtual, or real? Which microphone? Which peripheral? Which platform? Which MIDI device? Which monitors? Which integrated studio? Can I do it all in software? (Yes.) What are all these acronyms? (When can I start creating?)

In other words, where am I? Walk into any audio or music equipment supplier and, above the din and background noise, they will expect you to know. The Internet, meanwhile, is brimming with thousands of software patches, VST plug-ins, virtual instruments, microphone modelers, and a bewildering array of other apparent essentials.

SO WHERE AM I NOW?

Left: Often hailed as one of the more user-friendly synthesizers, the Novation KS5 offers a series of powerful filters and what Novation calls "Liquid Analog Sound." As with all good quality keyboards, you can incorporate the synth with your computer or with other components—in other words, it can filter, control, or be controlled.

By now the solution ought to be obvious: cut out the background noise.

There's much talk about the digital world, and most of it is rubbish. "Being digital," to use Nic Negroponte's phrase (he's one of the culprits at MIT's Media Lab), is really a simple matter of making a handful of unique choices, and forming a strategy for where they might take you.

To cut out the noise, just put yourself first. Ask yourself what you want, and what you are trying to achieve. The following chapters will ask these simple questions, and guide you to some possible answers.

Below: **Pro Tools** hardware components are designed to incorporate fully with **Pro Tools** software; indeed, many studios opt to use a combination of hardware and software. From an "ease-of-use" perspective, it can certainly be argued that real buttons, switches, dials, and faders are much easier to adjust than mouse-controlled ones in a computer program.

NUMBER ONES, OR ZEROS? The one certainty in all this is that audio has become part of a broader data stream, whose output and access points are numerous, and often beyond our control.

We might spend weeks crafting a dynamic, rich audio environment for a video, website, or musical composition, only for someone to experience it in a noisy room on a tiny laptop speaker, or via an earpiece connected to a palmtop. And if your target market is office-based, those speakers are probably switched off. We'll look at mastering and at monitoring on a range of speakers on pages 166 and 170.

Alternately, the deficiencies in your first DVD might be all too obvious when revealed on an average home cinema surround-sound system. In this way, the consumption of digital audio is far more complex and unpredictable than of any other type of digital content, such as photography, animation, or video. Turn to page xx for more.

But why is this? If you've taken the time to glance through our timeline of audio history, you're probably surprised by how much "contemporary" technology was actually developed two generations ago (multiply that by five for the number of technology generations).

But if surround sound was developed for motion pictures such as Disney's *Fantasia*, why has it taken several decades to reach the living rooms of non-hi-fi obsessives? The reason is simple: economics.

It was in the interests of movie-makers to pour money into in-theater technology to set their products apart from the rest, creating "one-off" experiences that a captive audience would never forget.

Audio-makers such as musicians, however, rarely had any level of control over listeners' technology. On the contrary, they were (and are) motivated by exposure, which today means mixing audio for radio, Windows PCs, Macs, digital TV, the Web, or any other output medium you care to mention.

Below: **Will your sounds or music be heard through hi-fi speakers, or a pair of headphones? On television, or over a car stereo? Through an earpiece on a mobile phone, or streamed over the Web on an audiophile's desktop computer?**

But things are changing. Now companies such as Sony own the content, the software, the hardware, the distribution network, and the gaming platform, the race is on to produce audio that plays a co-starring role in a multimedia, widescreen, broadcast-quality experience. One that's either streamed, published to DVD, or is available as part of a game environment. And because they own it, you can own it too.

We'll take an exclusive, insider look at how Sony's technology is converging around games, music-making, licensing, and content distribution later in the book. If Sony is successful, albums and games will become one and the same thing, and software will be given away. Impossible? Turn to page 176 to find out more.

Until recently, if we wanted to record audio, we bought an audio-recording device. If we wanted to play it back, we bought a playback device. It was all about hardware that was designed to perform one or two functions well. Those choices remain open.

Nowadays, however, our decisions will almost exclusively be about software, about applications. PC or Mac hardware can serve whatever purpose you want it to serve—if you decide to go that route. And what about the Linux community? Lots more about this from page 134 onward. So, you've got the talent. But just how do you turn your creativity and ideas into polished, up-to-the-minute, professional sounding audio or music? What are the hints and tips from the professionals to bring your work to life? How do you make and master a broadcast-quality recording? And what are the insider cheats to turn your occasional lapses into pitch-perfect, brilliant sounds?

The following chapters are where it all happens. We'll examine the key technology issues and strategies for creative people, and lay out some pointers for a safe journey ahead. So, if you're itching to get started, jump to page 72 right now.

But if you're interested, here's a personal view of the digital world. It offers a context for all this bewildering choice, and puts the rest of the book's decision-making strategies into perspective.

As you will see, the digital debate has implications for our work as creative audio- and music-makers—just follow the links in the text. So, read on, or jump ahead? Like all the decisions in the book, that is up to you.

01.06

It's a cliché that the wired and wireless worlds have turned a handful of certainties on their heads. "Mine is smaller than yours!" is now the boast of chattering classes on the move. The more upwardly mobile we are, the more downward the size of our mobile or PDA.

In audio, however, this is almost certainly a good thing. Roomfuls of dust-magnet gear can, if we wish it, be boiled down to a few lines of invisible code. What Laurie Anderson calls the "arms race" of bigger, faster, better, more, is over. But there are problems.

Text has become hyper, active, and hyperactive, where before it was discreet, passively consumed, and easy to control. Information has escaped its containers, its formats, to roam free on a vast network of networks. Or so the network tells us.

Entire corporations' fortunes now rest on their ability to put data back into its containers and sell it, preferably with low production and distribution costs. And then resell it in different containers, preferably to the same people ("completists"). Audio is at the forefront of all this.

Single media have become multiple media, and we can choose to consume or interact with audio via digital radio, the Internet, mobile phones, our games and home cinema systems, or the red button on our TV remotes.

Until recently, content and storage format have gone hand in hand. The success of any format was rarely to do with its technical superiority. More often than not, it was about whether it presented content in a form that people liked, or took pleasure in using, storing, or putting in their pockets: a cassette tape, a vinyl album, an enhanced CD.

PART 01. TUNE IN

CHAPTER THREE

AUDIO IN THE DIGITAL WORLD: A PERSONAL VIEW

Left: **Many organizations are working toward a future in which all media, including music, video and feature films, will be distributed online.**

Above: The record album continues
to define the way many people
experience recorded music—for
now, at least.

Usually a format adds something to an experience, such as eye-catching artwork, or a pleasing design. Occasionally, it defines a new experience: you could fit, say, ten or 12 songs onto a piece of vinyl before sound quality became a problem (the data had to be packed into a limited space). As a result, the "album" was born: ten songs on a piece of plastic, an A-side, a B-side, a double album. Many diversified organizations are now working toward a future where content of any kind—be it music, audio, video, text, photography, software, even movies—is distributed digitally, and entirely online.

As a result, all forms of digital content are converging around the Web and multi-purpose devices. Would you like your audio on a phone, a laptop, or a games platform? The access point is entirely yours to choose. But once you've paid for your content at one access point—let's say your desktop computer—the debate is raging about whether you will still be able to move it to another device, or burn it onto disk. You can influence this debate.

Above: **Should we be able to copy digital content to other devices? The debate rages, thanks to a legal system designed to protect the pre-digital world.**

In short, once audio content has become a digital data stream, some providers would like you to treat it like any piece of software, like any other stream of ones and zeros. Many pundits claim that this runs counter to the whole point of digital content—that it can be reproduced with little or no quality compromises.

One side of the argument says that audio file sharing cannot be theft, as the original content is never "taken away"— in fact, it is propagated. The other side says that digital duplication is not a victimless crime, merely an opportunity never to face your victim. We'll explore digital rights management for audio on page 140 onward.

As a result, licensing, lock-up, and intellectual property are king—but on a network that is designed for content that's "free," in every sense of the word. Digital technology is about ons and offs, ones and zeros, and many switched-on businesses would like to see analog technology switched off. The future is always on, then off again. And so is our romance with digital technology.

But why is this important in a book about digital audio? That's easy. The above debate is the reason why many creative technologists, and audio- and music-makers are examining the issue from completely new perspectives. They're looking at defining a new musical and audio language for the digital era; content that makes intelligent use of the unique ways in which we can interact with it, and the unique ways in which computers process information.

We'll take a look ahead with one of the pioneers of generative and vector audio on pages 176; at realtime performance sequencing on page 114; and at digital audio band and Internet radio on page 174.

THE LOST SUPERHIGHWAY

The "information superhighway" used to get all the blame for this frenzied unpacking and repackaging. Now, in the decade or so since it was first discussed, people have stopped talking about it. Why?

The reason is that the concept was always naive, reductive, and absurd. You might say that the superhighway was more a sidestreet of analog thinking than a statement of intent about how digital technologies might evolve. In retrospect, the abandoned baggage belonged to the very people who rushed onto the highway without looking, and not to the people who were "left behind." Highways don't move; people, traffic, and markets move, and not always in the direction we want them to go.

Think about it. Highways are linear, gray, and ancient distribution networks, which have a habit of connecting big communities and destroying small ones in their march from A to B.

The Internet, on the other hand, is by definition complex and interconnected. It allows communities of any size to thrive and locate each other on a network that changes shape with every log-on, or -off. But the initiative and enterprise rests with creative people to bring it to life.

This much we know, and we like to imagine that we have never known it before. But the same claims were made about the telegraph over a century and a half ago. And, arguably, the dot-dash, on-off conversations of morse code were the true beginnings of digital communication and commerce.

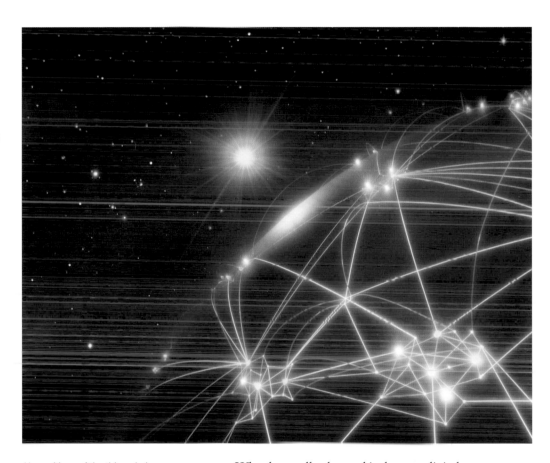

Above: **Many of the things being said about communication over the Internet were said about the telegraph over a century and a half ago; what has really changed is the speed, prevalence, and efficiency of our digital conversations over our analog ones.**

What has really changed is that our digital conversations have simply become faster, more prevalent, and more successful than our analog ones. And this has given rise to one of the paradoxes of the digital age. Just as the bandwidth and storage capacity to deal with vast amounts of digital information has become widely and cheaply available, so people are losing interest in storing it, or in fixing it in any format. But advances in storage and processing power have opened up professional-quality audio to the home user.

TUNE IN, LOG OFF Analog technology enables us to communicate simple, quantifiable, finite pieces of data—stories that have a beginning, a middle, and an end. When we store information in this way, it effects a change in a tangible medium.

Many analog technologies remain superior to their digital counterparts, or produce desirable effects and artefacts. Even when there is "parity," most experts still mix and match technology types and play to their strengths.

However, analog storage media are characterized by their limited shelf lives—indeed, by the fact that they sit on shelves at all. In short, they decay, or are easily damaged, which is why we regard them as precious and hang onto them for decades.

Digital technologies have destroyed those boundaries, if only because content has become something that can be infinitely re-edited, re-purposed, re-sampled, and re-mixed at source, then re-distributed with a click. We can interact with it, rather than merely make it, or consume it. It's never been about "e-;" it's always been about about "re-."

In the digital environment, every story changes with the retelling; each piece of content changes with the redistribution. Arguably, this makes it a more personal experience.

When we store audio digitally, then, we capture it for a moment before it moves on somewhere else. We turn it into a stream of ones and zeros. And if it's not perfect, we can always fix it later. Some pundits point out that, taken to its logical extreme, digital technology means that nothing is ever finished, that everything is a work in progress. Others reply that this is precisely the point.

In fact, digital storage media decay only marginally more slowly than most analog media. Optically etched media, such as CDs and DVDs, begin to decay after about 15 years. Digital content, meanwhile, could have an indefinite future when it resides on a server or hard disk because we can always move it somewhere else, from one container to another, without compromising quality. However, if the data is corrupted, or the file format becomes obsolete, our content is lost forever.

Writer Stewart Brand of The Long Now Foundation (www.longnow.org) argues that we are living in an "information dark age" of lost information, dead formats, and rapidly obsolete technologies: information that might still exist, but which can no longer be read. We looked at media types on page 54.

In the pre-digital age, then, the value of information was defined by its scarcity. In the digital age, it is defined by the speed at which it moves. But we are, as Brand says, used to living arithmetically (1, 2, 3, 4, 5), not exponentially (4, 8, 16, 32). The digital world runs on exponential technology—our world is spinning faster.

Above: Digital data can last forever without compromising quality if it is moved continuously to new disks—but only if the digital file itself does not become corrupted or obsolete. However, most digital media itself decays only marginally more slowly than analog media.

MOORE'S LAW VERSUS MOORE'S WALL

In 1965 Gordon E Moore, later co-founder of Intel, observed that the number of components on a microchip doubles every 18 months (he originally said every year, but the figure was later adjusted).

Moore accurately predicted the cyclical doubling of computer power, and the concomitant halving of cost, which continues unabated today. "Moore's Law" soon became shorthand for the IT industry endlessly offering "more bang for your buck" with each generation of processor.

But writer Stewart Brand observes in his book *The Clock of the Long Now—Time and Responsibility*, that as faster computers are used to design faster computers (and so on and on), humans will soon hit what he calls "Moore's Wall," the point at which they can no longer keep up with digital technology and the creative possibilities it offers.

The concomitant of this, Brand observes, is that technology becomes increasingly worthless, while at the same time the value of the work we produce on it lasts for shorter and shorter periods of time. The lesson? Concentrate on what you are creating, not what you are creating it on. And formulate a strategy for preserving your work beyond the lifespan of your equipment.

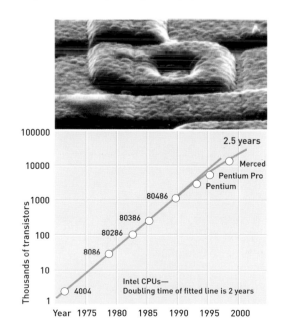

100000

10000   2.5 years
         Merced
         Pentium Pro
         Pentium
1000   80486
         80386
100   80286
         8086
10
                Intel CPUs—
                Doubling time of fitted line is 2 years
1   4004

Year 1975 1980 1985 1990 1995 2000

Thousands of transistors

AUDIO ARCHIVING STRATEGIES

DO THEY STILL KNOW IT'S CHRISTMAS?
REAL WORLD TECHNICAL MANAGER GEOFF PRYCE;
STUDIO MANAGER OWEN LEECH

GP: Damp and humidity are the enemies of audio. Most big studios who still use tape bake their tapes in an oven to keep out the moisture. But when it comes to digital, you really need an archiving strategy. Archiving is big business, but it no longer means consigning data to one format and just leaving it there—you need a re-archiving strategy to migrate your data onto each new technology as it comes along. We're aiming for a 100-year timeframe to preserve all our recordings for. As long as all the ones and zeros remain intact, the archive will survive. But that means ensuring that audio is archived with incredibly accurate clocking today—more accurate than the atomic clocks that keep world time.

OL: You'd think that record companies would be good stewards of their own material, especially given that backlist is so important to them. But so many big companies throw out their master tapes. Or they just lose them. A few years ago there was a skip outside Olympic Studios in London that was full of master tapes—they belonged to record companies, but they never bothered to ask for them back! Maybe they had nowhere to store them.

We hosted a big event recently, in honor of Band Aid's *Do They Know It's Christmas?* The BBC were here, and the record company sent the master tape of this huge worldwide hit that spawned the whole Live Aid thing. There was a big fanfare, and the tape machine was switched on. It was the wrong song! They'd lost the master tape! I don't think they ever found it.

God knows what some of these companies do now stuff is mastered on Pro Tools or Logic Audio. Just leave a box of CDs in the corner?

THE CRUNCH At heart, computers are still designed to crunch numbers; to digitize different types of data; and to move them from one place to another. Since the 1980s, they have also been designed to provide a graphical means of organizing and interacting with data.

All technologies, including storage media, are defined by their limitations. Given enough time—normally a couple of technology generations—limitations that were once perceived as drawbacks become attractive and sought-after: the compression and saturation of analog tape; the warm crackle of vinyl; the graininess of celluloid; and so on. They make us nostalgic for the time a recording was made, and if the technology wasn't up to the task, then so much the better.

In the case of digital technologies, the acceleration of processor speeds (roughly doubling every 18 months) together with the mass availability of cheap memory and storage mean that computers can crunch, organize, and store types of data that they were incapable of processing just a few years ago. (See page 65, Moore's Law versus Moore's Wall.)

Computers can now be used as standalone audio recording devices. Previously, large file sizes meant that desktop computers were best used as an interface for organizing and editing audio information, before recording it off onto an external device. A computer—PC or Mac—can sit at the heart of a digital audio studio; but it can also now *be* your studio. We'll explore the pros and cons of this on page 72, and look at different studio setups on pages 148 and 149.

In other words, memory capacity and processor speeds are fast becoming resources that we can waste, rather than push beyond their limits until our computers freeze, crash, or fall over. When a resource becomes plentiful enough to waste, we can safely assume the technology behind it is good enough to use.

So, we know where we've come from, and where we stand today. Now, it's time to log on, punch in, drop out, and find out where *you* want to go. As Peter Gabriel says, "Turn up the signal, wipe out the noise."

REAL WORLD TECHNICAL MANAGER, GEOFF PRYCE; CHIEF ENGINEER MARCO MIGLIARI; THE AUTHOR

GP: Music is about passion, creativity, collaboration. There are no rights and wrongs: there's no "right way of doing things" in audio recording. You simply learn by your mistakes. But the data industry is driving so much. We are at their mercy—IT companies are taking over music companies. Now there's a real crossover between IT and audio. The music industry is personal; but IT is impersonal.

When everything is reduced to ones and zeros, it doesn't matter to the medium whether it's music, software, or text—it can be anything. There's a convergence, the boundaries are blurred.

My background is in electronics. I'm used to repairing things if they don't work—I'm used to attaching longevity to pieces of hardware. With digital, there's less serviceability. If it doesn't work, bin it—just throw it away. Everything is unitized.

MM: So we shouldn't focus on technology! Some great music's been recorded on dictation machines.

THE AUTHOR: And that brings us full circle back to Edison.

ALIASING

Distortion in a digital waveform due to difficulties in processing higher frequencies. As in digital photography, it is removed by means of an anti-aliasing filter.

COMPRESSION/ COMPRESSORS (AUDIO)

Compression packs a signal into a smaller dynamic space. Compressors work by lowering a signal's transient peaks—the higher the peaks, the more they are packed into a tighter space. Modern pop production uses compressors heavily on vocals. Not because modern vocalists are too powerful, one suspects, but because compression makes quiet vocal passages seem much louder. It evens out a performance, sometimes to the point of making it sound unnatural. A related device is the limiter, which sets a threshold on the dynamic level of signal it will allow through.

DAC

Digital to analog convertor. The component in any digital audio device, such as a CD player or your PC, which converts the digital stream of bits into analog, changes in voltage that your speakers turn back into soundwaves. In cheap soundcards, the DAC can be noisy or hissy. As a result, it is better to have a sophisticated 16-bit card than a cheap 24-bit one. An A/D convertor turns analog data into a stream of bits. Home studio, USB-based A/D convertors are cheap and commonplace, operating at 96 kHz to 24-bit.

DITHERING

Intelligent reduction of the bit rate of an audio file by adding small amounts of white noise (noise that covers the entire frequency spectrum). Apogee UV22HR dithering is a standard dithering process adopted by Cubase SX and other audio production software.

PCM

Pulse code modulation, the uncompressed data format used in most standard digital audio file types. Standards body the Audio Engineering Society (www.aes.org) recommends a sampling frequency of 48 kHz for the origination, processing, and interchange of audio programs employing PCM, but recognizes 44.1-kHz sampling rates.

SIGNAL TO NOISE (RATIO), OR S/N

The gap between the strength of the signal and the noise floor. A higher signal-to-noise ratio is best, as noise is less noticeable. S/N is measured in decibels.

TOTAL HARMONIC DISTORTION (THD)

Absolute tape saturation or circuit overload. Three percent THD is the point at which tape saturation or circuit overload introduces audible distortion. Three percent THD is measured in the number of decibels above 0 dB at which this distortion occurs, normally using a 1-kHz (mid-range) reference signal. The gap between 0 dB and 3 percent THD on any recorder or audio format is called its headroom, while the gap between the noise floor and 3 percent THD is its overall dynamic range.

CHANNEL TWO

MATCHING NEEDS TO TECHNOLOGIES

02.01

Surprisingly in a book about digital audio, this is the most important question to ask before you embark on any audio or music project. The answer lies in three further questions.

First and foremost is the simple one: what are you trying to achieve? Next, what is your work's destination: theater, video, radio, CD, DVD, MP3, website, video game, animation, or all of the above? And finally, is it intended to synchronize with other elements, be imported into other programs, or exist independently of other content?

There are several basic approaches to bringing digital audio and music-making into a home studio setup, and making original audio recordings.

■ First is what we might call the "studio in the computer," in which you seize your computer's compelling price, storage, processing power, and space-saving advantages to build a virtual studio within its four beige walls.

■ Second is the computer in the studio, in which your Mac, desktop PC, or high-end laptop becomes the main component of a hybrid audio setup, linked to dedicated audio, music, and MIDI hardware. In this kind of setup, you might consider including an external controller hardware, linked to your preferred software package.

Such controllers, for example Digidesign's Mbox, Digi 001, and Digi 002 for Pro Tools LE, give audio production software a friendly face—or more accurately, an external interface with some analog-style knobs and sliders. These mean you can interact with your recording system more like a human being and less like a mouse-operator. We'll also look at the pros and cons of virtual mixers and instruments versus their hardware counterparts.

PART 02. MATCHING NEEDS
TO TECHNOLOGIES

CHAPTER ONE

DO I NEED A COMPUTER?

SOFTWARE VERSUS INTEGRATED STUDIO SOLUTIONS

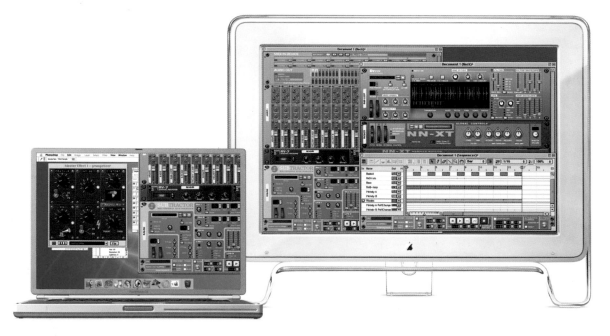

Left: While notebook screens are becoming bigger all the time, you will need a separate monitor to get the most on-screen "real estate" for all those digital components.

■ Third is the networked studio, where the advanced user might be running two or three computers, dedicated hardware, a portable integrated studio device (sometimes called a digital audio workstation, or DAW), and any number of other digital and analog devices. These devices might be linked by audio or MIDI across USB, M-Lan, or FireWire protocols.

■ Fourth, there's the high-end portable integrated studio. As the name suggests, these hardware devices are complete digital recording studios in a box, the highly evolved offspring of the cassette-based portastudios of the 1970s and 80s. Some hardware manufacturers like Korg, Yamaha, Roland, Akai, and Boss refer to their machines as DAWs (digital audio workstations), while software companies such as BIAS and Steinberg also call their products DAWs. In either case, it avoids using the less flattering acronym "PIS."

Below: **The Akai DPS24 is an excellent all-in-one option that may cost you a little more than a computer, but which offers frequent updates to its software and firmware.**

Analog is everything that's going on outside the box.

Marco Migliari

Above: **If you already own a computer, but you want to add a portable integrated studio (to use as a mixing desk, for example), be absolutely certain that the model you plan to purchase will interface directly with your system.**

Portable studios give you all the rollercoaster digital attractions of uncompressed 16-, 24-, or 32-bit audio, multi-Gigabyte storage capacities, cut and paste, and intuitive audio software, all presented in a self-contained unit. It does one thing: multitrack CD-quality audio, without leaving you riding the bumper cars of a computer's drivers, interfaces, glitches, and latency problems.

But most importantly, portable studios throw in an integrated mixing desk complete with faders and parametric EQ. On many midrange to top-quality machines, you might also find one or more expandable digital effects boards, offering reverbs, delays, other effects, and professional standard input compression. Turn to page 162 for more.

However, integrated studios' built-in software may be impossible to update, and your new machine may or may not interface directly with a computer. Low-end devices may also lack a digital I/O (input/output), a major design flaw on some budget machines.

In a home studio setup where you are already running a Mac or PC, having an additional midrange portable studio to hand can be a real benefit to audio work, especially in music composition.

You can use it in place of a mixing desk to route and equalize audio signals before they hit your soundcard, trim levels, add more effect and compression options, and, of course, record several gigabytes' worth of audio.

It's also reassuring to have an interface with real panpots, switches, and sliders, rather than a virtual one that forces you to make fine adjustments onscreen with a

Above: **Hot on the trail of some very popular four-track Minidisk (MD) recorders comes the Yamaha MD8, an eight-track version. Merging the convenience of random access with portability makes this a good choice if you want to use MDs. However, data minidisks can be expensive and unreliable.**

mouse. And, like any mixing desk, it's an interface that allows you to group complex audio feeds into a single stereo signal. In other words, it feels like "proper recording," and hardware like this can be a useful stepping stone towards understanding how professional studios work. But once you have invested in a standalone solution, you have effectively locked yourself into a way of working.

For a portable integrated studio, you can expect to pay anything from a mid-three-figure sum up to the same price as a fully-fledged multimedia PC or Mac. However, for a couple of hundred dollars you could pick up a "pocket studio" four-track machine that records onto removable 32 MB–128 MB SmartMedia cards.

Some of these budget microstudios offer incredible value in the form of built-in reverb, compressors, and other digital effects. They're great for sketching ideas on the road, or location recording (within the limitations of the media). They could be an ideal addition to your arsenal, if not perhaps your weapon of choice.

So, if you decide to go for a portable integrated studio, then you need to track down your local (rock) musical instrument store, or a specialist studio supplier. Shops like this might seem cramped, noisy, and occasionally intimidating, but they are usually staffed by people who want to be there. Ask their advice, and you'll quickly find someone who knows what they're talking about and their knowledge is very helpful—however young they might seem.

- ■ "Flying"/motorized faders—they're far from essential, but having flying faders means that your mixer will set itself up automatically for each song, moving each fader to its correct position in the mix
- ■ At least 10 GB of onboard storage—go for 20, 40, or more if you can afford it
- ■ An integral CD-R/CD-RW drive

NB: Mixers are usually described using a set of numbers, such as "16: 8: 2," or "24: 8: 2." This means that, in the first example, your mixer can handle 16 separate channels of audio, route them into eight mono groups (or four stereo groups), and then into two channels of stereo on final mixdown.

THE DAWS OF PERCEPTION?

What to look for in a portable integrated studio.

Whether you are using it in place of a computer, or alongside your desktop or laptop in a home studio setup, select from features such as these:

- ■ **24-bit, 96 kHz recording. Many machines give you the option to record either eight tracks to 24-bit, or 16 tracks to 44.1 or 48 kHz 16-bit to economize on processing and storage**
- ■ **At least one built-in effects board. You may find your model is expandable up to four effects boards**
- ■ **Input compression and limiting as standard—allowing you to record vocals professionally, without using up effects from the main board**
- ■ **Virtual tracks—these allow you to store alternative takes of each track**
- ■ **COSM mike modeling—a filtering system that emulates the dynamic signature of a range of top-quality professional microphones**
- ■ **Three- or four-band parametric EQ—explore all those frequencies in the mix**
- ■ **A range of digital and analog outputs—eg S/PDIF**
- ■ **A number of effects Sends and Returns—these are your routes to and from external signal processors**

Above: The Yamaha AW16G allows you to record 16 tracks of audio to the internal hard drive, then burn it to CD using the built-in CD-RW drive. Importantly, it is magnetically shielded, so you can use it alongside your regular computer system without a danger of electromagnetic interference from computer monitors or speakers.

Right: Digidesign's Mbox is an inexpensive add-on for your desktop or notebook if you want a reliable means to record 24-bit stereo audio from any type of source, such as guitars or microphones. With a copy of Pro Tools LE included, it is a worthwhile option for beginners, hobbyists, and even professionals. Singer Craig David uses one.

ANALOG VERSUS DIGITAL

**REAL WORLD TECHNICAL MANAGER GEOFF PRYCE;
CHIEF ENGINEER MARCO MIGLIARI;
STUDIO MANAGER OWEN LEECH**

GP: It's vital to remember that digital is not "a technology." When you talk about digital, you are really talking about storage media—and they're all different. Analog tape colors the sound in an aesthetically pleasing way. On analog, the frequency range is pretty much infinite. In the digital world you need petabytes of data before it's indistinguishable from the "real thing." But a sampling rate of 384 kHz and a 24-bit word length is a good approximation of audio vérité.

OL: Analog is like osmosis, but digital is archeology. It's a very serious point if you're considering mixing a track in a professional studio. When a musician does preproduction work on tape before coming into the studio, you can just put the tape on and see what you've got. But with Pro Tools or any audio production system, you have to spend days sifting through all the data.

MM: PCs are the cheapest way to record. They're also a fantastic way to make your product more powerful. But with audio it's crucial to go back to basics. It's not just about "computers in bedrooms." Analog is everything that's going on outside the box—literally.

Also on offer in your local music equipment store will be a variety of digital recorders, which record either onto an internal hard drive, or onto a removable format—CD, MD, DAT, and even S-VHS tapes in the case of "ADAT" machines. ADATs are popular eight-track digital tape recorders manufactured by the Alesis Corporation, and still popular in studios today.

Multitrack recorders like the ADAT allow you to overdub separate tracks of digital audio. They can be useful if you don't want to fill up your computer with audio files, or take a valuable laptop or sampler on the road. ADATs have the advantage of being modular. Linking two will give you 16 tracks, and three will give you 24 tracks, and so on.

But these days, of course, you can take your studio on the road simply by packing your laptop. Be prepared, however, to lose your studio forever if you take your eye off it and head for the bar. (This happens even in the IT world. The CEO of intellectual property company Qualcomm once lost his laptop at a security conference. The person who ended up with it effectively held the entire company in his hand. The technical term for this is a "multiple irony.")

If you're interested in making digital recordings on the move and want to know what kind of recorder or device to go for, we'll look at the options in more detail on page 84.

But ultimately, if you do want to post or broadcast your audio on the Web, add audio to video in Premiere, Avid, Final Cut Pro, Logic 6, Cubase, BIAS Deck, and Cool Edit Pro, or synchronize it with Flash animations, then a computer is indispensable, regardless of how you record or multitrack the audio to begin with.

So, let's start making some choices about working methods, hardware, software, and technology environment.

DIGITAL VERSUS ANALOG What, then, are the unique advantages of working digitally as opposed to working in analog space? Let's look at them one by one before deciding which type of solution—purely digital or hybrid, computer software- or integrated studio-based—works best for you.

THE DIGITAL ADVANTAGE
Cost and space

While computers and other digital audio equipment are not cheap, sophisticated audio-editing technology is within the range of most people's pockets. The march (or sprint) of technology generations means that yesterday's leading-edge solutions might be today's trash, so you can always pick up a bargain.

But as we've already seen, storage, memory, and processing power are resources that are plentiful enough to waste, so high-end computing is cheaper than we imagined would be possible five, ten, or 20 years ago. Go for it if you can. Few could have imagined even ten years ago that 24-track digital studios would find their way into thousands of homes.

If you opt for a computer-centric studio, or a completely virtual studio on your desktop or laptop, then the more powerful your computer, the better. Ignore Windows, Mac, or Linux "minimum" requirements, and go for "recommended," or higher.

And if your computer is dedicated to audio or music work, then you will encounter far fewer problems than if you're sharing space with office tasks or graphics work. We'll look at why later in the chapter.

But whatever your preference, quality digital recording technology is far cheaper and more commonplace than studio-quality analog equipment.

Above: **Your digital studio could be a single computer, or a series of linked digital components with or without a computer. These days, high-end processing, memory, and storage are relatively cheap, so you should invest in the most powerful gear you can afford. Shown here is a Pro Tools control surface.**

Below: Analog recording is still an option for many styles of music, and it is offered in many studios, but it is no longer really a cost-effective or realistic solution for the home-based studio.

PRODUCTION TIPS: JOHN LECKIE

REAL WORLD TECHNICAL MANAGER, GEOFF PRYCE

John's approach is never to bust zero. Never let the meter go into the red. Don't slam it: be conservative. You get a better sound by not thrashing it. The headroom will be good, and noise will be low. And, you know, John gets a pretty good sound!

WHY DO PEOPLE RAVE ABOUT ANALOG RECORDING?

The real world is analog. As Marco Migliari says, at the end of the day everything is analog; we couldn't hear it otherwise. At the high professional end, analog recording is at least as good as digital, if not superior (as many of our spokespeople believe).

The important thing to remember, then, is that digital is not "better" than analog, but it is quantifiably different. More specifically, it presents a unique set of choices and opportunities.

For home recording, there's no contest: it has to be digital. While many home-based musicians still praise the warmth and responsiveness of multitracking onto analog tape, they almost certainly lack the means to do it. The gulf between digital and analog is far wider in audio than it is in other technologies—particularly photography, where each discipline is as accessible as the other.

Indeed, it's a fair bet that the same people who have bemoaned the rise of digital technologies since the 1980s, have never possessed an analog recorder more sophisticated than a personal stereo or a cassette deck. So, it's a case of put up, or shut up.

True, a high percentage of rock music is still multitracked to tape, but it is usually mixed down and mastered onto a digital medium, such as DAT, long before it leaves the studio. And the chances of laying your hands on the unmixed 24 track tape are zero—it'll either be wiped and reused by the studio, or your record company owns it. Whichever way, you lose.

So, however noble your analog objectives might be (however much you might want to honor where you've come from), you still have no control over how your work will be consumed.

Even if your audience shares your principles, it almost certainly lacks the technology to respect them. But that is not to dismiss analog recording, or the thousands of devotees who rave about the authentic 1960s "analog sound" pumping from their CD players.

A pure analog solution of multitracking onto two-inch tape, producing a stereo half-inch mixed master, mastering this professionally in a mastering suite, then taking the result to a vinyl pressing plant, is not really an option for the home recordist.

DJ CULTURE Ironically, the people who have kept vinyl alive—dance music acts and DJs—are usually working the system in reverse: recording and mastering the track digitally, then pressing it to analog. But either is a valid approach, and you'll find a great deal of expertise locked up in those vaults of analog technologies.

Real World's Marco Migliari believes that people who leap straight into digital frequently have scant knowledge of sound or engineering principles, and might even be proud of that fact. "A lot of 'deep knowledge' is being lost in the rush to digital; there's a glossing over of the basics, an over-simplification. Just thinking that audio is about computers is dangerous: it makes for soulless sound and takes away from the performance."

Migliari accepts, however, that when it comes to creativity and cost-effectiveness, digital is the only way to go. Analog can never be as cheap, practical, and efficient, as doing it digitally in the home—and you will remain a hostage to the studio's fortune, rather than be in a position to "do it yourself" for a fraction of the outlay.

But the real cost advantage of digital audio, of course, is the opportunity to boil a roomful of dusty, depreciating hardware down to a few thousand lines of code that sit invisibly on your hard drive.

Below: **A major consideration in going digital is the ability to save space by using a computer instead of a roomful of big hardware components.**

If your computer has five years' life in it before the temptation to upgrade becomes irresistible or simply practical, then you can upgrade your studio as many times as you wish without upgrading your computer—at a tenth of the cost of replacing all that hardware.

CUT AND PASTE

All software-only recording solutions, such as Cubase SX/SL and Cubase 5 VST (page 100), Logic (page 100), Cool Edit Pro (page 115), Ableton Live (page 114), Reason (page 110), Deck (page 115), ACID-PRO (page 108), Cakewalk SONAR, Making Waves, Spark, or MOTU Digital Performer (see also Pro Tools, page 118), offer one killer application. That is, the graphical representations of every single aspect of your audio recording, right down to each event, every control, every waveform and effect, and every input and output.

This means that, like every pixel in a digital image, every event in a digital audio recording can be individually addressed, cut, pasted, cloned, edited, sampled, stretched, and filtered. Its relation to every other element, or group of elements, can likewise be shifted, shuffled, enhanced, or destroyed to your heart's content.

As you might imagine, these processes are known as "destructive editing," which irreversibly changes the integrity of the original signal, and "non-destructive editing," which does not.

Below: While dance music acts usually create music almost entirely digitally, the analog vinyl format has endured due to the turntable-based mixing techniques used by club DJs. You can even DJ now on your PlayStation! But vinyl's dominance is weakening now, as digital turntable emulators are sounding more realistic than ever. For DJs, a major benefit of switching to computer files from 12-inch singles is the ability to shed the weight of a full record bag!

If the event is a purely "digital" one—a MIDI "note on" event (see page 124 onward), or an instruction to trigger a sample—then it can, to all intents and purposes, be transformed into a completely different, unrelated event, or dragged to a new location.

Most integrated studio devices also offer this same cut-and-paste, graphical killer application, usually via a built-in LCD touch-screen, or similar.

Some top-of-the-range models allow you to bolt on a VGA monitor and work with a mouse, so the experience becomes similar to using a Windows PC or a Mac, albeit with a different interface and logic. Many high-end machines also interface with digital video cameras, and external editors such as your PC.

Modular recording software and hardware suites, such as Digidesign's legendary Pro Tools, offer the best of both ways of working, but lock you into an upgrade path and a slightly different technical environment.

That said, they can work with and beneath other audio-production software environments, such as Logic Platinum. But you may find this level of sophistication is far beyond your needs. Thankfully, Pro Tools is available in a cut-down "LE" version.

Obviously, the key is never to lose sight of what you are trying to achieve with your virtual landscape or portrait in sound. We'll talk about stereo images, ambiences, mixes, and so on throughout the course of this book.

That said, the cut-and-paste advantage also encourages play. For many people, play, fun, and experimentation are the fastest routes to learning. Don't underestimate them.

In particular, virtual studio packages such as Reason 2 (page 110), and simple PC sequencing packages like Making Waves are great fun to play with, and you can work out their logic after just a few minutes of play.

On the other hand, the "big" packages such as Logic Platinum, Logic, Cubase can take weeks of experimentation to second-guess—without looking at the instruction manual. It is unfortunate, but it is true: you *are* going to have to read the directions in the manual.

NON-LINEARITY

Despite being timeline-based, with the timeline usually broken down into musical bars or timeframes, software-based audio editing is not a linear process; the audio resides in RAM, and sometimes even in ROM. This means you don't have to spool through untold feet of tape to locate the first beat in a bar; you can jump to a locator point or mark instantly. This also means you can swap out sounds, samples, loops, and submixes and replace them with new content—without having to record new audio information.

More, you can marquee select a whole section of audio, across as many audio or MIDI tracks as you wish, move it somewhere else, or duplicate it and paste it into a different piece of work. In fact, you could edit a five-minute music composition down to three-and-a-half minutes in half as much time again.

Using software like this, a purely digital methodology becomes more about assembly, and less about performance. Video-makers know this, which is why for them an edit *is* the performance.

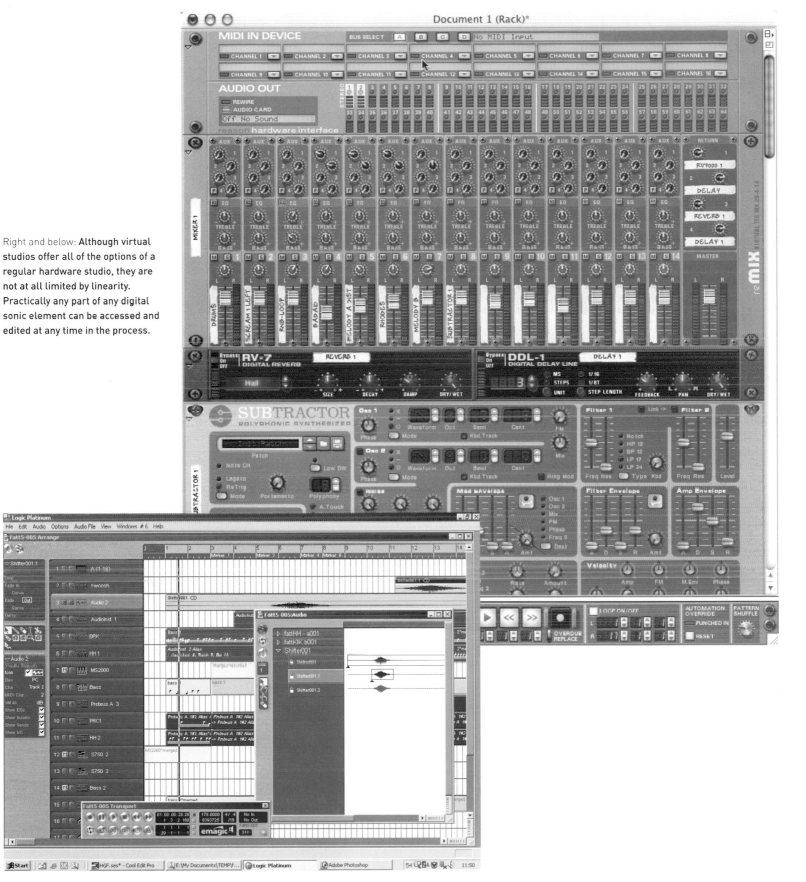

Right and below: **Although virtual studios offer all of the options of a regular hardware studio, they are not at all limited by linearity. Practically any part of any digital sonic element can be accessed and edited at any time in the process.**

THE STUDIO THAT FORGOT TIME... The denizens of analog facility Toe Rag Studios in London's East End are not Luddites or eccentrics rejecting the digital age. Far from it. By setting out to limit their technology options, they return recording to an age where it is solely about capturing one performance in one space on one day. Bands rehearse, spend most of their time setting up a sound, then recording and mixing takes place very swiftly.

It's the brainchild of white-coat-clad boffin Liam Watson, who has designed his baby around 1960s gear abandoned by studios like Abbey Road. It's a strategy that's met with success, as acts like Billy Childish, the White Stripes, and other "back to basics" groups now call it home.

Watson limits his capability to eight-track tape, and as much valve-run kit as he can lay his hands on. "Sometimes I get managers of big bands or record companies phoning up because they've heard some recording I've done and they like it. Then they ask me how many tracks I've got. I say 'eight,' and that's the end of the conversation."

In the digital realm, the multitrack separation of, for example, individual drums in a kit, encourages an assumption that you can fix any performance in the mix later on, rather than record a good sound at source.

Even for the most ardent digital fan, there is a lot to be said for Toe Rag's challenge to the cut-and-paste orthodoxy. Digital code might not decay like magnetic flux, but spontaneity and inspiration atrophy if you obsess about detail, plug-ins, and upgrades to the exclusion of all else—such as getting it right the first time.

The creative audio- and music-maker should beware of joining what Laurie Anderson calls the technology "arms race" and losing track of their peace of mind, or of spending so much time faking something that they might as well have bought the real thing.

So, if you want to go the digital-only virtual studio route, then make each edit and your production job the performance of your life. Be the conductor of your virtual musicians, samplers, and effects boards with every sweep of your mouse. (If this sounds pretentious, then you haven't tried it yet.)

PLUG AND PLAY

One of the great sound-engineering proverbs (apart from "If you can't fix it, make it loud") is: "Whenever two leads are gathered together in one place, they shall form a tangle."

Anyone who has spent hours on their hands and knees with a soldering iron trying to track down a loose connection and fix it, run feet of audio cable behind furniture, work out what dozens of different sockets are for, and then find the "On" button, appreciates software that self-installs. (Ah, if it were only that simple!)

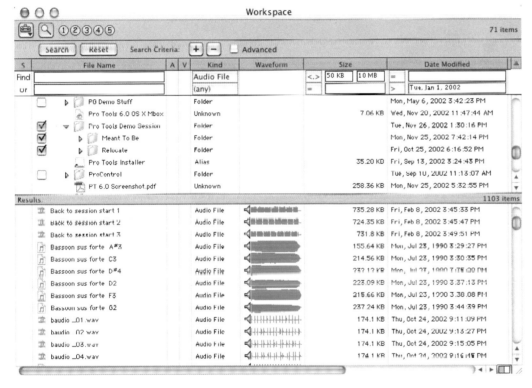

Above: **Most digital audio software has the capacity to provide a listing of all original files and a comprehensive, usable version history at a level of detail unmatched by the analog process.**

AUDIT TRAIL

Digital audio provides you with an audit trail that analog technology can never match. For example, most big audio production packages like Cubase SX and Logic create workfiles for you, into which the software automatically saves samples, WAVs, and other elements of your work.

PCs and Macs (and Linux machines running interfaces like Nautilus) are designed from the ground up to manage files and to allow you to interact with graphic representations of your data.

So, get your work organized into file hierarchies: work in progress, sound patches, samples, VST plug-ins, MIDI files, audio elements, and so on. Back these up onto CD by project, and/or by date, and save all the elements of each song as you go.

Marco Migliari adds: "A good tool is one that's an extension of yourself. It's absolutely vital that you start organizing your work early on."

Working this way allows you to backtrack and recompile your work into its original form, or break it down and remix it from the ground up. There are no limits except in your imagination: remember, it's not about achievement, it's about concept.

But back in the physical world...

Wherever you stand in the debate, you will almost certainly need some analog (true audio) input, unless you intend to work solely in simulated space, in which case jump to the sections on virtual studio software (see page 110), virtual instruments and effects (page 138), realtime sequencing instruments (page 114), and ambiences and acoustics (in Channel Three, page 150).

But remember sound engineer Marco Migliari's words: "Analog is everything that's going on outside the box—literally."

Here are some common problems, together with just a few solutions from the hundreds of competing options out there. Turn to pages 100–140 for in-depth analysis of the software.

Remember: this is by no means an exhaustive hardware or software guide. There are dozens of main audio and MIDI sequencing applications, and several hundred smaller applications and plug-ins. All of the main applications, and some of the smaller ones, have lengthy, in-depth books written about them. But you are better served by keeping your eye on digital audio magazines for more up-to-date information. Check out their websites too. All are excellent at offering advice and building like-minded communities of users. They are all highly recommended.

MATCHING SOLUTIONS TO NEEDS

I have a desktop computer, but I want to record quality audio on the move, such as interviews, ambient sounds, location reports, and so on. I just want to press Record, and go.

OPTION ONE

You could consider replacing your desktop with a laptop. This would enable you to run Logic, Cubase SX, Cool Edit Pro (PC), or BIAS Deck (Mac or PC)—plus an external A/D convertor and audio interface, such as the Apogee Mini-Me. This will allow you to capture audio from the big, wide analog world out there and turn it into data that your computer can process and then store.

**PART 02. MATCHING
NEEDS TO TECHNOLOGIES**

CHAPTER TWO

HELP ME, I WANT TO...

Left: **Expensive audio production units are not only impractical for location recording, but the risk of damage to these expensive components is simply too great.**

Alternately, your Mac OS X or Windows XP laptop could run Pro Tools LE, and use Digidesign's Mbox external control surface. The Mbox also works with earlier Mac iterations and previous generations of Pro Tools. If you want this level of functionality (and it's highly recommended), go for the Mac environment, as Digidesign and Apple are collaborating on high-profile product releases. In a PC-centric world, such a public relationship can only be taken as a statement of intent and a mutual badge of quality assurance.

Either way, just plug an omnidirectional mike into the XLR socket of the Mini-Me or Mbox (use directional mike for interviews), monitor through headphones, and you're away. If you can afford it, invest in a pair of mikes for stereo recording. A good microphone will always be a solid investment. After all, it is your link to the real world. No amount of mike modeling and EQ will compensate for inferior input. Think of your mike as being the audio equivalent of a high-quality lens on a camera.

Both the Mini-Me and Mbox have two XLR inputs, and the devices connect to your laptop via the USB port. (Remember, do not buy a laptop for audio work unless it has at least two USB ports.)

Simpler packages such as Cool Edit Pro or BIAS Deck are probably easiest to use in location environments, as long as you use an external A/D convertor to get the sound onto your

Above and below: **For location recording, remember that you will have to consider your power source. Any external A/D converters will need to be powered through the USB port—as opposed to a wall outlet—so you will have to keep a careful eye on your notebook battery.**

laptop. But remember, the "big" packages are also available in cut-down versions, such as Logic Gold and Cubasis.

Far from being frustrating peripherals, A/D convertors and mike pre-amps such as the Mini-Me and Mbox add an extra level of control to your software, plus valuable checks and balances in terms of input level.

There are several 24-bit, 96 kHz A/D convertors out there in the budget price bracket, such as M-Audio's Duo, but they are not all suitable for location work, as most of them require an external power source. Both the Mini-Me and the Mbox are powered up via the USB port and your laptop—so keep an eye on your battery life!

OPTION TWO

If location recording is the primary source of your digital audio work, and onscreen editing is not a realistic option, you could opt for a dedicated audio recorder. Many professional journalists and broadcasters—when they are not linked directly to the studio via a broadband connection—still use DAT recorders. (Never underestimate the advantage of a tape recorder's moving parts. Being able to see the machinery of your digital recorder working is a boon in a face-to-face interview.)

You could also consider purchasing a portable integrated studio or microstudio, but bear in mind the time limitations imposed by using SmartMedia cards or MDs in budget models.

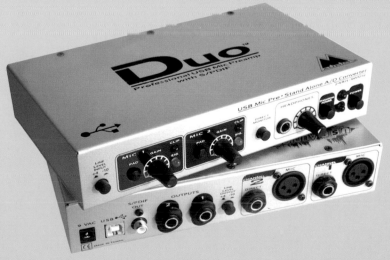

I'm a guitarist, and I find it difficult to record my electric or acoustic guitars onto my computer. It's impossible to monitor what I'm doing, and the sound quality is usually disappointing.

OPTIONS

First the electric. Rather than mike up your amp in a home studio setup, consider buying a "direct box," such as the Pod, by Line6. Devices like this emulate the acoustic signatures of a range of classic guitar amplifier and speaker cabinet combinations, and are designed to sit between your guitar and your PC, or digital multitracker. The Pod v3.0 connects your guitar to your computer via USB. Earlier versions need the intervention of an A/D convertor.

But you don't have to go for a hardware solution. As you might imagine, virtual direct boxes and amp simulators are commonplace too. At the time of writing, IK Multimedia's Amplitube is first among equals. Like many task-specific software tools, it works either in standalone mode, or as a VST or Pro Tools HTDM plug-in (see Jargon buster, page 91).

You can try either approach with an acoustic guitar as well. But to get a better source recording from an acoustic, try close-miking it near the sound hole and recording it onto three audio channels—panned to nine o'clock, 12 o'clock, and three o'clock—to create a wider spread of sound at greater amplitude. Then try adding compression to the center channel, and subtle reverb to both of the wide channels. This is a subjective solution.

If you're still not happy with the results, consider recording the room sound as well with a pair of mikes, then mixing all of the results together. As ever, there is no "correct" solution—experiment until you hear something that makes you smile.

Above: **If you use "virtual amplifier" software to add distortion or other effects to a recorded guitar track, make sure you have a full-sounding, clean recording in the first place. Otherwise, you will find the plug-in algorithm does not have enough sound to work with; remember, no amount of EQ tweaking can invent sounds that aren't there.**

I'm a non-musician, but I love music, especially dance music, and I want to play with loops and beats in real time, and do some mixing on the fly. Then I want to save off my work, share it, and perhaps try my hand at performing in a club environment.

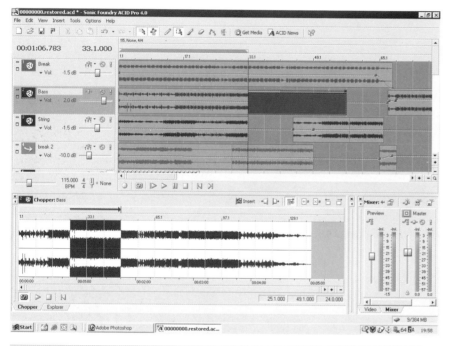

OPTIONS

You're very well served by the market—and by the future direction of live music and clubbing. ACID PRO and Ableton Live (see pages 108 and 114) allow you to drop in loops, then time-stretch and beat-match them in real time. Ableton Live in particular is aimed at the "laptop jam" scene, where DJs and sample-based bands network their laptops together and jam in real time.

All the beats and loops you need are available commercially, online, or via cover-mounted CDs. Making your own loops is easy, once you've got the hang of it—and there are dozens of communities of like-minded people out there for you to join.

For more musically-minded people, Reason (which you'll find links well with Ableton Live) is the most accessible of the "virtual studio" packages. It includes a raft of pre-prepared loops and samples, which can be topped up by visiting www.reasonsrefills.com, and similar sites (do a Google search).

At the lower end of the sequencer market, Making Waves is a budget package that is as simple as dropping icons onto a timeline and pressing "Play." At the opposite end of the market, packages like Pro Tools LE and Logic Audio now have the DJ market in their sights.

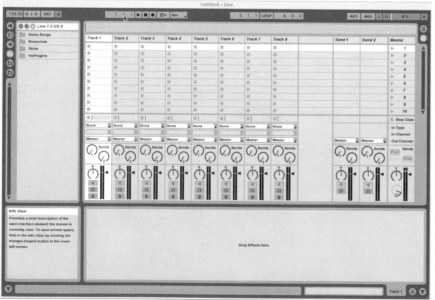

Left: **Both Mac and Windows users who want to perform live sets with laptops are well served by programs such as Sonic Foundry Acid or Ableton Live, but you will need a powerful processor, plenty of memory, and a fast hard drive.**

part 02. matching needs to technologies

I'm not a musician at all, but I have a digital video camera, and I want to play around with audio in a video environment, and maybe publish the results on the Web, or onto DVD. I'm not a professional—I just want to have fun.

Right: BIAS software packages serve the budget end of the Macintosh market, and are more than suitable for merging sound with video.

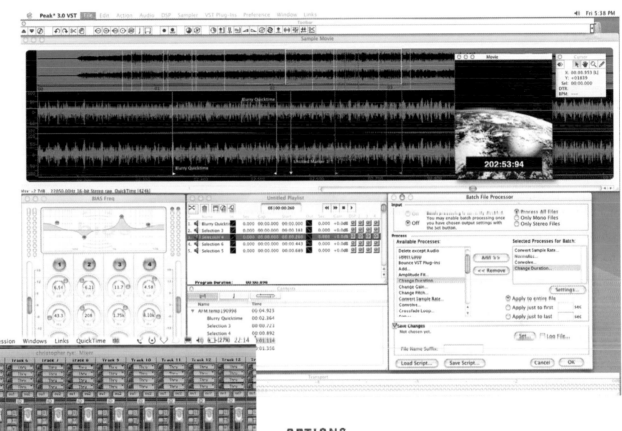

OPTIONS

As technologies converge, you are increasingly well served by both the budget and professional ends of the market. At the budget end, both BIAS Deck and Cool Edit Pro assume that you may be dealing with video as well as audio elements.

But among the "pro" packages, Logic Audio has perhaps made the biggest moves toward a fully integrated audiovisual environment. Its Video Thumbnail track shows thumbnails of your video feed at key stages within the Arrange window. In Mac OS X, both Steinberg's Cubase SX and Nuendo offerings allow you to output a QuickTime movie via FireWire.

JARGON BUSTER
AUDIO/DATA INTERFACES AND DRIVERS

ASIO

(PC/Mac) Audio Streaming Input/Output. A Steinberg-developed soundcard driver with low latency times. An extremely powerful and reliable system for software synthesis that sits outside the operating system. Recommended, and supported by most sequencers and soft synths. Use it if you can.

AVOPTION

This is Digidesign's Plug-and-Play compatible, two-card interface that enables the importing of video and audio from high-end Avid video workstations, or any NTSC or PAL sources such as video tape, directly into a Pro Tools video track on a Windows or Mac OS system.

CAKEWALK DXI

(PC) DirectX Instrument. Plug-in interface for soft synths based on Microsoft's DirectX architecture, currently supported only by Cakewalk's SONAR audio production package. Allows routing of MIDI tracks, realtime control of synths, and so on. (See DirectX.)

DIRECTCONNECT

(Mac) Digidesign, maker of the Pro Tools software suite and its associated hardware interfaces, developed this data interface for the Mac (let's call it a dataface) to stream audio directly into the Pro Tools environment. Allows up to 32 separate channels from a soft synth or sampler to be independently routed and mixed in Pro Tools.

DIRECTSOUND

(PC) Microsoft-developed driver for Windows 98 onwards, that is often regarded as causing problems with certain soundcards at low buffer settings. If you are experiencing audio glitches or dropouts, this may be the problem—or you may need to change your latency time or buffer settings to compensate.

DIRECTX

(PC) Microsoft plug-in standard, which allows DirectX plug-ins, such as effects modules and soft instruments, to run in the host application. However, as is sometimes the case with Microsoft initiatives, the standard has been muddied by proprietary versions, such as Cakewalk's DXi—which will not run in Cubase, for example. Non-proprietary DirectX plug-ins will run in any compatible host application, including Cubase. Needs DirectX Support.

FREEMIDI AND MAS

(Mac) Two standards developed by MOTU (Mark of the Unicorn) for its Digital Performer audio production software. MAS (MOTU Audio System) allows audio routing from a soft synth into Performer's mixing environment, while FreeMIDI allows you to mix MIDI tracks from a soft synth within Performer.

MEDIAMANAGER

Avid Unity MediaManager is an "asset management suite" that allows production assistants to access and manage bits of digital media from any networked or Internet-ready computer, thanks to a browser-based interface. The Select version of the software manages video clips on a LAN (Local Area Network); both versions are available for Mac or Windows systems.

MIDI

(n/a) Musical Instrument Digital Interface. The lingua franca of digital music. 1980s-developed asynchronous serial protocol that allows compatible devices, including most hardware keyboards, synths, samplers, and signal processors, and many multitrack recorders and portable studios, to exchange musical and nonmusical instructions. Audio and MIDI sequencing applications and virtual studio packages accept and manage MIDI data, and allow you to control soft synths and other virtual instruments via an external keyboard.

Send Effect 1 - Karlette

Left: Virtual Studio Technology instruments—or VST instruments—are compatible with many major audio or music software packages. VST synthesizers can also often be used on their own, but the effects plug-ins are especially handy when mixing or mastering your work in a program such as Cubase or Logic. This one does a fair job of imitating an early tape delay.

MME

(PC) Microsoft standard wave driver for soundcards. Like DirectSound, it may cause problems with sophisticated virtual instruments.

QUICKTIME

(Mac) Apple's media player. This is mentioned here because you may find that your Mac defaults to QuickTime at every given opportunity when you are saving off work. Approach with care, unless you are dealing with multimedia files in Logic, or Cubase SX, where it will be your best friend.

SOUNDMANAGER

(Mac) The standard audio driver on all Macs—the Apple counterpart to MME and DirectSound. While a solid, swift, and reliable system, it might not be up to the task in a very high-end system dealing with ultra-low latency times.

VST Send Effects

TDM/HTDM

(Host) Time Division Multiplexing. The Digidesign architecture beneath its Pro Tools software and hardware environment (Mac/PC). The HTDM evolution allows compatible virtual instruments and plug-ins to be bolted onto the Pro Tools family. In the Mac OS X environment, non-TDM-compatible instruments may work with the use of the authorizing system iLok.

VST/VSTI

(Mac/PC) Virtual Studio Technology (Instrument). Arguably the main plug-in standard for effects and virtual instruments, supported by Steinberg (Cubase SX), Emagic (Logic Audio), and others. Soft synths can work as standalone instruments, but if they are VST-compatible, simply add them to the VST directory and they will appear as options in your VST-compatible host application. VST, DirectX, and HTDM have enabled audio production software to become fully integrated and expandable studio environments.

NB: Many software packages, especially soft(ware) synths and samplers, will run in most of the environments listed here. Check the packaging for details of what will and will not run with your main audio application.

02.03

Earlier in the book, we mentioned that the audio technology landscape is complex and hard to map. This is mainly because the access points to digital content are converging. The availability of cheap storage and fast processing means that your software can now offer you a single point of interaction with the worlds of sound, music, video, animation, broadcasting, and the Web.

A few years ago, it would have been easy to single out a simple MIDI sequencing package and music composition tool; a standalone audio recording program and editor; or a product that turned your off key dabblings into a professionally printed music score. Today, those distinctions are blurred. That same cheap storage and fast processing power mean that your PC or Mac can now realistically act as fully functional, 24-bit audio recorders, as well as manage all that MIDI and multimedia data that you might decide to throw at your work.

All bets are off, and into the mix the software industry has also thrown loop-based music creation tools, virtual studio packages, realtime sequencing programs, and virtual instruments. All of these products recognize that once audio has been digitized, it can be sliced, diced, output, and consumed in as many ways as there are digital devices. Your task is to find the package you are most comfortable with.

But first, the creative audio- or music-maker has to establish what it is that they are trying to achieve. Most software packages either lean more toward audio recording, editing, and management (perhaps with a limited MIDI facility), or more in the direction of music composition and/or MIDI sequencing. So the first thing to do is work out what suits your needs.

**PART 02. MATCHING
NEEDS TO TECHNOLOGIES**

CHAPTER THREE

SOFTWARE-ONLY SOLUTIONS

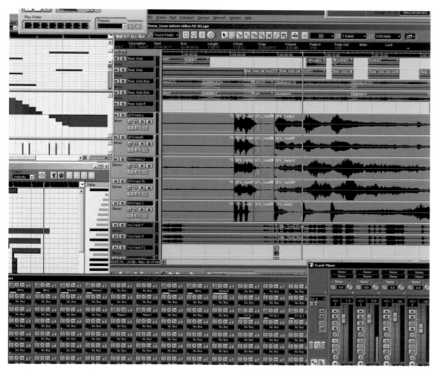

Left: **Nuendo is a good example of
a powerful, all-in-one recording,
mixing, mastering, and CD
production environment.**

A handful of programs, such as Logic Audio, Cubase, Pro Tools, and Cakewalk SONAR, offer all of these options and much, much more. Others do one thing, and do it brilliantly. Your first step therefore lies in deciding whether you are most interested in recording audio for audio's sake—and perhaps synchronizing it with video or animation—or whether you are primarily interested in writing and recording music, with or without any analog input from the outside world. (Remember, too, that audio-editing packages can still deal with music when it has been saved in an audio format.)

Your second choice is perhaps the more difficult one, as it involves deciding how far you want to progress in any of these areas. It's an important choice to make early on, as it means thinking about whether your technology needs to match the scale of your ambitions, or whether your ambitions will ever match the scale of the technology. If you go for a big,

Above: Cakewalk SONAR is a relatively new addition to the digital audio production market, and it is rising rapidly in popularity by offering good value for a relatively low price.

expensive piece of software or hardware, that choice will be hard to undo later on.

Some of the "all-in-one" programs offer far more than you will ever need if you just want to dabble and have fun. But if you want to record, mix, and professionally master complex audio or music compositions as just one element in a multimedia environment, then Logic Audio, Cubase, Nuendo, Pro Tools, MOTU Digital Performer, and Cakewalk SONAR exist for the very purpose of putting commercial CD and DVD production firmly in your hands. But what is a sequencer?

SEQUENCERS Sequencers' roots lie in the analog synthesizers of the 1960s and 1970s. Early synthesizers, like the suitcase-style VCS3, were really patchworks of oscillators and filters, which worked rather like old-fashioned analog telephone exchanges. The player—more accurately, the operator—connected oscillators or filters together by using a series of patch cables.

Those of you who have read the sections on sound, waveforms, and synthesis know that voltage, frequency, and pitch are interrelated in an analog process. Knowing this, it wasn't long before engineers in the late 1960s realized that a synthesizer's oscillators (its sound generators) could be triggered in a rhythmic or melodic sequence by routing timed voltage pulses into them. The first sequencers were born.

Today, the defining principle of sequencing lives on in the "arpeggiator" function of some hardware keyboards and synthesisers, where the player holds down a chord and the arpeggiator generates rhythmic sequences from the individual notes of the chord.

But as recording and music-making became digital in the 1980s, and GUI-based software became more sophisticated, the definition of sequencing gradually evolved. Today, sequencing mainly refers to the generation, recording, management, and editing of both audio events and MIDI events in a timeline-based software package.

That said, workstation keyboards, such as the Korg Triton range, contain basic MIDI sequencers that allow you to multitrack, arrange, and edit musical passages, but they offer a limited graphical representation of the information you record.

But what is a timeline?

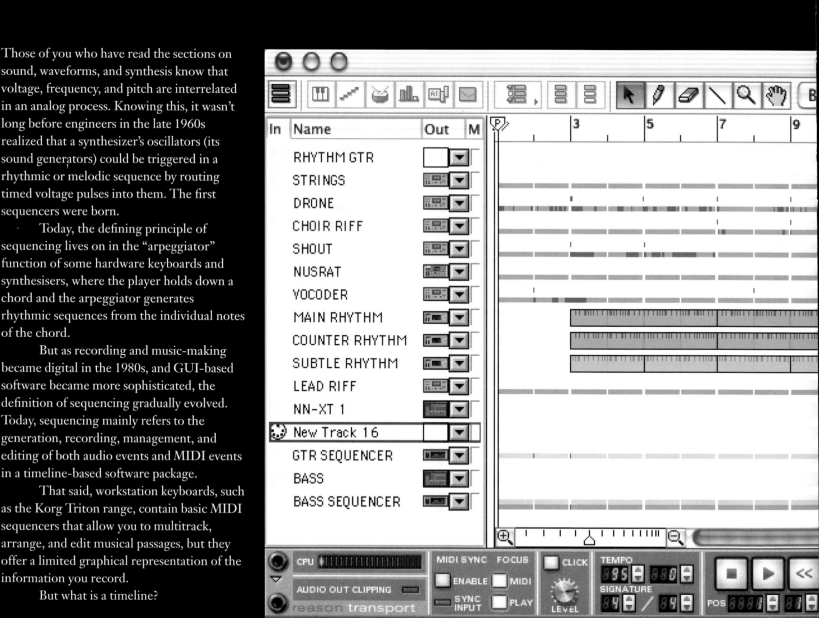

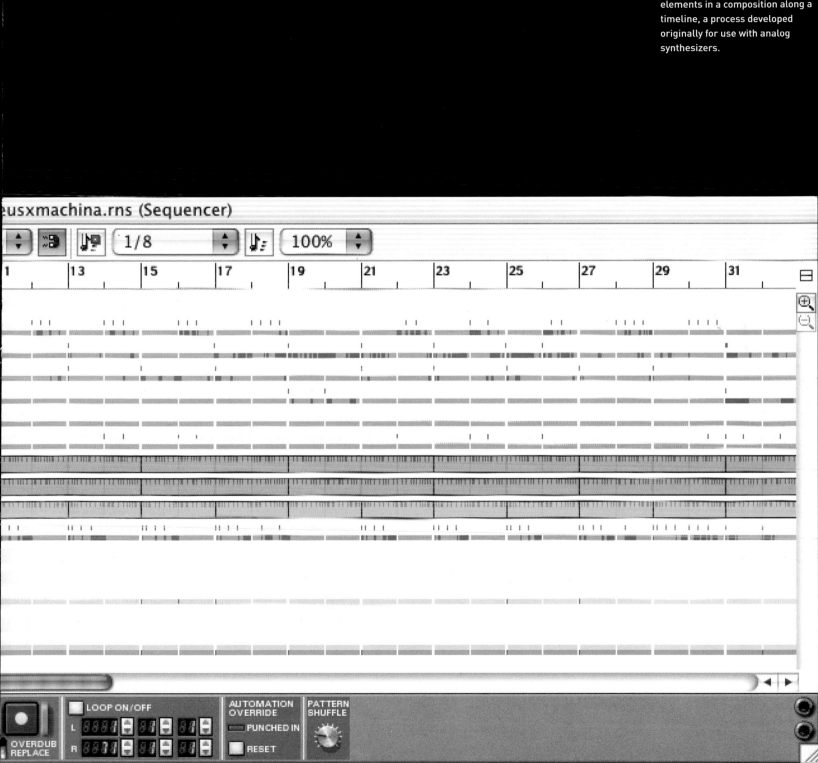

TIMELINES AND "ARRANGE" WINDOWS

All audio- and video-editing packages are based on the principle of the timeline, because audio and video content is defined by its duration, and by events that happen at every point during that duration. The timeline is a scrolling graphical track that enables you to view and interact with each and every event that you add to your work.

Assuming that there are four beats to the bar, we can calculate that in a 120-bpm (beats per minute) song, the default tempo of most sequencing programs, the cursor will move through 30 bars in one minute.

In audio-only software, and in sample-editing programs such as BIAS Peak, the default time division will be Min:sec:ms. However, you may also be given the option to view your audio files in divisions of frames per second (fps), which correspond with those used in video and film.

Common frame rates are 24fps (film), 25fps (PAL/SECAM), 29.97fps (NTSC), and 30fps (DVD players). Packages that allow you to edit music and sound to video clips or feeds, such as Pro Tools, BIAS Deck, and Logic Audio, give you the option of viewing your work in a variety of time divisions. Portable integrated studio devices work with both Min:sec:ms and with frames. Timelines in programs such as BIAS Peak also allow you to view the escalating number of samples that each track contains.

Uniquely, a timeline allows you to see, manage, and edit the events you have created before they are played back (or triggered) in real time, and to jump to events instantaneously—things that are impossible in any meaningful sense with analog technologies.

Timelines break down audio, video, and animation into time divisions: "this event happens here and has a duration of x." In a pure music-making environment, the default time division will be the number of musical bars (through which the cursor moves at a speed set by the tempo of the song). However, you will also be presented with a counter that gives you the corresponding readout in minutes, seconds, and milliseconds (mins:sec:ms).

Above: **Most programs now go beyond simple sequencing, and combine editable, pre-recorded audio tracks with sequenced instruments, filters, track EQ, and many other mixing parameters.**

In all audio- and music-production packages, each track generates, and can be viewed on, its own timeline. So, in a 24-track piece of audio or music, there will be at least 24 separate timelines. You can view any or all of these in the Arrange window, along with MIDI and other "event" tracks, such as loops, edits, fades, effects, automated events, and drums patterns. For example, the MIDI event window lets you see and edit all of the note on/off events, controllers, and commands that you have generated.

And that's all there is to it. Once you've got to grips with the principles, you'll find it makes a lot more sense in practice. Your *Complete Guide* recommends at least two helpings of play and experimentation with every helping of your instruction manual.

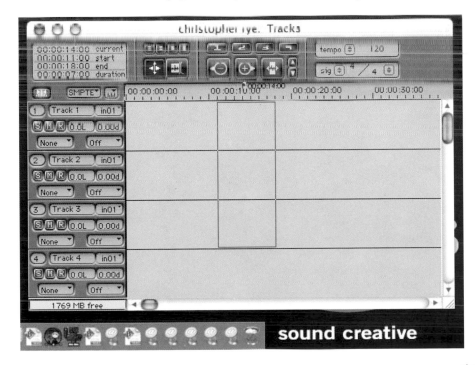

Above: **Many virtual synthesizers can be used on their own as instruments, and not just as plug-in modules. With a MIDI keyboard connected to your computer, they can be played and recorded live, which gives your synth parts a more natural feel because minuscule timing errors humanize the resulting track.**

Below: **Nearly all audio software, no matter how simple, offers some kind of timeline-based interface for arranging and mixing tracks.**

WHAT ARE PLUG-INS?

Plug-ins are single-purpose pieces of software that can, as the name suggests, be plugged in to your main application, adding new functionality, a new set of tools, or a whole new instrument to play with.

In our realm of software-based audio recording, it's best to think of plug-ins as being the software equivalent of buying a new toy for your real recording studio, such as a new effects unit, the latest keyboard or guitar amp, or an entire box of microphones.

For example, IK Multimedia's AmpliTube is a virtual "direct box" and amp simulator for guitarists (see also "Help me, I want to...," page 86), while most virtual instruments and soft synths (see page 138) can be run either as standalone or as plug-ins to your main audio/music application.

Plug-in standards, such as VST and HTDM (see Jargon buster), exist so that you can shop around for a studio-full of professional gear. But rather than bring it home in a truck, you can simply slip a CD into your computer and fire it all up in one go, without worrying about cables and mains leads—or whether you have the space.

Here's a rundown of a handful of the most common packages in the home, semiprofessional, and professional studio environments. A product's appearance here is not an indication of its superiority over competing offerings, nor is it any guarantee that it will work for you. Rather, this section is designed to give you a flavor of what's out there.

Obviously, many professional studios offer a range of software, as clients may have preproduced work in any number of programs. That said, most studios standardize on a couple of suites—for example, Real World uses Logic and Pro Tools—set up to interact and to offer the best possible range of options.

**PART 02. MATCHING NEEDS
TO TECHNOLOGIES**

CHAPTER FOUR

SO WHAT ARE THE PACKAGES?

Left: **Most packages consist of a series of modular parts, and many offer their own special variations of existing functions, like MOTU Digital Performer's surround-sound filter. Do not be lured by the sheer quantity of features—it is important to find out about the quality of each before you pay for them, and this can usually be done by trying demo versions.**

Below: **Cubase** is one of the complete audio and music production suites whose roots lie in MIDI sequencing on the old Atari platform.

COMPLETE AUDIO AND MUSIC PRODUCTION SUITES
LOGIC AUDIO (Emagic Software, a division of Apple)
LOGIC (MAC OS X); LOGIC 5 PLATINUM, LOGIC 5 GOLD (MAC/PC)
CUBASE (Steinberg, now part of video specialist Pinnacle)
CUBASE SX/SL (MAC OS X, WINDOWS 2000, XP); CUBASE 5 VST (MAC/PC)

FULL AUDIO AND MIDI MUSIC PRODUCTION AND MASTERING SYSTEMS

Since their appearance as competing MIDI sequencers for the old Atari platform, Logic Audio and Cubase have matured into virtual audio production studios at the highest professional level. For many recordists and musicians, they form the "big five" along with Pro Tools (see separate sections, page 118 and 148), Cakewalk SONAR, and MOTU Digital Performer.

Both are solid, their audio engines are powerful, and sound quality is exceptional. Arguably, Logic Platinum 5 and 6 are both friendlier packages than Cubase 5 VST, which can be daunting and counterintuitive at times. Cubase SX, however, is a successful reinvention, and it solves some of the audio engine and interface design problems of its earlier incarnations.

Cubase is now rooted in Steinberg's Nuendo engine, a product rated by many professional studios. When sometimes a package grows so far above its original functionality, it reaches a point where it needs a radical redesign: Steinberg have pulled it off.

More significantly, Apple's 2002 purchase of Emagic leaves Cubase as the only one of the two whose development is likely to continue on both Mac and PC platforms. For PC-based studios who have standardized on Logic, this means either crossing over to the Mac if they want to upgrade from Logic 5 Platinum, or switching to a competitor, such as Cubase.

Like most software of its kind, Logic Audio and Cubase revolve around an Arrange window, featuring the familiar timelines where you can edit and interact with audio and MIDI data (simultaneously, if you wish) using a set of dedicated tools.

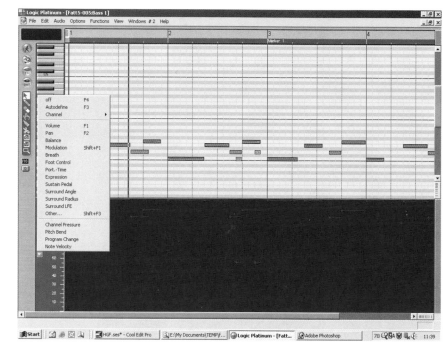

Above: **Apple's purchase of Emagic means that development of Logic Audio is not likely to continue on the Windows platform, but Mac users will undoubtedly benefit from improved compatibility and stability.**

Among Logic Audio's offerings is a collection of virtual analog-style synths. You can supplement these with any of Emagic's range of standalone soft synths (including the EXS24 sampler) in plug-in mode, or with any third-party VST instrument. (See FM7, Kontakt, Reaktor, Absynth, and Halion, page 138.) Similarly, Cubase SX gives you the Waldorf A1 virtual analog synth, VB1 virtual bass unit, and LM7 virtual 24-bit drum unit, and it can also accept any (platform-compatible) VST plug-in.

Unique to Cubase SX, however, is the VST System Link, which enables professional users to network computers running VST software and ASIO hardware, across both PC

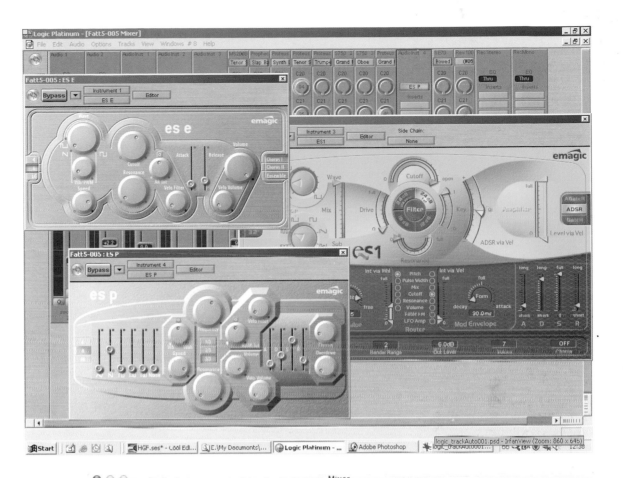

Right: **Logic Audio** offers a collection of virtual analog-style synthesizers which can be used on their own or as VST instruments.

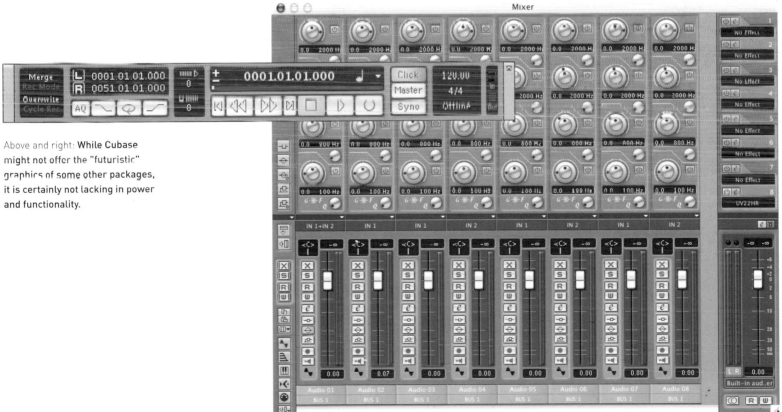

Above and right: While **Cubase** might not offer the "futuristic" graphics of some other packages, it is certainly not lacking in power and functionality.

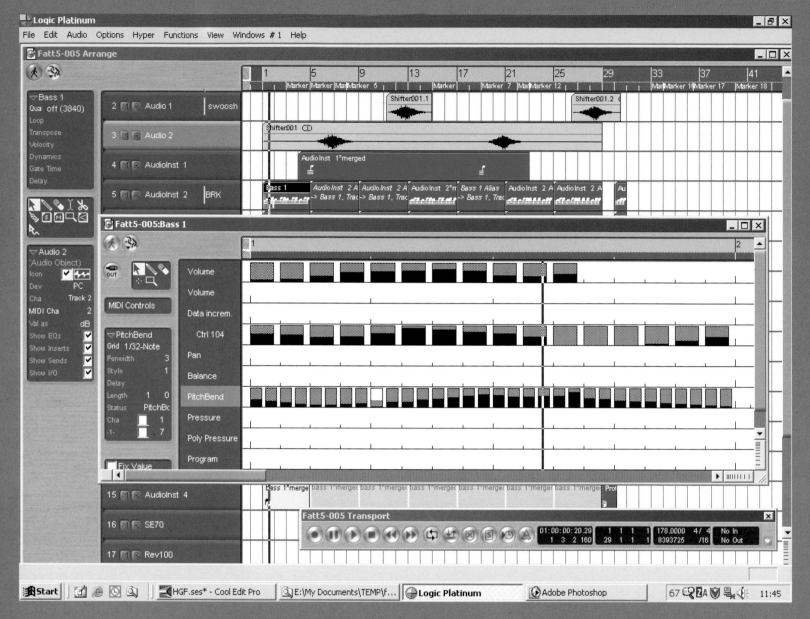

Above: **Logic Audio's Hyper Edit** feature offers an alternative to the usual MIDI-editing tools.

and Mac platforms. Harnessing the System Link unleashes the potential of each computer: an engineer could decide to run all audio tracks on one machine, all VST effects on another, all MIDI functions on a third, and so on.

All recent versions of Logic and Cubase boast a wide range of sound effects and signal processors that you can apply either as Inserts, or as Auxilliary Sends/Returns, just as you can on a mixing desk in a real recording studio.

Inserts are "inline" effects that apply to an individual audio channel. They are added before the signal is equalized. Auxiliary effects sit outside the mixer. Any number of audio channels can be routed to them by individually assignable amounts. This is done via each channel's Send control.

part 02. matching needs to technologies

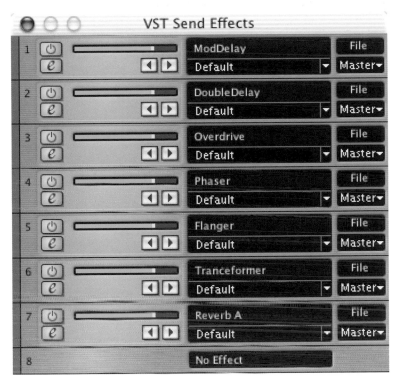

Send effects are routed back into a mixer by two or more Return controls. In this way, you can control the amount of Send from each channel to your auxiliary effect, and also the amount of Return from the effect overall.

Cubase SX, for example, permits the use of eight Insert effects per channel, and presents you with up to eight Sends (to a total of eight Auxiliary effects in any given song). Logic Audio, however, is particularly strong on those all-important mastering tools, which can give your mix an overall gloss as you master the file to CD or DVD.

Routing audio and effects in either program is easy. Logic offers "sidechain inputs" to its mastering processors (compressor or gate settings that can be applied across the board). A sidechain input enables you to use an external audio signal to control your compressors or gates, creating pumping bass lines, for example, or "ducking" effects on a delay.

Full automation of track settings and effects has been available in Logic for some time, and the parameters are easy to access and edit. Meanwhile, Cubase SX offers radically improved automation for the first time. Automation events can now be drawn graphically into the Project window using a Pen tool. Each audio and MIDI track now has its own automation track, containing all the relevant audio or MIDI parameters.

Clearly, Logic Audio's and Cubase SX's strengths lie in their range and depth of features. For example, Logic Audio's Hyper Edit window provides an intriguing alternative to the usual Edit tools for manipulating MIDI data.

Above: **Just like in a real recording studio, effects in Cubase can be routed through an Auxiliary Send/Return, and then back into the mixer. This allows you to control the amount of Send to the auxiliary effect, and also the amount of Return to the mixer.**

In Hyper Edit, MIDI events are represented by a succession of columns, which can be assigned to any MIDI controller and edited (or created) with a sweep of the mouse. A similar feature is found in Propellerhead Software's Reason virtual studio.

But perhaps the most powerful tool for playing with MIDI in Logic is the Transform window, where existing events can be altered en masse according to definable parameters. Once set up, custom parameters can be saved and reused in later projects—a boon when you're doing laborious or complicated work across a number of pieces, or you want to build up a repertoire of "signature" edits.

Logic Audio's Groove Machine— under the Audio Editor—creates "groove templates" based on audio files. It's a facility that works best with drum loops and other audio samples that have a strongly defined rhythm. Once you've created a template from a drum loop, for example, you could choose to apply it to a MIDI pattern. The effect would be to move the MIDI note data to match the rhythm of the audio sample.

Groove templates can be found as MIDI tools in other software, such as MOTU Digital Performer, but Logic can apply the templates to audio files as well. Rival package Cakewalk SONAR offers the Cyclone groove sampler, one of the outstanding features new to version 2.

As you might expect, Cubase SX has its own Groove Template facility, along with some new sample-editing features. One is the Hitpoint, found under Sample Editor. Using Hitpoint, you can take a slice out of a loop or other piece of audio (similar to image-slicing in Photoshop), and apply a range of parameters to it, such as setting it to adapt to a tempo change without affecting the pitch of the sound.

Unique to Logic Audio, and one of its most powerful features, is the Environment. Initially devised as a platform for setting up and controlling MIDI devices, the Environment has developed into a comprehensive tool for customizing the flow of MIDI data within the program. If you want to find out more, go to www.swiftkick.com, where you will also find some free tools.

Unique to Cubase SX is the optional 32-bit TrueTape recording technology, which emulates the warmth of analog tape saturation. Also new are Cubase's Unlimited Undo and Redo facilities—a bonus for anyone who has gone off on a tangent (perhaps following one of Eno's *Oblique Strategies*) without saving a copy of the original mix.

But one aspect of recent versions of both Logic and Cubase is their shared emphasis on a multimedia environment, rather than pure audio production and music composition. Both programs now offer video monitoring in the Arrange window, including thumbnail previews of frames, alongside the standard synchronizing functions such as SMPTE encoding (see Jargon buster, page 121).

Cubase SX has taken a step further into the realms of home cinema and recordable DVD with its six-channel surround-sound mixing window. The circular window (sound describes a sphere, remember) illustrates the ideal surround-sound field. You can position an audio object anywhere within this and move it in virtual space, spinning sounds around your listener's head, perhaps, or following the onscreen action in your first video feature.

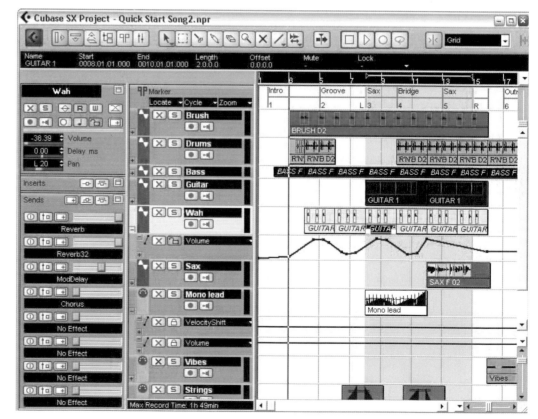

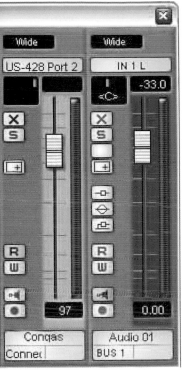

Above left and left: The mixer in Cubase is a separate window with a corresponding track for each of the instruments and auxiliary effects or processing sends from the Arrange window. Note the surround sound.

Above: Master effects can be applied to the entire mix using separate Cubase components, or plug-ins

BIAS Deck and Cool Edit offer less comprehensive surround-sound facilities, while Pro Tools, of course, has had the professional end of the market boxed up for a generation or two.

In summary, both Cubase and Logic are equally effective as the centerpieces of a home studio (real or virtual), or as standalone virtual studios in themselves. But if you are a novice in home recording, audio, or music composition, you should be wary of the steepness of the learning curves and the bewildering number of features on offer.

Simpler audio packages like Deck or Cool Edit, or more intuitive music-creation tools such as Reason, might be better starting points, and the results will be just as "professional." But if you're thinking big from day one and you're prepared to invest the time and the energy, either Cubase or Logic could be the perfect tool—the extension of yourself that creative professionals need.

The future for both packages will be fascinating to watch, as Apple gives Logic a taste of the "iLife," and Cubase looks to scale the Pinnacle of multimedia. But whichever way you jump, both packages reward installation on highly specified computers (min. 1,000MHz processor, 7,200rpm hard drive, 256–512 RAM, and a good soundcard).

MUSIC-CREATION TOOLS If you buy any music-making software, you should consider purchasing an external (piano style) MIDI controller keyboard to enable you to play your software's internal synths. Controller keyboards are inexpensive "dummy" keyboards designed to be the musical interface to your data-crunching Mac or PC.

If you already have a hardware MIDI synthesizer or sampler, use that. If your music-production software has MIDI functionality, it will be able to trigger sounds from your external MIDI synth. If you are working solely with loops, you may find you can work with your mouse and QWERTY keyboard, if you are comfortable in that environment.

Below: **The Nord Lead 3 is an example of a modern hardware synthesizer that is also available as a rack model, which means it can be controlled with an external MIDI keyboard, sequencer, or equivalent computer programs.**

Below: **Most hardware synths are virtual-analog—that is to say, they use electronics to emulate the warmer analog sounds. Access produces one of the most popular models, the Virus (above), renowned for its over-the-top sonic possibility. The indigo model (lower) combines the Virus synth engine with workstation capabilities.**

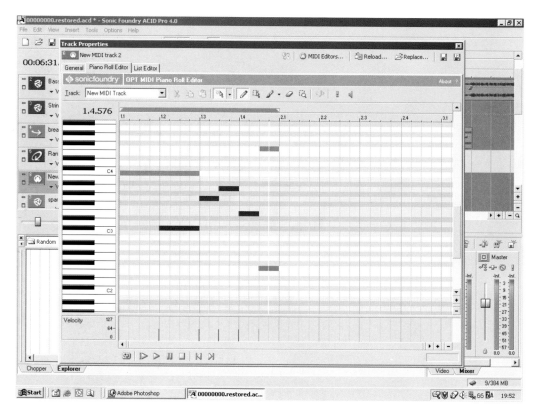

You can add realtime effects to each track, and automate them using Envelope Control—there are over 20 onboard effects, as well as the standard support for third-party DX and VST plug-ins, and so on. (Envelopes apply just as much to effects added to a signal as they do to the original signal itself.)

New to recent versions of ACID is the addition of MIDI tracks for controlling external hardware synths and internal software synths. Although the MIDI-editing tools lack the elegance of some high-end packages, all essential features are easily accessible. With the addition of a few hardware or software synths and effects, ACID gives you all the tools to produce original music, or to remix tracks to a highly professional level.

ACID is equally at home in the multimedia and Internet realms. It supports a wide range of audio and video formats, plus 5.1 surround-sound mixing, and you can import video files into a project for audio synchronization.

That said, there is only a single video track with limited editing functions, but frame-accurate synchronization nevertheless makes it a workable tool for creating video scores. (If you like the ACID interface but want deeper video-editing functionality, try Sonic Foundry's Vegas Video, which adds all the necessary functions for video production.)

Of particular interest to the Web developer are a handful of unique features. For example, you can embed metadata into your audio and video streams and use it to launch websites, display captions, or trigger URL flips, opening up exciting possibilities for dynamic websites.

This software is an audio sequencer/music composition tool, with added video, Web (metadata), and MIDI functionality.

ACID PRO is a loop-based music creation tool that is intuitive to use and packed full of features for audio, video, and Web projects. Audio files can be cut and spliced to create loops, as is common to all audio sequencers. But a more intuitive working method is to edit loops directly on the timeline by dragging the start and end points of the sample to the desired length in musical bars—a feature also of Ableton Live and Logic Audio as well.

Automatic time-stretching will beat-match your samples—but obviously, this will change the tempo and pitch of the source audio files. It is even possible to pitchshift individual sections of a loop to generate original melodies and drum patterns from any sound source.

Above: **ACID is a popular program among hobbyists, remixers, and DJs because it is easy to learn and easy to use. However, it is capable of producing professional quality music tracks. Its relatively low price is partly due to the fact that it lacks advanced wave-editing features, but it integrates well with any of the industry-standard wave editors.**

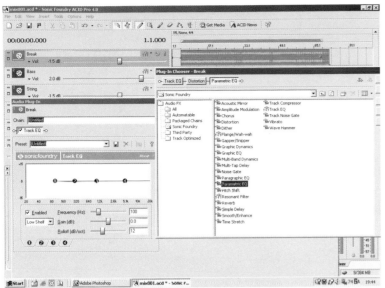

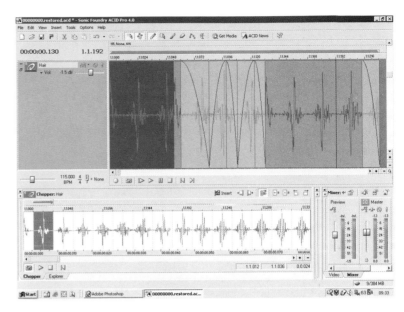

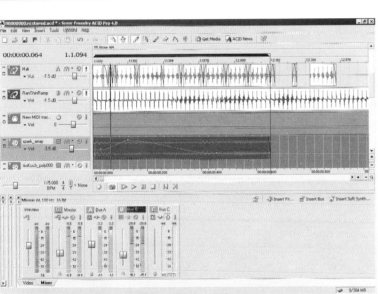

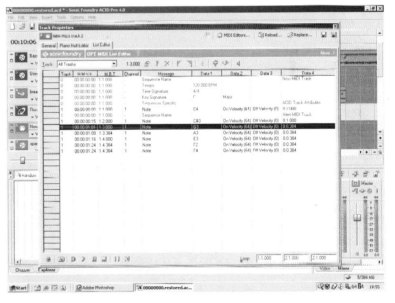

Metadata formats, such as XMF—eXtensible Music Format—are essentially sets of "data about data." They are like "data envelopes" that contain various different data types. In a converging online environment of mobile devices, different computer platforms, and so on, metadata will be the lingua franca that allows all of these technologies to interact and to talk to each other. With all those ones and zeros containing audio, video, images, and Flash animations, the interconnected world will be exciting indeed.

It is also worth investigating ACID's Regions function, which adds markers to your files that are recognized within Macromedia Flash and Director movies as Cue Points for triggering events.

One limitation is the lack of full wave-editing features, but ACID integrates perfectly with Sonic Foundry's own

Above: **ACID's user-friendliness** is largely a result of the fact that almost all of the features can be viewed in a customizable main window. For example, the mixing and panning sliders are integrated into the Arrange area rather than appearing in a separate window.

Sound Forge, or it can be used with a third-party wave editor, such as Steinberg Wavelab.

With all of this functionality, you might imagine that you'd get burned by using ACID. Quite the opposite: it is intuitive, and enjoyable. What it lacks in depth, it more than makes up for in the accessibility of its interface, and the wide range of cross-media applications. (In the rush to add more and more levels to software—the afflictions of "featuritis" or "bloatware"—many developers lose sight of fun and simplicity, two signs of a well-designed product.)

REASON (MAC/PC) Propellerhead Software

This is a virtual music studio environment that's as big as your imagination—but it lacks audio.

Taking its name from a firearm in the novel *Snow Crash*, by cyberpunk guru Neal Stephenson, Reason certainly packs a punch, but it is far from life-threatening. Quite the opposite: the cyberpunks at Propellerhead Software have designed the most elegant, simple, and creative tool on the market for anyone new to digital audio.

The virtual studio is what Hollywood would call "high concept." Reason presents you with a rack of virtual instruments, samplers, drum machines, a mixer, and some digital processors and effects. In the simple Arrange window, you can edit your timeline, and interact with MIDI data, patterns, and controllers. Finally, it presents you with a set of sequencer controls that resemble those of an analog tape recorder ... and that's it.

Propellerhead even has the temerity to label things "Record," "Click," "Tempo," and so on. It says much about the complexity of today's software that such simplicity appears so radical. That said, the company has had the luxury of developing its tool from a standing start, rather than adding layers of functionality as technologies have evolved, which is the case with most of the "big five."

The beauty of the product is that its potential is limited only by your hardware's ability to cope. The Reason "rack," which resembles the racks of processors and sound modules you might see in a real studio, is infinitely expandable. As you add instruments to it, Reason wires them automatically through to the mixer, and labels the track for you. Indeed, you can spin the rack around and reroute all your virtual cables by simply unplugging them, then plugging them in somewhere else.

Go to the Create dropdown, and you will see the options to add a sequencer track, a 14:2 mixer (14 channels into stereo master), six different instruments (two synths, two samplers, a REX loop player, and a drum computer), plus four processors, four effects, a step sequencer (see below), and an "input machine" for managing external data sources. This might seem frugal, but the key is that you can add as many of these to your rack as you wish, including mixers (each of which could have four Sends and Returns).

That said, Reason is a quirky product. If you wish to add a new loop to your piece, you have to create an additional machine to play it. And although Reason can accept WAVs in any of its instruments, including the Re:Drum computer, the program does not offer beat-mapping or time-stretching in the

Below: The Matrix step sequencer enables you to create musical parts on your choice of instrument, which can then be triggered by the main sequencer. You can add as many other modules, such as the NN-XT sampler, as you like.

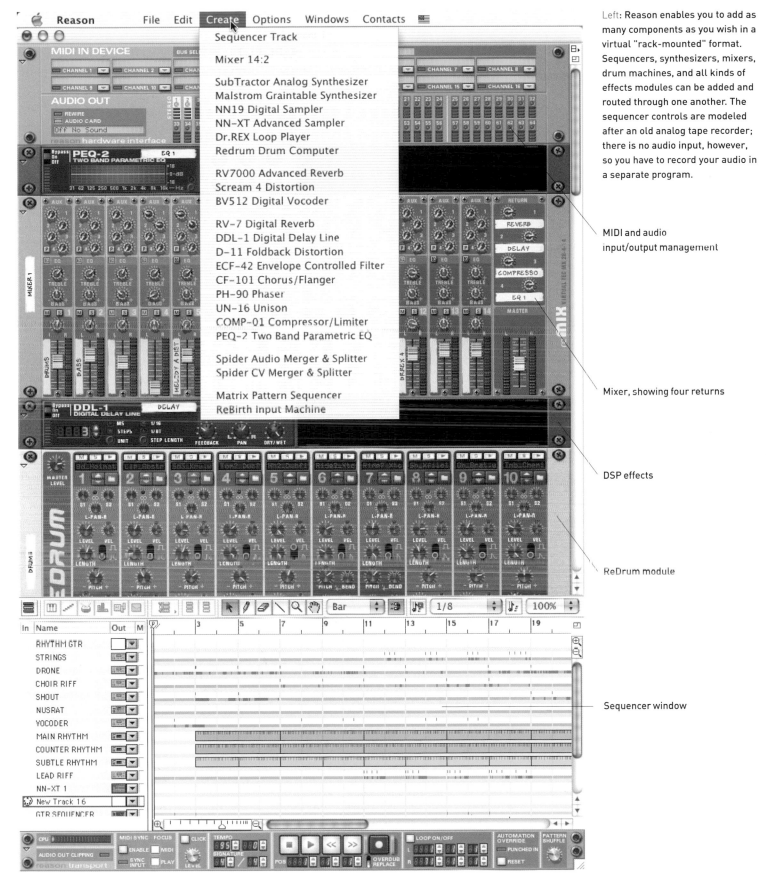

Left: Reason enables you to add as many components as you wish in a virtual "rack-mounted" format. Sequencers, synthesizers, mixers, drum machines, and all kinds of effects modules can be added and routed through one another. The sequencer controls are modeled after an old analog tape recorder; there is no audio input, however, so you have to record your audio in a separate program.

MIDI and audio input/output management

Mixer, showing four returns

DSP effects

ReDrum module

Sequencer window

chapter 04

111

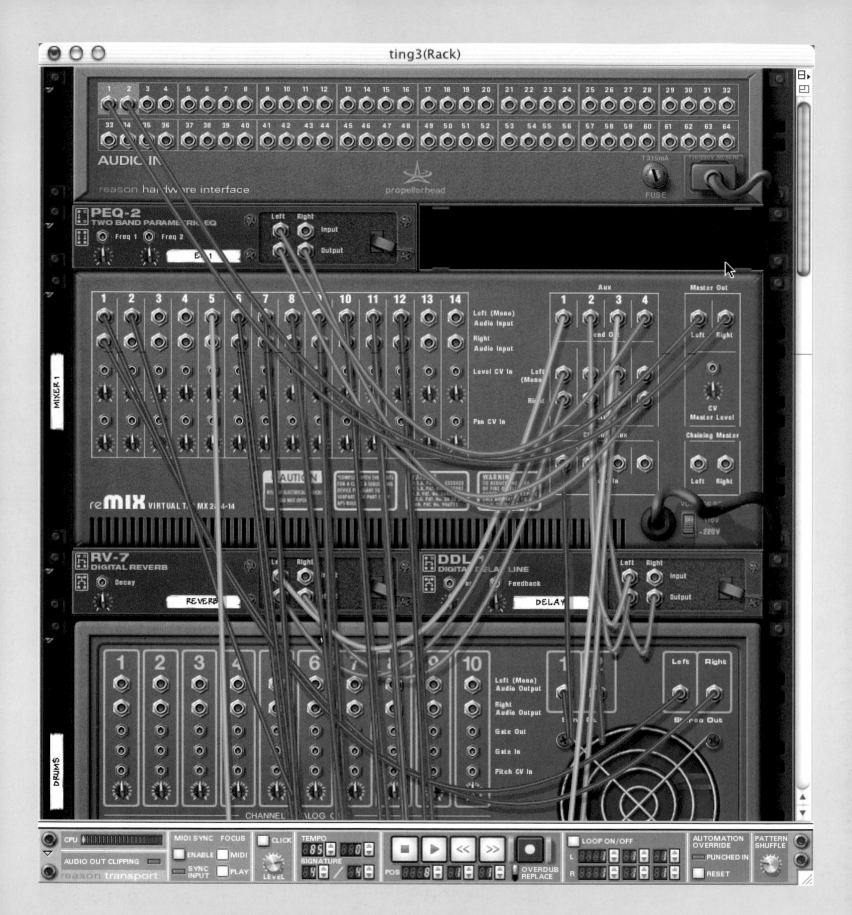

conventional sense. Instead, the REX loop format locks any number of loops to each other and to the tempo of the song. However, loops and samples are fully editable and sliceable.

By far the most powerful of its instruments is the Malström "graintable" synth. And this is despite the fact that, unlike the other instruments which are 99-note polyphonic (you can play up to 99 notes through a single oscillator), it offers only 16-note polyphony. Malström combines two types of synthesis: granular (where sound is created from minute pieces of audio, each of which has its own "signature") and wavetable (based on a look-up table of rudimentary samples).

Even a glance at Reason confirms one thing: it appears very "analog." Indeed, Propellerhead has thrown in a variety of tools modeled on the days of predigital synthesis, where control voltage (CV) was king. This noble ancestry is most evident in the Matrix step sequencer, where you can draw in simple or complex patterns, then route them through to any of Reason's instruments.

The only drawbacks with Reason are that, despite being a virtual studio, it is not VST compatible—you cannot plug in any third-party effects or instruments. However, there are dozens of websites where you can download new Reason loops and samples.

More significantly, however, there is no audio input, so if you wish to add vocals or "real" instruments as audio, you will have to export your Reason track into another program, such as Logic, Cubase, Pro Tools, or even Ableton Live.

■ Reason's vocoder, Reverb 7000, sound destroyer, equalizer and other new modules added in 2003 give the program a broad range of functionality to rival even a fully featured VST suite.

Left: With a click of a button, you can spin the virtual rack around to see how it is wired up, just as in a real studio, minus the irritating tangles and cramped rack space. Reason hooks everything up for you automatically as it is added to the rack, but you are free to re-route cables as you see fit.

Right: Indeed, sequencing just one of Reason's powerful synthesizers can be enough to put together an interesting piece of music. While the software itself is not VST compatible, there are many components included out of the box, and many more available for free download on the Web.

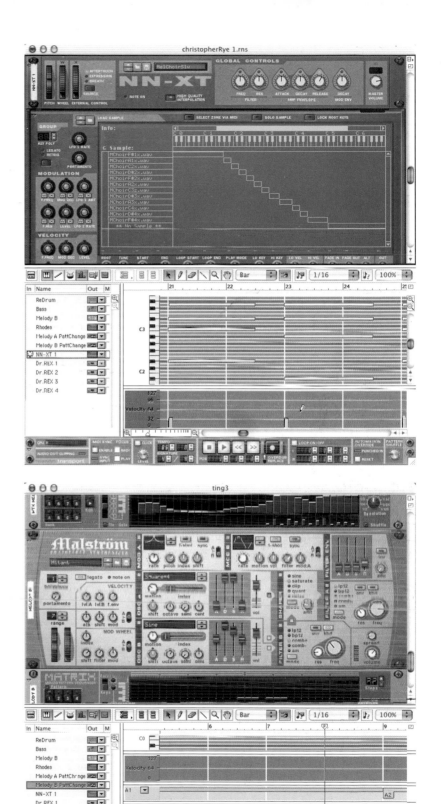

Above and below: **Ableton Live is a good package with much of the same functionality as the competition, but geared toward live performance, hence the name. Note the simple, flat interface of the Effects window (top), the Session window (middle), and the Arranger window (bottom).**

This is a realtime audio sequencing instrument that can be played like an instrument.

Like Reason and Acid, Ableton Live is another of those high-concept products that has emerged since laptops took digital audio mobile, and fast processors matched the e-beats of clubbers, screenagers, city-zens, and the latest in-car nations. Live (or Ableton, as it has become known) takes a DJ's beat-mapping requirements to their logical conclusion, by doing it on the fly.

Ableton's Timewarp engine grabs common audio file formats and time-stretches them in real time as files are read off the hard disk, locking everything into the session's tempo, or reading tempo from an external source (such as MIDI Timecode or MIDI Clock). In other words, you can jam with it, which makes Ableton the ideal tool for the emerging "laptop jam" movement in smaller clubs and bars.

Another unusual feature is that you can chain an open-ended number of effects together for each track, and for each Send channel (similar to Reason's infinite rack, but without the need to add additional mixers).

Each effect can be edited on the fly, by drawing in effect curves and envelopes. But in spite of all this, editing remains nondestructive, and there are infinite Undos.

If you are looking for an easy option to add audio to Reason tracks, Ableton Live is a good one. Indeed, with both products pitched at dance music-making (although Reason is far from limited to that), it may be the perfect companion. As you might imagine for a tool aimed at dark rooms and, perhaps, hazy focus, the interface is brightly colored, and simple to the point of being flat and 80s GUI inspired. But this, of course, could be the first example of truly retro GUI design.

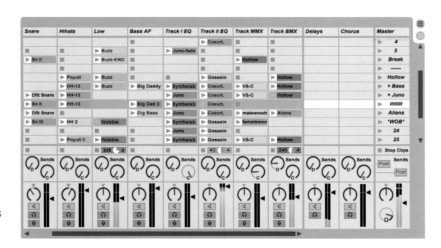

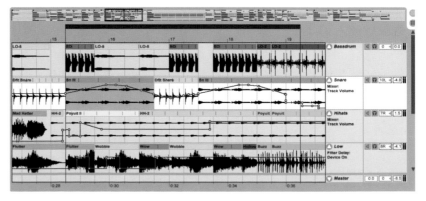

MULTITRACK AUDIO RECORDERS/MULTIMEDIA EDITORS
COOL EDIT PRO (PC) Syntrillium Software
BIAS DECK (MAC OS 8, 9, X)

BIAS (Berkley Integrated Audio Software) Inc

Software multitrack recorders and multimedia editors can clean up analog recordings.

Cool Edit Pro and BIAS Deck are dedicated multitrack recording studios that provide a virtual alternative to hardware systems such as the Alesis ADAT, or the high-end portable integrated studios made by Tascam, Fostex, Akai, Roland, Yamaha, Korg, and so on.

Although the functions cover much of the same ground as the hardware, the visual interfaces are an improvement on the screens found on most hardware devices—particularly in the case of the very clean looking Deck. Your decision lies in whether you prefer working virtually to having a physical interface to play with.

Cool Edit Pro (there is also a scaled-down version called Cool Edit 2000) offers 128 stereo audio tracks and a familiar suite of editing tools. You can record or import audio into the multitrack window, then lay it out to produce new arrangements. It offers beat-matching/mapping as well.

Alongside its standard windows and editing tools, BIAS Deck offers up to 64 simultaneous stereo tracks, plus 999 "virtual tracks" (alternative takes of your performance that sit outside the mixing chain, rather like elements on a pasteboard in a wordprocessor or image-editor).

Like some of its hardware cousins, Deck includes full mixer automation. This enables you to record fader movements and EQ changes into the computer for automatic reproduction later. Automation can take place within "scenes," where a different

Above: **The main benefit in using multitrack audio recorders on your computer is that the interface is always better on your screen than it could ever be on the tiny window of a typical hardware device.**

mixer setup is loaded for key passages of audio, such as where there is a physical change of environment or scene in a video.

Both Deck and Cool Edit Pro include onboard sample/wave editors, a feature not often found in other audio-sequencing packages. In Cool Edit, the function is integral, whereas in Deck it's provided by free companion package, Peak LE. (Peak is also available as a full, standalone package.)

Equal in power to software such as Steinberg's Wavelab and Sonic Foundry's Sound Forge, the wave editors allow you to permanently alter a sample, whether you simply want to trim off unwanted audio to save disk space, or completely transform it to create new sounds.

CLEANING UP OLD RECORDINGS IN COOL EDIT PRO AND BIAS DECK

In both packages, there is a wide range of DSP effects on offer, which can be applied permanently in the wave editor, or as real-time effects in the multitrack window. The noise-reduction tools for removing hiss or crackle are particularly good.

Even the dustiest of old records can be cleaned with remarkably little loss of audible sound quality. You can easily import noisy analog recordings into either wave editor, and remove noise, hiss, and unwanted artefacts, and also normalize volume levels and apply fades and edits.

Once you have done this, there is nothing to stop you applying EQ and compression until you have breathed new life into your old recordings. But remember: you are not adding original information, you are merely enhancing what is already there. You may be able to "dig out" specific frequencies, as sound engineers say.

Neither of these packages offers sophisticated MIDI editing, so neither is of use as a pure music-composition tool, unless you are recording everything as audio. That said, both can import MIDI data into their libraries of elements to put at your disposal. So, if you set up a song in Reason, for example, and export it as a MIDI file, both Cool Edit Pro and Deck will be able to read it, including each of the individual MIDI instruments in the file.

Both Cool Edit Pro and Deck offer sophisticated video synchronization. Cool Edit Pro in particular supports a huge range

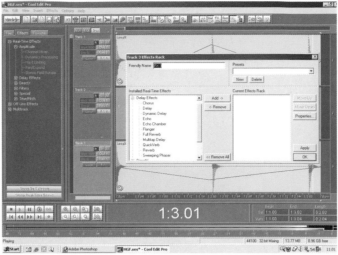

Left: Adding and mixing tracks and effects is a simple process in Cool Edit. However, unlike seqencer-style software, modifications made to individual audio tracks and sounds are permanent unless the Undo function is enabled.

Above: **BIAS Deck is a multitrack recorder with an interface that more closely resembles arranger software. Like Cool Edit, it offers a basic video import utility for multimedia and synchronization projects.**

of file formats. These are all votes in favor of virtual rather than hardware workstations, because integrating video and audio elements via a single interface (your computer) is a lot easier than working with separate pieces of hardware, such as a portable integrated studio and a DV camera.

At the time of writing, BIAS Deck offers 48kHz sampling to 16-bit, whereas Cool Edit Pro supports 32-bit processing, and 192kHz sampling to 24-bit. However, the bonus in BIAS Deck is a powerful 5.1 surround sound mixing facility, with joystick control.

In summary, both products flaunt the beauty of doing a small number of tasks well. As each product is platform-specific, the choice is made for you if you are already in either the Mac or PC environment. But if that choice has yet to be made, make it by looking at which video-editing and music-creation tools you might want to go for as well.

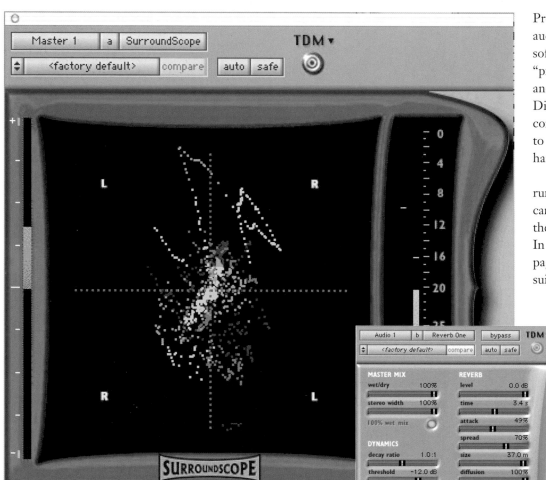

Above and right: **Pro Tools** offers very powerful and complete tool sets for surround-sound editing, reverb, and many other functions.

Pro Tools has a unique place in the digital audio and music pantheon. It is not just a software suite at the consumer and "prosumer" ends of the market (Pro Tools 5 and 6 LE, used in conjunction with the Digidesign Mbox, 001, and 002 USB controllers). Pro Tools scales all the way up to an end-to-end studio facility of integrated hardware, software, mixers, and modules.

The Complete Guide will give you a rundown of the Pro Tools range and what it can offer you in the home and in the studio in the next section of the book: Channel Three: In the studio, present and future. So, turn to page 148 for more on this industry-defining suite of tools.

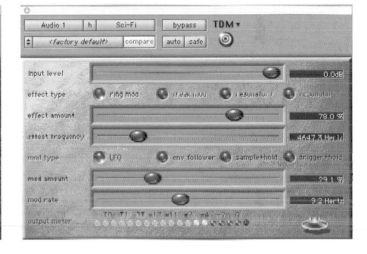

Above, right, and below:
Software components in
Pro Tools are fully integrated
with a series of hardware
components for easy
adjustments and an efficient
work environment, which is
helpful as the virtual side of
the suite has a wide variety
of features and windows.

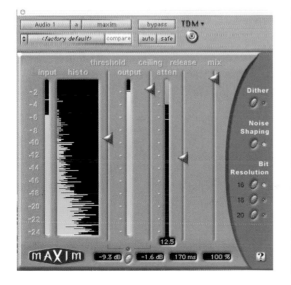

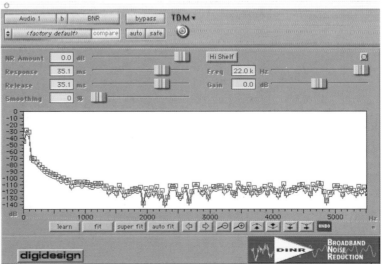

AIF/AIFF Audio Interchange File Format. Standard audio file format on the Mac platform.

AVI Windows PC-centric video format.

CEL Not to be confused with Autodesk Animator Pro's native file format, CEL stands for "Cool Edit Loop." These files are loop tracks that have been compressed as MP3 data, and which contain Cool Edit-specific information on the number of beats used, tempo, key, and stretch method (if applicable). Also, while MP3 files usually contain a few samples'-worth of silence on either end —making them unwieldy to use as loops —Cool Edit eliminates this silence automatically from CEL files.

DLS The self-explanatory DownLoadable Sample format.

DWD The native format for DiamondWare Sound Toolkit which is meant for games and multimedia, and is supported by some other software, such as Cool Edit Pro.

MID MIDI file format. See SMF.

MOV Apple Quicktime movie format MP3 (MPEG Layer 3). Now standard compressed audio file format for the Web and dedicated player devices.

MPEG Motion Picture Expert Group compressed video format, of which MP3 is an evolution.

PCM A raw, usually uncompressed sound file with little to no header information, of the type produced by tone generating software (for example).

QUICKTIME Apple's excellent multimedia player, which may make its presence felt as you work.

RA, RM OR RAM RealAudio or RealMedia streaming audio or multimedia file which requires a Real player or browser plug-in for playback.

RIFF Resource Interchange File Format, an owner-definable mix of MIDI, WAV, AIF and other files in a portable format.

REX Loop format developed by Propellerhead for its Reason virtual studio and ReCycle loop editor.

SKD Sseyo Koan Design. Native instruction set format of Sseyo's generative music composition program, Koan (now owned by Tao Group). It tells your soundcard what to play, and also builds the "instrument" to play it.

SMF Standard MIDI File format. There are three types. Type 0 contains one track of information in one song; Type 1 contains all the original track structure of one song (one track per channel); and Type 2 contains all the original track information for an unlimited number of songs.

SND Alternative file extension to AIF on the Mac.

WAV Wave file format. The standard audio file format on Windows PCs.

WMV Recent Windows-specific video format.

XMF eXtensible Music Format. A music-specific evolution of XML (eXtensible Mark-up Language), XMF is a metadata file type (see below), and contains MIDI files, rich media files, samples, and so on.

OTHER TERMS

ADR Automated Dialogue Replacement, a method of "voicing over" existing dialogue in a video soundtrack, for example.

BEAT-MATCHING /MAPPING Matching the tempo of an audio loop to the tempo of the track it has been pasted into. In most cases, this will alter the pitch of the sample, but some programs can now retain pitch information.

BUS A common connection between a number of circuits.

CLICK (TRACK) Optional audible click in audio software that counts out the tempo and time signature of a recording. It is not recorded as audio, and it can be switched on or off at any time.

DSP DIGITAL SIGNAL PROCESSING (EFFECTS) Group of processes that applies spacial, time, and other dimensions to a signal. See page 162.

KEY MAPPING The mapping of any digital function, sound, sample, or instrument, to a specific key on a keyboard, usually a real or virtual music keyboard. An example would be mapping individual drum samples to specific keys, so that playing each key in turn creates an entire drum kit.

MASTER/SLAVE The use of any hardware or software device to control another. In analog audio, this might be two tape machines, for example, and in digital audio one software program setting parameters for another, via a protocol such as ReWire.

METADATA Data about data, such as XMF and XML, which is embedded into differing technologies. The use of metadata allows different data sets, computing platforms, databases, and mobile technologies to share information and communicate, regardless of their provenance. In an audio environment, it means packets of different data types, including MIDI, samples, etc, can be sent to any compatible device.

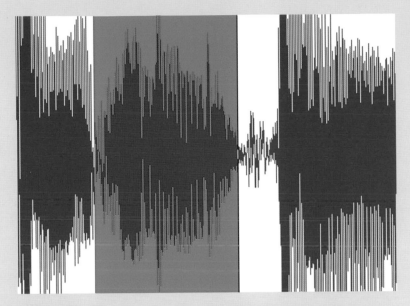

NORMALIZATION The process of increasing the amplitude of a wave's peak to a reference level in a wave/sample-editing package. For example, importing a WAV into BIAS Peak, and asking the software to locate the loudest point and increase the volume of the whole track until the peak hits 0 dB.

OMF Open Media Framework. Facility that permits the import and export of sessions from programs such as Digital Performer, Pro Tools, and Cubase/Nuendo, also from and to video suites such as Final Cut Pro Punch in/out Record function on most audio recorders (hardware and software), which enables you to drop in at any point of the recording with additional, or replacement recording, then drop out again, leaving the rest of the track intact.

QUANTIZE A standard function on all MIDI sequencers that allows you to move note data onto the correct beats of the bar. For example, if you have played a synthesizer line manually that is meant to be in accurate sixteenths, or in accurate triplets, the Quantize function will shift all of the note information onto those beats if you request it. On strong settings, use with extreme care if you don't wish your work to sound "mechanical." (A sound engineer told the *Complete Guide* that "feel" is just musicians playing out of time. You can prove or disprove that theory with Quantize, depending on your taste.)

REWIRE Mac/PC system common to most MIDI and audio software suites that allows you to transfer MIDI and audio data seamlessly between ReWire-compatible products. For example, you could import a Reason track into Cubase to add vocals and external audio

SMPTE (TIMECODE) Pronounced "Sum-tee," this stands for the Society of Motion Picture and Television Engineers. The SMPTE timecode is a standard method of synchronizing both audio and video devices. In a digital process, the software generates the code; in an analog process, the code is "striped" onto one track of tape. The EBU (European Broadcasting Union) also promotes its own synchronization standards.

SURROUND SOUND Six-or-more-channel sound: left, centre, right, left surround, right surround, plus low-frequency effects channel. It is essentially quadrophonic, plus the center and low-frequency (bass boost, subwoofer) channels.

TIME-STRETCHING The analogous process to beat-matching/mapping.

VIRTUAL TRACKS In both software and hardware multitrackers, virtual tracks allow you to store alternative takes of a performance, rather like the pasteboard on a wordprocessor or image editor.

LATENCY

We know that in the big, wide, analog audio world that sound travels at 344 meters/376 yards per second. Another way of looking at it, is that it travels at .34 meters/13½ inches per millisecond. In the switched-on, switched-off world of computers, however, digital audio is data that has to be buffered, just like any other data. It also has to be converted between analog and digital at the recording stage, then back again on playback and monitoring.

This can mean that you hear (and see) perceptibly slow response times when you are dealing with audio in real time, especially when you are monitoring via ASIO to external monitors, using a number of VST plug-ins, or watching the signal peaks in your virtual mixer. This is known as the "latency" of the system, and it is measured in milliseconds. The response times might only lag by these tiny amounts, but it is enough to cause problems at worst, or confusion at best.

Latency exists in a pure analog sense as well: monitoring via headphones does not introduce (significant) latency, whereas monitoring in a large room via speakers clearly does.

But in the digital audio world, you can minimize the problem by lowering the buffer size of your soundcard, or by going to the ASIO control panel in your main application. When using VST plug-ins, you can lower latency there in the Delay Compensation option under File→Preferences→VST.

We've heard a lot about MIDI, and we've covered one or two of the basics. But what is it in practice, and how does it work?

MIDI is the beating heart of digital music facilities. It stands for Musical Instrument Digital Interface. Since the early 1980s when it was developed, it's become the lingua franca that digital music devices use to talk to each other. It's also the way by which any MIDI device can control any number of other MIDI devices in a (daisy) chain, using any, or all, of 16 MIDI channels.

A MIDI channel is distinct from an audio track (which stores audio information), and an audio channel (which routes audio information). So what does MIDI do?

Effectively, MIDI files are both the "score" and the "performance," but they do not supply the instruments to play it. MIDI is a common language, a protocol, and, like most means of initiating digital conversations, it's also a set of specifications and controllers.

Strictly speaking, MIDI data is a set of binary instructions, transmitted, in serial, at relatively low speed (31,250 bits per second) from one compatible device to another. MIDI files contain no audio data. Rather, they contain information about how a MIDI instrument should play a note, chord, or sequence of notes, or about how a MIDI device should behave at any point during this process. Its primary function, then, is as a music description language, a set of directions about when and how to reproduce a musical event.

If you hit a key on an old upright piano, you are doing nothing more than switching on a note with a button, and

**PART 02. MATCHING NEEDS
TO TECHNOLOGIES**

CHAPTER FIVE

AN INTRODUCTION TO MIDI

Left: **The main feature of the Midiman Oxygen8 keyboard is that it can control several parameters of a software synthesizer, but it does not necessarily need a MIDI interface; in that sense, it has more in common with a regular computer mouse or keyboard input than a typical MIDI keyboard.**

Right: **Most multifunction music software packages, such as Cakewalk's SONAR, offers a graphical interface to edit MIDI information. This is usually in the form of a simple piano roll (pictured), but can sometimes take the form of a more traditional musical score.**

creating a musical event. If you hit the loud pedal, you are activating a controller to modify the note, adding expression to it. The directions concerning when and how to do this reside in a musical score, which is itself a linear code of fours, eights, sixteens, and so on. We could say that these are the footprints of someone else's musical journey. MIDI provides the means to follow them in the digital world, along a chain of connected devices.

MIDI is a rare (perhaps unique) example of an industry uniting early to agree on a standard, then preserving it through subsequent technology generations to maintain backward compatibility.

MIDI DEVICES

Keyboards, samplers, and sound modules are among the many types of standalone digital instruments that can play back MIDI information as music that you can hear. Non-sound-generating devices, such as signal processors, digital multitrackers, and integrated studio devices, can often be controlled by the same stream of data. They can be switched on or off, or be told to perform specific functions.

Within your computer, your MIDI sequencing program provides a graphical means of interacting with and editing that data. Turn to page 148 for diagrams of typical MIDI studio setups.

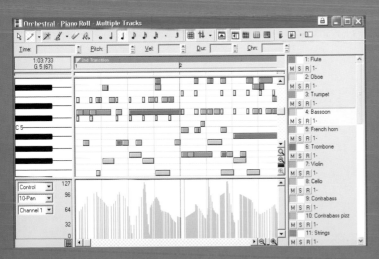

Above: Of course, using the Oxygen8 as a regular MIDI controller is also possible, with appropriate jacks on the back of the unit.

SO HOW DOES IT WORK?

Look at the back panel of any dedicated MIDI hardware device, such as a workstation keyboard, and you will see either two or three MIDI sockets. Together, these form what is known as the MIDI bus, or port.

The sockets are:

IN—which receives MIDI instructions from an external device, such as another keyboard, or from a sequencer application on your computer.

OUT—which sends MIDI data to an external device.

THRU—which receives and sends the same MIDI data, as an echo of the "In." It passes into the device, then simultaneously out again to any number of others in the daisy chain. Some devices and interfaces have just two sockets: "In," and "Out." If you have a PC or Mac whose soundcard lacks a MIDI port, you will need a MIDI to USB (Universal Serial Bus) interface, or a FireWire or M-Lan to MIDI interface.

M-Lan is an emerging protocol for linking networked audio and MIDI devices, and FireWire is the high-speed data transmission protocol found in many digital devices. Such interfaces are inexpensive, offer any number of individual ports, and are available from specialist studio suppliers and many mainstream stores.

ANY STORM IN A PORT A MIDI port can send or receive data on up to a maximum of 16 MIDI channels. Some devices have more than one built-in MIDI port, and your soundcard and sequencing software may enable you to configure multiple ports, each of which could send and receive data on a full set of MIDI channels. You will, however, almost certainly need a MIDI patch bay to get the best out of multiple devices.

This is a good time to mention that MIDI is not just about facilitating a digital conversation between like-minded devices. Any MIDI musical instrument, such as our workstation keyboard, will use some or all of its MIDI channels to route MIDI data internally, regardless of whether there are any other MIDI devices for it to talk to. It enables devices to talk to themselves.

So, let's take a snapshot of MIDI in motion by looking at a non-software example of how it works: the workstation keyboard. This is a "multi-timbral," polyphonic musical instrument that includes a built-in sequencer (and perhaps a sampler as well). This simply means that you can program several complete pieces of music into the keyboard, with several different "instruments," or "voices," playing simultaneously.

Let's say that this keyboard includes a 16-track onboard sequencer. You could decide, arbitrarily, to assign a separate MIDI channel to each of the 16 tracks available in the song. So, for example, Track one could be on MIDI Channel one, and Track 16 on MIDI Channel 16. In fact, we could set it up in any way, but this model is both logical and easy to manage.

Now let's say, for the sake of argument, that the "instrument" you have assigned to Track one is a sample of a string section. When you begin playing and record to Track one, MIDI information is created about the notes you're playing, as you play them, while the sequencer is set to "Record."

Although you can hear your performance as you play, you are not making an audio recording, as no sound is being recorded to tape, disk, or chip. The sequencer is simply compiling data about which keys you strike, how hard you strike them, in what manner, and for what period of time.

So, you are effectively writing the score in real time as you play, but as binary code rather than as musical notation. When you press the "Play" button after you've finished, the sequencer addresses the keyboard's internal oscillators or sound banks, triggers them, and the result is an exact reproduction of your performance.

The sequencer will have registered whether there is any sustain or vibrato on each note ("aftertouch"), plus a huge amount of other information listed under dozens of different MIDI controllers. These correspond to the note's on or off status, its attack, decay, bend, volume, and so on—as we examined in our section on waveforms and synthesis. The manual that comes with your instrument will list all of these.

All the data about your performance is now available on MIDI Channel one. You could switch the MIDI channel if you wished, and make the same information available on MIDI Channel two, 16, or any other, but let's leave it where it is.

Here's where MIDI's other advantage comes into play, whether you're recording MIDI data on a standalone device like a workstation keyboard, or using a computer-based MIDI sequencer and editor.

Once the data has been captured, you can move events, or correct them. Have you hit a wrong note in an otherwise perfect performance? Turn it into the right note, stretch it, move it, pitchshift it down an octave, or add sustain...it's easy. Software MIDI sequencers let you do all of this onscreen with your mouse.

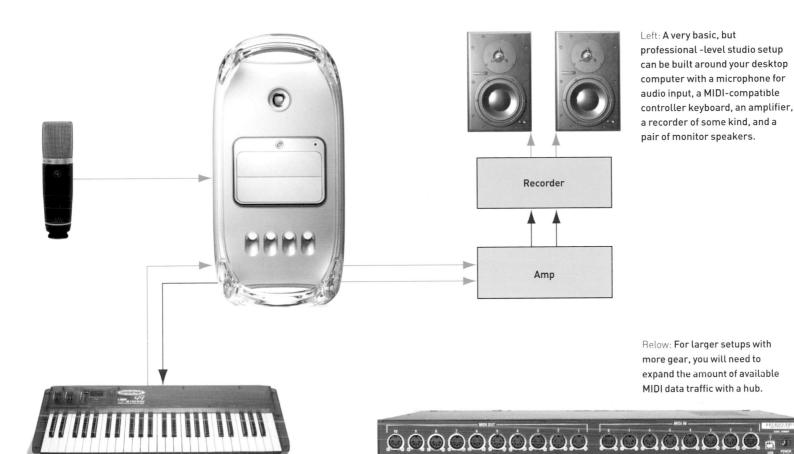

Left: **A very basic, but professional -level studio setup can be built around your desktop computer with a microphone for audio input, a MIDI-compatible controller keyboard, an amplifier, a recorder of some kind, and a pair of monitor speakers.**

Recorder

Amp

Below: **For larger setups with more gear, you will need to expand the amount of available MIDI data traffic with a hub.**

Now set up a second internal instrument (within the keyboard) to respond to, and on, MIDI Channel one. Let's say this instrument is a piano sample. Now when you press "Play," both internal instruments, piano and strings, will play the same information you originally recorded, but in the "voices" of two different instruments.

Now let's say that on the sequencer's MIDI editor, you switch the controller of MIDI Channel one from "Internal" (within the keyboard) to "External" (to control a separate device), or to "Both." Let's use the example of "Both."

Set up a third sound—let's use a saxophone sample—on an external keyboard or sound module, and tell the instrument to receive instructions, for that sample alone, on MIDI Channel one. When you press "Play" on your sequencer now, that external instrument will also play back the same information you originally recorded. Had you chosen "External," only the external instrument would play.

You can repeat the original process, recording new performances on "audio" Tracks two to 16, via MIDI Channels two to 16. In this way you build up, or multitrack, a complete piece of MIDI music. Separate instruments, on separate "audio" channels, are each controlled via separate MIDI channels.

Above: **Even larger studios with various digital and traditional components are often thoroughly integrated using many, many MIDI patch cables.**

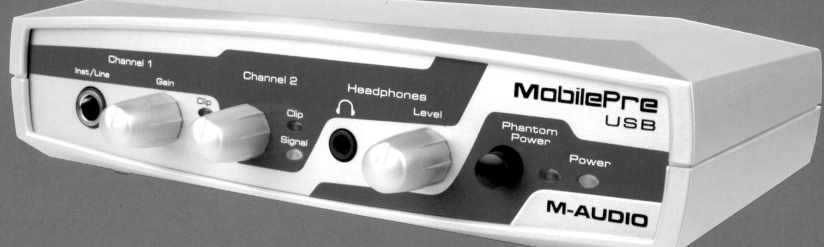

Above and below right: **Whether or not you have MIDI ports, you will probably need a USB hub. Both A/D converters and MIDI-to-USB converters use USB ports, and both types of input devices are handy for laptop-based portable studios.**

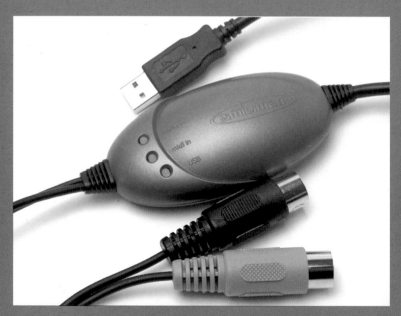

Above: **Strictly speaking, a mouse is the only input device you need to make music on a computer, and while it may be your only option on an older notebook, it is certainly not the easiest input device to use. If your soundcard doesn't have a MIDI port, and your motherboard doesn't have a USB slot, you should probably consider an upgrade.**

part 02. matching needs to technologies

PORTABLE MIDI Remember: MIDI data is compact and portable. You are not recording audio. The fat sound you hear has already eaten up your keyboard's or your computer's memory, and is simply being prodded into life by the few kilobytes'-worth of MIDI directions you've generated.

What you hear is an audio performance, but no sound has been recorded at this stage. You get the original performance every time you press "Play."

Each MIDI channel can also send and receive pure control information. So you could send a "program up" command to a signal processor, set to receive data on a specific MIDI channel, and direct it to switch to a reverb effect at a key point in your composition. Or you could send a program change command to your external sound module, directing it to switch from Voice 32, for example, to Voice 41. Your MIDI device or software will give you a list of relevant MIDI controllers.

Essentially, what a software MIDI sequencer adds to this way of working is to let you manage all this information via a graphical user interface, and to examine, slice, dice, and infinitely edit it to your heart's content. It also offers a means of managing the MIDI devices that are linked (directly or otherwise) to your computer— and of managing audio tracks as well.

Below: To conserve ports, you might want to consider a dual USB audio input and 16-channel MIDI interface like the AudioSport Quattro by M-Audio.

THE PAPERLESS PIANOLA

Perhaps the direct ancestor of MIDI is another invention that was around at the time of the telegraph: the pianola. MIDI is in many ways a digital version of the pianola's paper roll. The data is our 21st-century equivalent of the punched holes in the paper, and the instrument being played is whichever one you insert the roll into (or rather, send the directions to).

MIDI files of well-known songs are available to download off the Web, and these will tell your soundcard, or any external MIDI device connected to it, what notes to play, and in what manner. But MIDI files are dependant on the instrument they play at the user's end. The "performance" will be the same, but the data "plays" whatever instrument may be waiting for it. This was the impetus behind a further evolution of the MIDI standard: General MIDI (GM).

General MIDI (GM) is a set of 128 "sound sets," on which all manufacturers of GM-compliant MIDI devices have standardized. Essentially, these 128 GM patches will sound similar from device to device. The sound set is broken down into sets of eight sound patches under these categories: piano; chromatic percussion (for example, glockenspiel, marimba); organ; guitar; bass; strings; ensemble (for example, orchestral, including choir); brass; reed; pipe; synth lead; synth pad; synth effects; ethnic (sitar, bagpipe); percussive; and sound effects.

Your soundcard will be GM compliant. If your soundcard is wavetable based (and it probably is), then it will use minute samples of actual digital recordings to produce a more realistic sound. FM (frequency modulation) synthesis, as the name suggests, constructs purely synthetic sounds, and some soundcards use this principle.

For some examples of MIDI and other studio setups, turn to Channel Three, In the studio, present and future, page 144 onward.

Computers are not built, as musical instruments are, to be extensions of the mouth or hand that let us talk a universal language, or make gestures in sound, melody, harmony, and symphony. They are designed to crunch numbers, digitize information, and move data from one place to another. As we have already seen, however, this is a process that lies at the heart of music, that most mathematical of artforms.

But even in the first decade of the 21st century, a surprising amount of people still rage about Mac versus PC. Mac fans are passionate about their system of choice, while PC users and software developers are usually pragmatic. They cite safety in numbers, price, and availability as

incentives to throw in their lot with the 90% global majority. Most home users have a PC, while a majority of top professional studios lean more toward the Mac environment. But the economics of a PC-dominated world dictate that software developers at the "home" end of the market have to concentrate on Windows PCs. This is a prime consideration.

A 2001 ODYSSEY

In 2001, both Microsoft and Apple announced the availability of new versions of their operating systems, drawing up the battle lines for a renewed charge of the old warhorses, and occasional allies, through 2002 and up to the present day.

Both promised the abandonment of an old way of life, old code, and to varying degrees, legacy support. Both exhibited symptoms of a serious outbreak of "featuritis" (dozens of new audio, video, and other mini applications). Both also suggested that you upgrade your hardware to make the most of the new environments. In a technology economy of flat hardware sales, this was just what the stock markets wanted to hear. (Both Microsoft and Apple later added that their particular brand of "X" wouldn't make your old machine a "0.")

PART 02. MATCHING NEEDS TO TECHNOLOGIES

CHAPTER SIX

THE BATTLE OF THE Xs

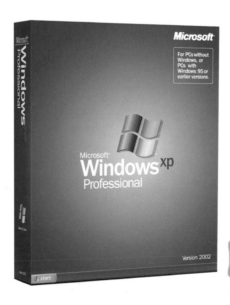

Left: While the Mac is often the system of choice for creative professionals, Windows is the OS for a majority of consumers. The stability of Linux makes it a favorite among a few dedicated users, however, and its audio software is beginning to evolve.

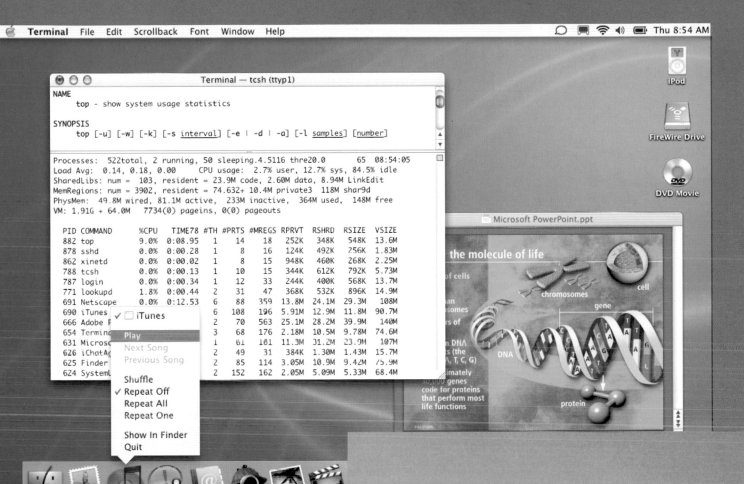

As far as you are concerned, the question is really: Windows XP, Mac OS X, or Linux? Classic Mac OS 8 or 9 (which also run within Mac OS X) or Windows 98 upward? Software developers often forget that you might not be in a position to upgrade. In most cases, the decision is made for you if you are buying a new machine, or by the demands of your chosen software. We'll discuss Linux shortly.

If you are looking into buying a new machine in the computer market, remember that you no longer need to be shackled to your desktop; laptops are every bit as powerful and reliable as the immobile PC or Mac, and battery life is acceptable for mobile audio work.

But which platform has the "X" factor for audio? *The Complete Guide* is going to stick its neck out and say that there is little to choose between either technology, and that the main deciding factors are simple practical ones, and matters of taste. Yes, there are differences in technologies, clock speeds, architecture, and so on, but the makers of those dozens of audio software suites have already thought about these problems and solved them for you.

Above: **There are significant differences between the Mac OS X (left) and Windows (right) operating systems used on Apple Macs and PCs respectively, but the working environment is similar.**

THE REAL PROS AND CONS The latest versions of the "big five" packages are built for OS X and Windows XP, with the sole exception of Logic Audio 6 upward, which is limited to the Mac OS X environment—there is no Windows XP support. However, Logic Platinum 5 offers most of the facilities you are likely to need for the foreseeable future, and it runs in Classic versions of Mac OS, as well as in Windows 98 onward.

Other software suites, such as BIAS Deck, have been "carbonized," which means they will run in both Mac OS X if you have it, and in earlier versions of the operating system if you don't. Others, such as Ableton Live, will run quite happily in Classic mode within OS X, as well as in Classic Mac.

Clearly, the only answer if you have a pre-OS X Mac or pre-Windows XP PC is to decide what functionality you want, then to see if your chosen software will run in your operating system. If it will not, consider upgrading your operating system. If you can't (see below), then either lower your sights, or raise your overdraft limit.

In the short term, another problem lies in third-party VST and other plug-ins. Not all currently work with Mac OS X, so if you do upgrade or buy a new machine, you may still find yourself running your suite of plug-ins via an application in Classic mode.

SYSTEM REQUIREMENTS

For Windows XP Home Edition, Microsoft recommends Pentium III, 4, AMD Athlon, or Duron processors; at least 1.5 GB of free disk space (Windows 98 required 300 MB), and 128 MB of RAM. For OS X, Apple makes similar recommendations to Mac users: a G4, iBook, iMac, or Powerbook machine, 128 MB of RAM, and 1.5 GB of available storage.

Ignore all minimum requirements. This is audio, and the above figures are just not good enough. Creative audio- and music-makers should up their minimum requirements to 256 MB of RAM, with 512 MB highly recommended, whether they are running a Mac or a Windows PC.

Standalone packages such as Reason, ACID, and so on, will run quite happily on lesser systems, but if you are also running Cubase, Logic, or Pro Tools, your machine will begin to slow down unacceptably for audio work.

Remember, anything approaching 20-millisecond latency or higher will make your system inadequately responsive to real-time audio tasks, and glitches will be irritating. There's no reason to put up with anything greater than low, single-digit latency figures.

It has to be said that this is one advantage of portable integrated studios: they are built and optimized to record audio, and tend to be far more robust and reliable than either computer-based platform.

Below: **If you are on an older OS and are planning to upgrade, you should make sure your existing software will still work.**

Above: **Cross-platform compatibility between Windows and Mac is becoming more and more common, even for the native file formats of specific software programs. Apple, however, seems to be staking its claim on next generation audio, and rebuilding the company around music and multimedia.**

MORE PROS AND CONS

Since co-founder Steve Jobs took another bite at Apple, the hardware and software maker has regained its shine. But Apple's strengths are simultaneously its weakness. First, the company produces machines that are more and more seen as exclusive design icons, at a time when fast processors and cheap storage have made PCs into consumer goods. So if cost is a deciding factor, a new, high-specification Mac might be out of the question.

But part of that design-led approach has also been to make Macs into self-contained "plug and play" devices that are designed as docking stations for a series of portable audio, video, and lifestyle devices. Apple's commitment to digital audio, music, and video is clear. In fact, the company sees its future as being at the core of the expanding world of creative digital arts and "personal space" technology.

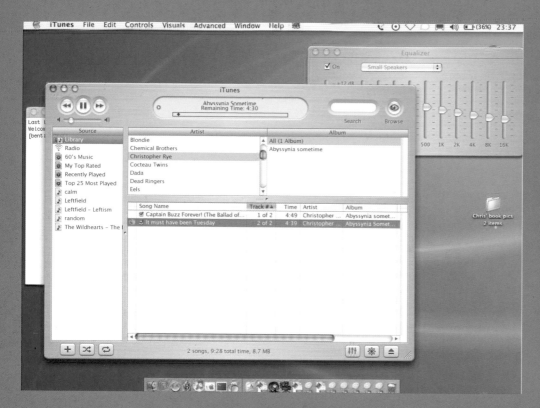

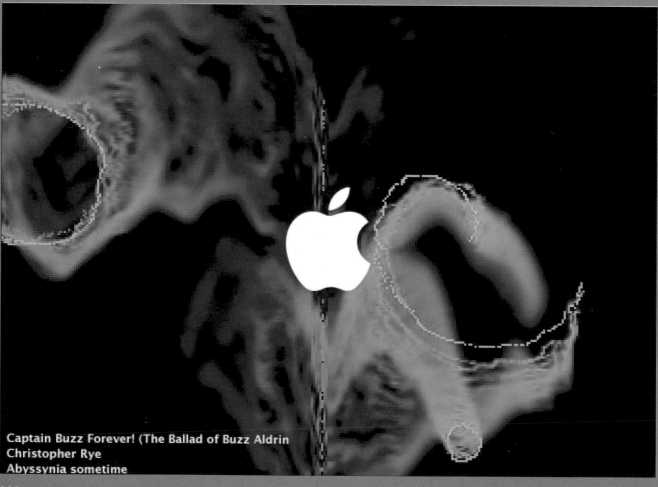

Captain Buzz Forever! (The Ballad of Buzz Aldrin
Christopher Rye
Abyssynia sometime

As a roadmap technology, Apple will take you to where you want to go. Not for nothing has OS X's sophisticated iTunes MP3 player been integrated into Apple's suite of "iLife" products.

Like Windows Media Player, iTunes can generate freeform animations based on analyzing the frequencies in your audio track. The separate iPod portable MP3 player can hold thousands of songs.

Apple's online iTunes venture and its ambition to acquire a music publisher or record label have been further indications that technology companies understand the content market better than many content publisher.

If any of this is a deciding factor, go with the Mac. As in any well-designed item, its form and function are one and the same, unlike PCs' (improving) mix of technologies, protocols, and compatibility problems. Note: Microsoft makes the operating system, dozens of other companies make the hardware, and still more companies manufacture software, drivers, peripherals, and so on.

Pick up an iMac and you have a single device, a single mains lead, two or three USB ports, and a FireWire connection. Having a computer that is a well-designed unit rather than a sprawl of boxes, leads, ports, and peripherals is a boon in an audio environment of USB and FireWire compatible devices—and in a home studio that may already be "spaghetti junction."

But this brings us to the downside: all those boxes and peripherals. The fact is that these are far easier to buy for the PC than they are for the Mac. Pop down to any mainstream store, and you will see shelves stacked with PC-compatible DVD-R drives, speakers, printers, and so on. (A printer might be useful if you want to print a musical score from Cubase, for example.)

Next, there's the Apple brand itself. Since Apple does not license its products, only Apple makes them. This too is a potential boom or bust economy. When you purchase

Apple hardware, Mac software, or one of Apple's growing line of audio devices, you can be sure you're not going to get internal compatibility problems, or a driver pileup. On the other hand, if Apple hits the skids, support will vanish overnight.

That said, for Apple the "X" actually means something. In iteration terms, it refers to version 10 of the Mac environment. But Apple's "X" also marks the spot where it attempted its own "Think Different" campaign—paradoxically, by jumping onto a piece of technology whose roots lay in the 1970s.

OS X is based on Unix, the Bell Labs-developed operating system (it's that telephone company again). More specifically, it is based on Darwin, the Unix-based system that grew out of Apple's acquisition of NeXT, in the late 1990s. Darwin is the theory behind Apple's evolution.

So what? Well, with more than thirty years of development behind it, Unix is as solid a foundation as you can get in an operating system. Linux too is a Unix derivative, as we will see. It also opens the door to a much larger developer community of hardcore techies. But the move has annoyed a handful of software developers who have been loyally making products to run under the Classic Mac environment.

■ At the time of writing, VST plug-ins were not fully compatible with OS X, but Fxpansion (www.fxpansion.com) had produced a software solution that turns VST plug-ins into OS X Audio Units. Check online or with your supplier for up-to-date information.

Below: The functional similarity of audio player software between the two platforms is at least partly due to the wide acceptance of MP3 as the main compression format for audio.

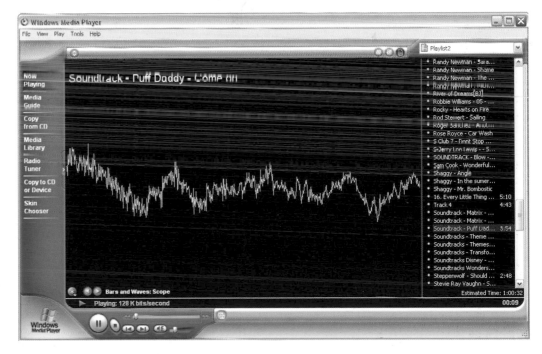

LINUX FOR AUDIO AND MUSIC People still think in terms of Mac versus PC, but these are far from the only operating systems for home users. It's also worth considering Linux, the "open source" OS. Linux is a derivative of Unix, and it takes its name from Finnish student Linus Torvalds, who helped develop it in the early 1990s. Creative audiophiles can run it on their PCs or Macs, either in place of their operating systems, or within a partition.

The difference between Linux and the other major operating systems is that the source code—the kernel of computer code at the heart of any operating system—is "open." In other words, it is freely available, and shared between a global community of tens of thousands of developers worldwide. The code underlying Windows, on the other hand, is proprietary (closed, owned by a proprietor), a piece of intellectual property that Microsoft shares with few organizations outside of US government agencies.

In many senses, then, Linux is "free." Developers share the source code and, under the terms of the license to do so, they are committed to pooling their work back into the global community of developers. The source code is freely available if you wish to use it or run it. Alternately, you could buy or download a branded distribution of it at very low cost, from distributors ("disties") such as Red Hat, Debian, SuSE, and dozens of others. For your money, you'll get support as well as manual.

At present, Linux's presence is most strongly felt behind the scenes on servers and within corporate computer networks—not a bad achievement for the new kid on the block. But all that may change between now and your next major hardware/software upgrade in three to five years.

The attraction of Linux is that there are hundreds of thousands of developers working on it at any one time, with the shared intention of unlocking all the proprietary doors of the software industry. Indeed, they call their collaboration "copylefting," to highlight their stand against copyright.

The result is that the market might seem unfocused today in terms of headline-grabbing software, but what is there has the work of tens of thousands of people behind it, even if it is a lone developer's tool for cleaning up your guitar sound.

The next five years or so could see the biggest upheaval in the software industry since the late 1980s, with several audio workstations, MIDI sequencers, wave editors, and other big ideas for audio buffs and music-makers set to filter down from public license to public consciousness.

Linux may be a risky basis for your audio studio today (none of your existing plug-ins will work on it, and support will be patchy at best), but there is no doubt that it will be the one to watch when the time comes for your first major upgrade decision. If you are planning ahead on a five-year timescale (*The Complete Guide* acknowledges that this is an outmoded concept), then you should factor in a potential crossover to Linux. This could mean, ironically, going for a Mac OS X-based solution today.

Among the emerging players are: multitrack audio sequencer Ardour (http://ardour.sourceforge.net); the similar Audacity (http://audacity.sourceforge.net); another multitracker, GSMP (http://sound.condorow.net); digital mixer Mix (http://sound.condorow.net); MIDI sequencer Anthem (http://anthem.sourceforge.net); audio/MIDI sequencers MusE (http://muse.seh.de) and Jazz++ (http://www.jazzware.com); step sequencer Hydrogen (http://hydrogen.sourceforge.net); MIDI sequencer and notation editor Rosegarden (http://www.all-day-breakfast.com/rosegarden/); and the high-concept AGNULA project, spearheaded by Red Hat among others.

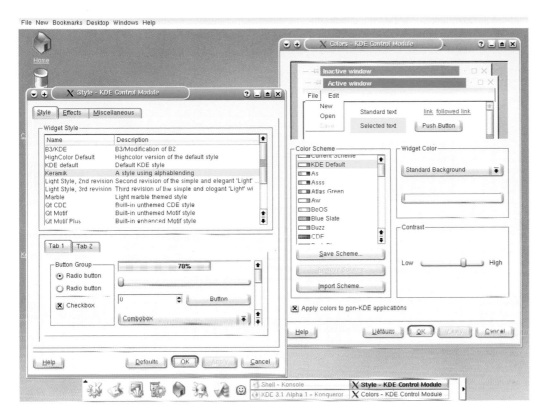

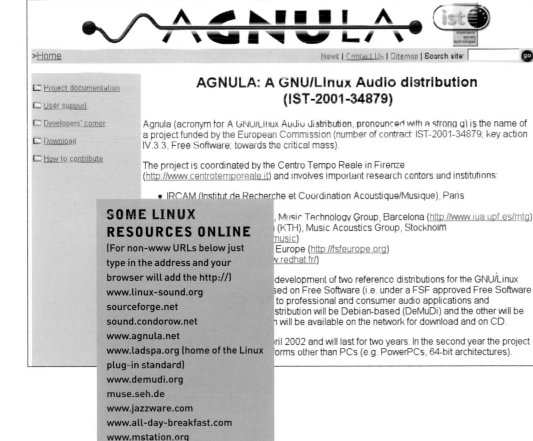

SOME LINUX RESOURCES ONLINE

(For non-www URLs below just type in the address and your browser will add the http://)

www.linux-sound.org

sourceforge.net

sound.condorow.net

www.agnula.net

www.ladspa.org (home of the Linux plug-in standard)

www.demudi.org

muse.seh.de

www.jazzware.com

www.all-day-breakfast.com

www.mstation.org

intended as the first audio-specific distribution of Linux (http://www.agnula.org). *The Complete Guide* says: watch AGNULA over the next two to three years, and then make your decision.

With Apple's OS X shift to Unix, the leap for the "big five" software packages into the world of Linux would be small in terms of code, but massive in terms of business model, as each company comes from the proprietary, intellectual property-based world. But in this day and age, business models and five-year plans are not what they used to be.

That said, Apple's purchase of Emagic makes more sense when viewed in the light of a low cost, "free" Unix alternative. There may be more to Apple's strategy than meets the eye. OS X to Linux – a small leap (for you); Windows XP to Linux = a different planet (for Microsoft).

But the real impetus may come from the film industry, where big-effects, blockbuster movies are often put together on powerful, Unix-based workstations. A high-end Linux audio product which takes off in that rarefied realm would make the medium-term future very interesting indeed, should the repercussions filter down into the "prosumer" end of the audio software market.

There are thousands of Linux resources on the Net. But for audio, you would do well to check out these URLs, then follow the links from there. Alternately, check out the excellent *The Book of Linux Music and Sound* (plus CD-ROM), by Dave Phillips (No Starch Press).

SOUNDCARDS There are nearly as many 24-bit soundcards out there as there are software packages that rely on them. But at the time of going to press, these were some of the popular, or highly rated, product lines and the manufacturers to watch. (*The Complete Guide* recommends that you keep your eye online and on computer music magazines. Alternately, talk to your local dealer.) Expect to pay in the region of $100–$200, on average.

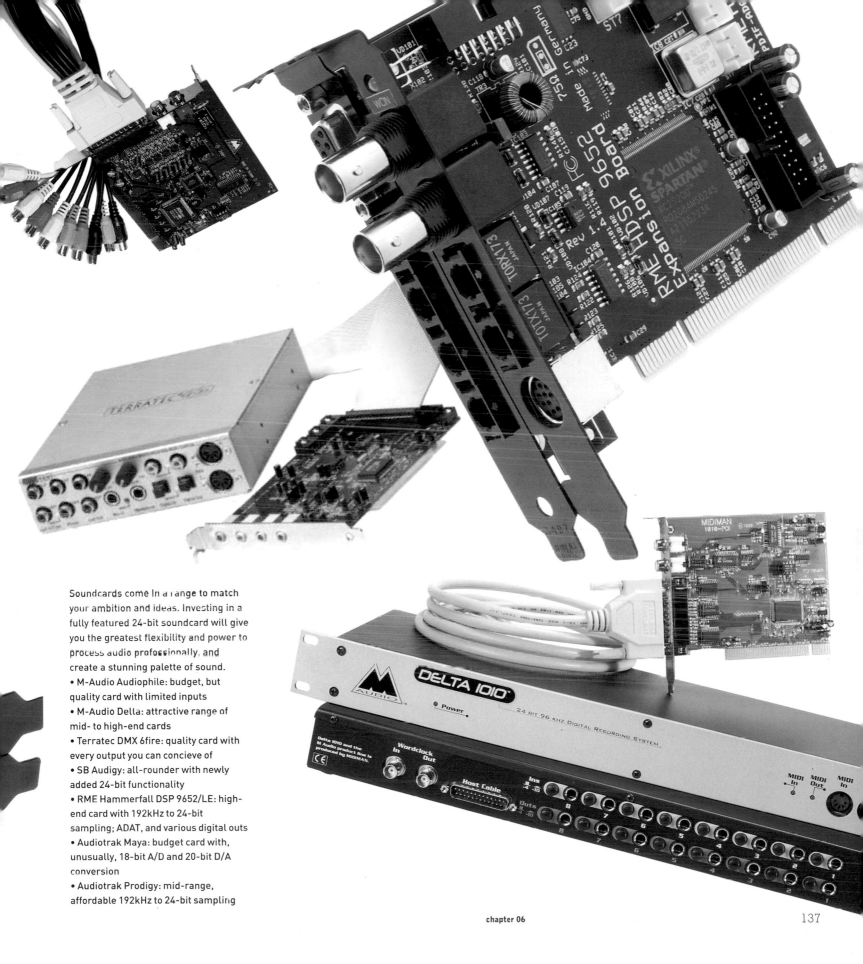

Soundcards come In a range to match your ambition and ideas. Investing in a fully featured 24-bit soundcard will give you the greatest flexibility and power to process audio professionally, and create a stunning palette of sound.

• M-Audio Audiophile: budget, but quality card with limited inputs
• M-Audio Della: attractive range of mid- to high-end cards
• Terratec DMX 6fire: quality card with every output you can concieve of
• SB Audigy: all-rounder with newly added 24-bit functionality
• RME Hammerfall DSP 9652/LE: high-end card with 192kHz to 24-bit sampling; ADAT, and various digital outs
• Audiotrak Maya: budget card with, unusually, 18-bit A/D and 20-bit D/A conversion
• Audiotrak Prodigy: mid-range, affordable 192kHz to 24-bit sampling

VIRTUAL INSTRUMENTS Virtual instruments have been the software success story of the past few years, and have contributed to musicians' acceptance of computers as being more than just boxes of processors. Most musicians possess one or more physical keyboards, but the move to virtual instruments and soft synths persuaded even hardware giant Korg to release some of its classic keyboards in a software-modeled form, early in 2003.

HERE IS A SMALL SELECTION OF THE DOZENS OF VIRTUAL INSTRUMENTS ON OFFER...

FM7
Native Instruments
www.native-instruments.com
FM-based soft synth that reproduces the classic sounds of synths such as the Yamaha DX7, DX11, DX21, DX200 groove box, and so on, but with an extended sound architecture that accepts audio inputs as operators for FM sounds, modulation, and effects. But unlike the classic synths it emulates, the FM7 offers an intuitive graphical interface for the creation of sonic envelopes and complex, evolving sounds. Supports VST; DXi; DirectConnect; MAS; ASIO; FreeMIDI; OMS. Mac/PC.

ABSYNTH
Native Instruments
The third of four NI products here shows this company's dominance of the market. Absynth makes the heart grow fonder with a handsome modular interface offering the chance to construct "everything from organic textures to rhythmic madness." Includes six oscillators, four filters, three ring modulators, and a waveshaper for each voice. Supports VST; DXi; DirectConnect; MAS; ASIO; FreeMIDI; OMS. Mac/PC.

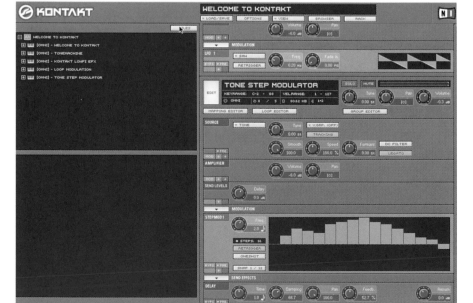

KONTAKT
Native Instruments
Powerful sampler offering drag-and-drop sound environment for the creation of new instruments and effects. Comes with six CDs of samples, including piano; drums and percussion; bass, acoustic, and electric guitars; and classic synth patches. Also offers granular time-stretching and pitchshifting functions, 17 filter types, dozens of integrated effetcs, and up to 256 stereo voices. Supports VST; DXi; DirectConnect; MAS; ASIO; FreeMIDI; OMS. Mac/PC.

REAKTOR
Native Instruments
Modular 96kHz, 32-bit sound studio offering a bundle of tools for realtime synthesis, sampling, and digital effects processing, reading and writing audio files direct from the hard disk. Includes FM and analog-modeled synths, realtime compression and expansion, dozens of effects, and up to 16 channels of surround sound. Supports VST; DXi; DirectConnect; MAS; ASIO; FreeMIDI; OMS. Mac/PC.

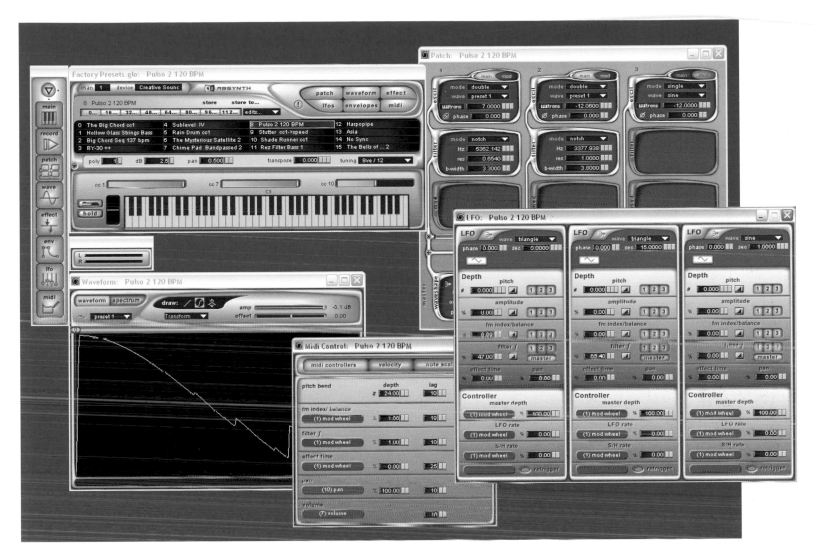

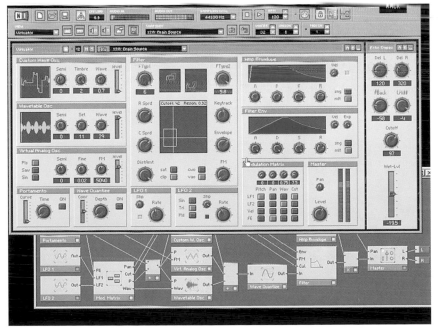

Many musicians have augmented their keyboard hardware with racks of sound modules, which are essentially dedicated boxes of sounds governed by the MIDI environment. Nowadays that whole way of working too is being replaced by virtual instruments, and soft(ware) synths and samplers.

There are several advantages. First, you can comfortably run perhaps a dozen separate virtual instruments within a high-specification laptop, along with the instruments that you might already have within a package such as Logic Audio or Cubase. Second, most virtual instruments can run either as standalone or as plug-ins to your main application. Third, they are all expandable and sit at the front end of a global community of creative programmers who release new patches week in, week out for your listening and playing pleasure. Fourth, they open the doors to classic sounds and to the advantages of classic pre-digital synthesis, but with all the accessibility and manageability of the digital world. Fifth, they occupy a fraction of the space of their real-world counterparts. And sixth, they cause a fraction of the damage to your bank account!

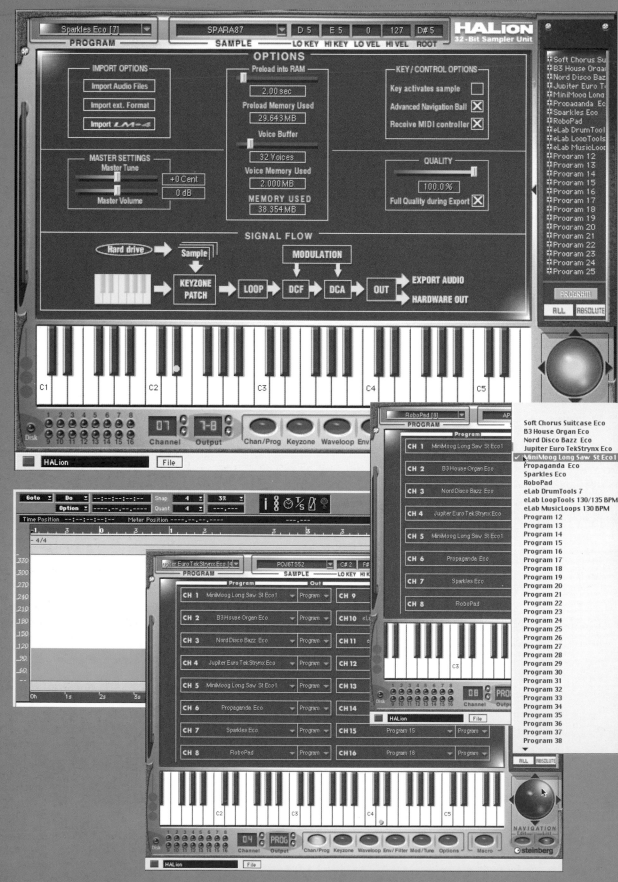

HALION (VST)

Steinberg
www.steinberg.net
VST 32-bit sampler with intuitive
and imaginative graphical
interface, two envelopes, up to
eight edit points, drag-and-drop
functionality, and an embedded
"Waveloop Editor." Comes with
four CDs of samples, loops, and
original content. File formats: WAV,
AIF, Akai (samplers), E-mu
(samplers), SP2, REX.

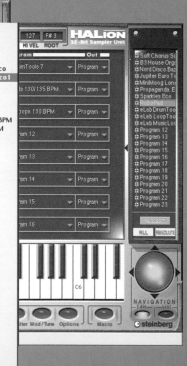

part 02. matching needs to technologies

SOFTWARE SECURITY AND DIGITAL RIGHTS

The Internet is sometimes seen as a modern-day equivalent of the Great Library of Alexandria, that lost repository of human knowledge that was destroyed by warring civilizations between 88 B.C. and A.D. 645. But what is rarely acknowledged is that the Great Library was partly stocked by pirates who robbed ships of manuscripts, bullion, and goods.

The Web has its own warring civilizations: software empires and diversified multinationals on one side, and occasionally, some of us on the other. Software companies pour millions of dollars into antipiracy initiatives, but the wired population still finds itself tempted by the prospect of a free music track here, or a cracked audio software package there.

Digital technology's unique advantage means that anything capable of being digitized can be, and will be, pirated—especially software. As discussed in the introduction, digital piracy is often seen as victimless theft because the "owner" never loses the stolen article. But when we talk about the "owner," those ever-present inverted commas show just how deeply the Internet has challenged the notion of owning a digital property, especially an intellectual property. "Licensee" is now the appropriate word.

But neither side is completely secure in its position. Privately, most software giants accept that professional software pirates have a knack of opening up overseas markets and of driving the purchase of legitimate goods. Just as privately, many individuals will give into the temptation to grab free goods. And if they do give in, they resent the implication that they are doing it for commercial gain (that they are, in other words, acting illegally).

The law will never move at Internet speed, which is why the debate over where legitimate sharing ends and piracy begins is perhaps decades away from resolution. It may never be resolved, and the system may have to live with an "acceptable" degree of abuse. But where does audio and music software stand in all of this? The answer is: in a dangerous position.

Few audio software companies are part of large multinationals, unless they have fallen prey to strategic acquisition, as was the case with Apple's purchase of Emagic (Logic Audio) in 2002, and Pinnacle's acquisition of Steinberg (Cubase, Nuendo) in 2003. Most audio and music-production packages are developed by much smaller companies whose finances are unpredictable, and whose profit margins are slim, given the huge investment in research and development (R&D) that they have to make to stay ahead.

One of the problems with cracking software for home use is the assumption that every company is a multinational that "deserves it," and that every code is there to be cracked. In an age where music hardware companies are going to the wall because of the prevalence of software studios and virtual instruments, those are dangerous assumptions to make. If you crack audio software, you may be the victim in the long run yourself.

Multinationals will always look after themselves, and many are moving toward a future where music software is given away in major retailers, and you will fork out the cash for packaged digital content to run on it. Smaller developers will never have that luxury.

That the legal system is still grappling with the repercussions of the Internet was demonstrated in April 2003 when a US court ruled that the Grotester and Stream Cast, makers of the Grokster and Morpheus file-sharing programs, were not legally responsible for the activities of users.

Despite this, the music and film industries claimed victory, saying the ruling established that file-sharing was "not sharing, but stealing." This debate has been raging now for nearly a decade, but seem no nearer resolution.

Below: **Software companies usually offer demo versions of their software with limited functionality or a time limit in an effort to let potential customers try it out before they pay for it.**

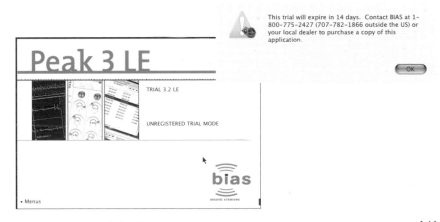

This trial will expire in 14 days. Contact BIAS at 1-800-775-2427 (707-782-1866 outside the US) or your local dealer to purchase a copy of this application.

OK

Peak 3 LE

TRIAL 3.2 LE

UNREGISTERED TRIAL MODE

bias

• Menus

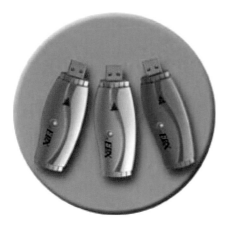

Left: **Dongles have the dual disadvantage of being easy to lose, and of taking up valuable USB port space.**

Below: **Pro Tools Mbox hardware only works with the software, and vice versa.**

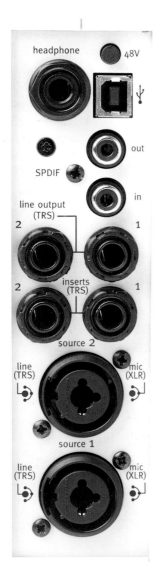

DONGLES

Recent versions of Cubase (SX upward), Logic Audio (Platinum upward), and other packages such as Reaktor sidestep the pirates by shipping with a USB "dongle." This is a small piece of hardware that slips into your USB port and authorizes the software, along with any associated plug-ins.

Without the dongle, the software will lock up. It's a worthy initiative, although dongles have the twin disadvantages of occupying a valuable USB port, and of being easily lost. They may also cause problems with plug-ins that you have sourced legitimately from magazine cover disks.

But the best example of the strategy is Digidesign's Pro Tools suite. Pro Tools is both a software and a hardware product range, so no piece of Pro Tools virtual kit will work without the associated piece of hardware, such as the Mbox, the Digidesign 001 and 002, or any of the high-end devices that the company supplies to studios.

This is a better strategy than the still-crackable dongle, as the quality of the hardware at even the consumer, "LE" end of the range makes it a good investment. And working in a hardware/software environment that is integrated from the ground up means that you avoid the compatibility problems of a more "open" system.

DIGITAL RIGHTS

Obviously, such measures only authorize the tools to make the content, and are of no benefit when it comes to protecting content itself, or enforcing licensing terms for commercial distribution. This brings us to the emerging, and controversial, area of digital rights management.

Much has been written about it in recent years, but the issues are essentially these. The laws governing traditional commerce were drawn up for the physical world of bricks, mortar, and tangible assets. Digital content, such as music released commercially online, is not a tangible asset, and neither does it behave like one, so there is no point in attempting to regulate it and lock it up as though it were a property of the pre-digital age.

Tangible commerce, in which physical goods are moved from A to B, is about distribution; digital commerce, however, is about "superdistribution," where information is able to flow freely between millions of interconnected access points. The technologies that are proposed to make digital content commercially viable in this environment are digital rights management (DRM), and digital libraries (essentially databases that behave like cashpoints).

DRM is about embedding the terms under which digital content can be consumed into an electronic license, in the form of a sealed envelope of data that holds the content itself. To open the content, it must have been paid for, and legally downloaded.

Apple is partnering with music companies to enable paid-for downloads to its iPod MP3 player, suggesting that, if the music industry cannot agree on Internet strategy jointly, then the way ahead seems to be piecemeal deals with individual manufacturers and service providers.

I said to people ten years ago that music would be sold by phone companies, but few believed me.

Peter Gabriel

The technology— essentially an extreme evolution of the serial number system that accompanies any piece of software—is controversial as some companies propose limiting digital content's consumption to the device onto which it has been downloaded. Others suggest time-limiting content so that it deletes itself from a user's system, offering buyers the option to "own" it for one month, for example, or two.

An alternative model is the hosted service. One example of this is Peter Gabriel's On Demand Distribution (OD2). "I said to people ten years ago that music would be sold by phone companies," says Gabriel, "but few believed me." (They obviously had no knowledge of audio's history.)

OD2 is a trusted partner and DRM venture which licenses "e-tailers" to use its services. "I'm delighted to bring the benefits of cutting-edge technology, while looking after artists and rights holders by revolutionizing the distribution system," says Gabriel.

"OD2 uses the Microsoft Windows Media platform to take digital content and encode it in a number of different formats, including MP3, and host it on secure servers. It is encrypted and served by us invisibly to the user, accompanied by an electronic license," adds OD2 CEO Charles Grimsdale.

"Stores used to be places that could turn you on to all sorts of stuff. We believe that e-tailers should now fulfill this role, and OD2 offers a service that enables them to add music to their product range," concludes Gabriel.

Gabriel has a respectable history of supporting the interests of content providers (to use Laurie Anderson's phrase) worldwide. But, arguably, this type of venture casts him and others who seek to be trusted technology partners in the role of intermediaries, something that superdistribution is designed to strip out.

CHANNEL THREE

IN THE STUDIO, PRESENT AND FUTURE

It is not unusual for beginners, hobbyists, or remixers to experiment for a while with some demo software, a few downloaded loops and samples, and perhaps a cheap microphone plugged directly into the soundcard. However, improving the quality of music or audio projects means improving the quality of your components and your home studio.

The size of your setup, and the number of components you will need, both depend on what you want to do with your system. Are you composing or recording music? What genre of music is it? Do you need to record any unusual instruments? What kind of space do you have, and does it have good acoustics? In some cases, you may find that you cannot do everything you need to do, particularly if you are living in a place that has very thin walls. In these cases it might be advisable to rent some studio time to lay down your vocal tracks, for example.

Whatever your practical or financial situation might be, a small range of digital home studio setups is provided here. You will need to shop around and compare individual components yourself. Prices will vary, especially when you are shopping for the right desktop computer to sit at the hub of your studio. If you're tempted to crack software, consider the implications outlined in our earlier look at DRM.

PART 03. IN THE STUDIO

CHAPTER ONE

HOME STUDIO SETUPS

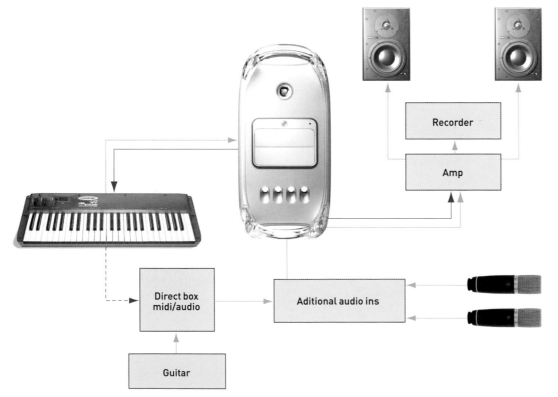

SMALL STUDIO

This is a basic system, but it still has everything you need to create professional songs. However, you will not be able to record a huge amount of instruments simultaneously, so you should be prepared to use synthetic or sampled drums rather than a full drum kit. You can record multiple instruments in multiple takes, however, and mix the resulting tracks on the computer.

MEDIUM-SIZE STUDIO

The main advantage of this slightly larger studio is the ability to use more inputs at once, which means you can record some material live off the floor with multiple musicians. However, the role of the computer here is primarily as an instrument rather than a recording device.

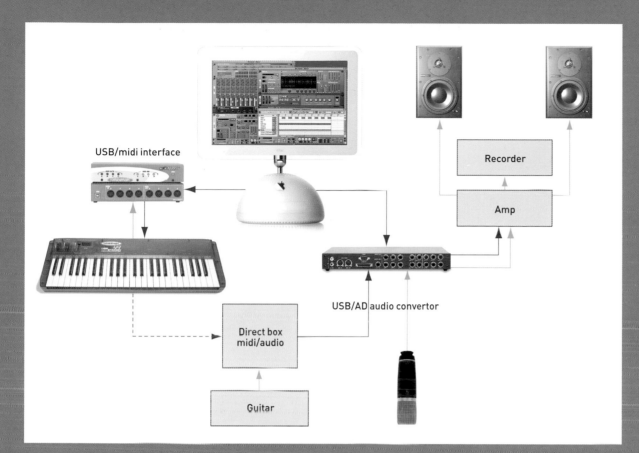

USB/midi interface

Recorder

Amp

USB/AD audio convertor

Direct box midi/audio

Guitar

LARGE STUDIO

This fully interconnected system incorporates several more instruments, and an external mixing desk or integrated studio for the most possibilities in terms of recording situations. With enough microphones, a full band could be recorded live in studio, and being able to mix before the music hits the soundcard is a bonus in this instance. Multiple MIDI devices could be connected to this system at the same time—this can mean that each device can have a person playing it, or that one person can control all the devices using one controller. Most large professional studios use more components than there are in this diagram, but the basic plan remains the same.

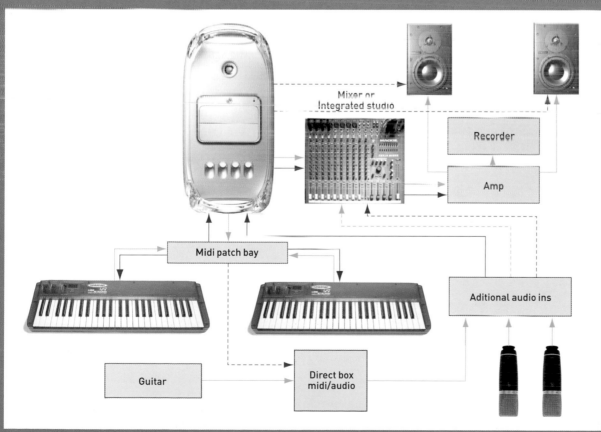

Mixer or Integrated studio

Recorder

Amp

Midi patch bay

Aditional audio ins

Guitar

Direct box midi/audio

Right and below: **A professional studio is not just about having enough cabling to link all the components together, but also a room with the right acoustics. In live situations you will need to separate instruments from one another to some degree; but even when just recording a vocal track by itself, your room needs to have a decent sound with a bit of natural reverb—but not too much! Unless that is the intention...**

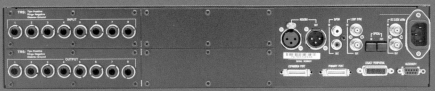

THE ALL-IN-ONE VIRTUAL STUDIO: DIGIDESIGN PRO TOOLS

Digidesign's Pro Tools software has, like Cubase, Logic, MOTU Digital Performer, and Cakewalk SONAR, become synonymous with digital audio. It is one of the names to drop.

What sets Pro Tools apart from its peers is that it is not just audio workstation software, from the "prosumer" LE version (Version 6, at the time of writing) upward. It is also a suite of hardware products, including audio control surfaces, cards, hard disk recorders, mixer modules, and so on.

Many albums, such as Massive Attack's *Mezzanine* and *100th Window*, have been recorded, edited, and produced entirely on Pro Tools suites, or within Pro Tools facilities. Digidesign is a division of video specialist Avid, based at Pinewood Studios, so the products are designed to integrate with a range of other professional media.

At the home and prosumer ends of the market, you can install Pro Tools software on your Mac or PC, attach the Mbox, Digidesign 001, or 002 control surfaces, and hit "Record." But the system will match whatever scale your ambition, imagination, and bank account is aiming for.

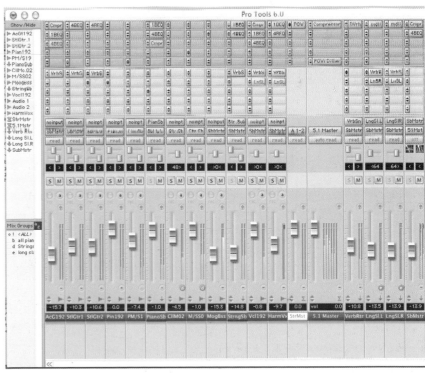

Above: If you do not want to shop for a bunch of separate components, especially if you are uneasy or unsure about whether or not they will function together as intended, then perhaps a Pro Tools suite is your best choice. These suites include high-quality, audio-specific components, such as fast FireWire drives and control surfaces that work together with a software interface.

DESIGNING A SPACE
This is one of the most challenging and fascinating aspects of recording audio, as it cuts to the heart of the question: what is a studio?

Left: **To work in the audio industry, you will have to be adept at dealing with a variety of people, creative individuals in particular. Even musicians themselves don't always get along—Crosby, Stills, Nash, & Young, for example, have endured a great deal of creative conflict during their original time together as a group, and in subsequent reunions. Pictured is Graham Nash in the studio.**

A recording studio is not just one empty room, and another one full of equipment. It is also the people who work there. Studios that have a "sound" are usually the ones that have attracted a group of people who share a passion, a vision, or a way of working, plus the speed of working that comes with true expertise.

No one considering a career in sound should ignore the fact that working with people is 90 percent of the job. If you spend your days nurturing a relationship with a computer, those skills will not transfer easily to an environment where complex, creative people require them. But what has this got to do with designing a space? Everything. It's true that studios such as Hansa in Berlin offer spaces that have a "signature"

acoustic—in Hansa's case, the brittle, metallic sound heard on David Bowie's *Low*. Large facilities such as SARM, Air Lyndhurst, and Abbey Road can also accommodate an orchestra, and work with audio across a range of media. But if you are collaborating with people, you must create an environment where they feel comfortable, as well as one that is sympathetic to what they do.

part 03. in the studio, present and future

You can hide an amazing, fully-featured studio in your home—even Abbey Road is not really that huge (see top left)—but you should be certain that your neighbors cannot hear you, or that they are diehard fans of the singers you are recording! Soundproofing can be a good first step to customizing the acoustics of your recording rooms, but you may not want to lose the original sonic character of a room with, say, a few large windows. Below: SARM studios.

SYMPATHETIC ACOUSTICS

If you work purely digitally with no audio input, then your space exists in a microchip. If you want to record audio, then your space is wherever you lay your laptop—if you have the right equipment. But for most people, creating a physical environment to work in is essential. So, what do you need?

■ For recording voices, instruments, and "spot effects," choose a space that is just "live" enough. In other words, one which neither adds so much room sound that it is impossible to take off, nor one which is so acoustically "dead" that it kills the excitement and sounds unnatural. (Unless, of course, you need either of those options.)

■ Most people like singing in the shower or subway because they experience the joy of hearing their voice in a sympathetic environment. You need to create a sympathetic environment in your home or studio, bearing in mind the reverberation of a subway may not be what you want to hear on disk.

■ Large rooms with hard surfaces and wooden floors are ideal: the sound will be warm and "reedy" and will give you the flexibility to record it ambiently, or to strip out the room sound with close miking. Stone rooms offer powerful reverb for high-volume sounds, plus a surprising amount of bass; metallic rooms are brittle; tiled or glass rooms highly reflective, sometimes warm and complex; rooms with soft furnishings absorb sound and can be acoustically neutral to "dead."

■ To test a space acoustically, clap your hands loudly and listen to the character of the reverberation. If you are recording vocals, sing "Ah" at a range of pitches and listen to how the sound behaves, and how it is reflected back at you. Can you capture that sound?

■ For monitoring and for the recording itself, try to situate your control room in a separate, acoustically dead space, away from the performance area.

■ Do you have sympathetic neighbors?

For more on monitoring, turn to page 166, and for a look at how to fake the acoustic signatures of physical spaces, turn to Effects and Processors, page 162.

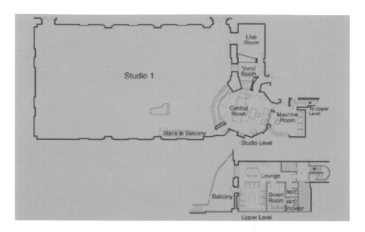

Left: You will need to plan your studio so that there is at least one room that is completely separate from all the recording gear. To test the acoustics in a room, clap your hands loudly and listen to the reverberation; then, try the same thing with your voice. Then, decide if the resulting "natural" effects are something worth capturing.

Above: The late Frank Zappa was a celebrated musician and social commentator, but he was also a major innovator in the studio. He worked in production and owned studios for most of his career and was always among the first few to embrace new methods. He consistently used existing devices and technologies in unusual and ingenious ways.

INSIDE AND OUTSIDE REAL WORLD

Real World has a range of physical spaces, from complex, wooden production facilities and workrooms, to a stone room with a glass floor. Most famously, it offers the "Big Room" (above and left), a flexible recording and rehearsal space built out over the mill pond of a converted watermill in Box, near Bath, England.

The room is concrete, glass, and steel, with a high ceiling. One unusual feature is the ventilation, via huge ceramic pipes. Although the room is sealed from the outside world, there is a distinct breath of fresh air. Peter Gabriel explains in his introduction to the studio that he "wanted the air to feel like someone had left a window open."

MICROPHONES AND MIKE USAGE

Let's rewind to an earlier cue point: we're back at transducers. Microphones are the main transducers for turning soundwaves into electrical impulses. There are many different types, and hundreds of models at every price point that you can imagine.

Invest in one good microphone at least, preferably a pair. But if you can only afford one for recording a voice, ambient sound, or perhaps a live instrument, have a look at our array of usual suspects.

Remember: your PC mike, or a $10 microphone you pick up in an electrical store, is the equivalent of wrapping a piece of plastic wrap over a camera body and expecting it to act like a lens.

If you want an all-round vocal mike that adds a kick to voices, consider an affordable, quality condenser mike, such as the AKG C1000S. This is a small diaphragm model—mikes like this will add an edge to voices—and you can switch the AKGs between cardioid and hypercardioid patterns.

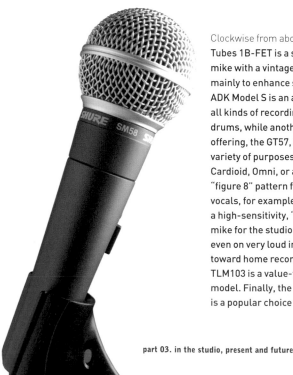

Clockwise from above: **The Groove Tubes 1B-FET is a solid-state cardioid mike with a vintage sound, intended mainly to enhance strong vocals. The ADK Model S is an all-purpose mike for all kinds of recording, from vocals to drums, while another Groove Tubes offering, the GT57, is also intended for a variety of purposes, and is available in Cardioid, Omni, or a Hypercardoid "figure 8" pattern for interviews or duet vocals, for example. The AKG C2000B is a high-sensitivity, "workhorse"-type mike for the studio and will work well even on very loud instruments. Geared toward home recordists, the Neumann TLM103 is a value-for-budget-price model. Finally, the rugged Shure SM58 is a popular choice for live vocals.**

MICROPHONE TYPES AND USES

Dynamic mikes operate by means of a moving coil to capture sound pressure. Small-diaphragm cardioid versions like the SM57, SM58, and Beta 58A are popular for live vocals, and they don't need powering. Large-diaphragm dynamic mikes are extremely rugged and can handle equally rugged sound sources.

Condenser mikes use the diaphragm method (as it were) of capturing sound. Such mikes can be "phantom powered" by many devices, such as a mixing desk, or run with an integral battery. Condenser mikes are highly responsive, but less rugged. They add a kick to voices, as they are sensitive to high and transient frequencies, but boost the bass with proximity. Small-diaphragm condenser models love high frequencies, while large-diaphragm condenser mikes add a unique warmth all round, especially for studio vocals.

Left: You could use a direct box such as the M-Audio DMP3 to record vocals directly into your soundcard.

MIKE RECORDING PATTERNS AND THE PROXIMITY EFFECT
CARDIOID (DIRECTIONAL)

Cardioid mikes, such as many small-diaphragm condenser models, grab sound predominantly from directly in front, but capture far less from either side, and nothing from behind (hence cardioid pattern mikes' popularity in live environments, or in less than ideal home spaces). The sound pickup pattern is an inverted heart shape, hence the name.

Cardioid-pattern mikes accentuate the bass frequencies of a sound when the source is closely miked. This is known as the "proximity effect," and led to the "crooning" sound in the 1930s, where singers such as Bing Crosby sang close to their condenser mikes to produce a rich, *basso* sound. Conversely, cardioid-pattern mikes can make the sound thin when placed at a distance.

HYPERCARDIOID (BI-DIRECTIONAL)

Similiar to cardioid models, they also pick up sounds from behind in a similar pattern— useful if you want to grab a little of the room sound in a close environment without picking up reflections from specific areas. The sound pickup pattern is thus a "figure 8."

OMNIDIRECTIONAL

These pick up sounds from all directions, with a good bass response, but no proximity effect. They are thus best suited for ambient sounds, capturing a room sound, or close-miking a voice without exaggerated bass boost.

Left: For a genuine, warm-sounding pentode tube mike, the Groove Tubes 1B is a good bet, but expect to pay a higher price.

MIXERS AND MIXING

Mixers are the devices that bring your audio to life. They give you the opportunities to "hear what's there," to turn your raw material into a fully realized stereo picture, or to immerse yourself in a dynamic surround-sound environment.

You can listen to each audio channel individually, place it at a desired point in the stereo or surround-sound picture, and move it relative to any other signal, or group of signals, in the mix. And, as we have already covered, you can manage the frequency and phase relationships between all the signals you've gathered.

In the physical world, analog and digital mixing desks give you all the advantages of an interface that you can touch and interact with. Whether you are recording to a digital multitracker or onto your Mac/PC, adding mixer hardware to your home studio setup enables you to manage complex inputs from music devices, microphones, and other audio sources into a single stereo feed before it enters the digital realm.

In the virtual world, the mixer sections of your main application either mimic their physical counterparts, as is the case with Reason, BIAS Deck, and so on, or add window after window of functionality, as you will see in the mixer windows of packages like Logic Audio, and Cubase.

But virtual mixers' real advantages lie in the fact that they can be infinitely expandable. Virtual mixers also give you automation as standard, and your software will save the mix with each track. Hardware mixing desks offer automation at a hefty price point (via motorized "flying" faders), while the majority of desks have to be manually set up for each piece of work—not easy if you have lost your notes.

Above: **Automation is standard on virtual mixers; on real mixing desks, "flying faders" are something you pay dearly for.**

These are the most common components of any mixer, real or virtual:
- **Channel Faders for managing the relative volumes of each channel of audio**
- **Master Faders for managing the overall volume and stereo output of the audio**
- **Group Faders for managing the relative volumes of groups of individual channels, routed from the Group Assign function, for example in a 16 (channel) : 8 (group) : 2 (stereo) mixer**
- **Inserts for sending single audio channels out to an external effects processor prior to equalization, then routing them back in at the same point. Mixers can have anything from one Insert point per channel, to multiple Inserts that are individually addressable and editable**
- **(Aux) Sends for routing any number of audio channels out to effects and signal processors by an amount that is individually assignable within each channel**
- **(Aux) Returns for returning the overall output of the external effect back into the mixer**
- **Gain controls for managing either the amplitude of the input signal into each channel,**

and/or for managing the amplitude of a signal within specific frequency bands

■ Meters presenting a visual readout in decibels of individual channel volumes, plus the master volume, usually showing a maximum of +6 dB or thereabouts (remember, this is a measure of relative amplitude)

■ Panpots for positioning signals within the stereo picture, from hard left through every degree to hard right

■ Mute and Solo buttons for muting individual tracks, or hearing them in isolation during a complex mix

■ EQ—The "meat" of your mixing desk, offering two, three, four, or more sweepable frequency bands within which the relative amplitude of a signal can be enhanced or diminished.

Above and right: Although newer-model mixing desks are becoming more compact, you can still end up with a fairly big workspace; this is fine, as long as you are comfortable working with your gear.

MIXING WORKSHOP In this illustration, a VST Channel Mixer in Cubase has been set up for audio Channel one. The EQ button has been activated, and the VST Channel Settings window shows the EQ and Effects settings for that audio channel.

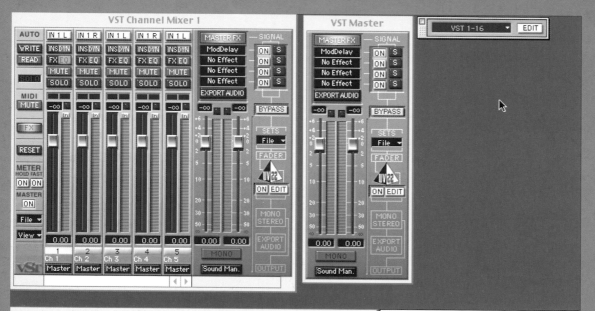

Each band of the four-band EQ section (bottom right in the Channel Settings window) has been activated. The first has added a Gain of +11.3 dB to the 20 Hz frequency band; the second, a Gain of –1.3 dB to the 688 Hz range (the signal has been attenuated); the third, a Gain of –1.7 dB to the (approx) 6.2 kHz band; and the fourth, a Gain of +4.7 dB to the 12 kHz band.

The readout above plots the curve of the EQ, relative to 0 dB (relative amplitude). Each of the EQ bands creates a graphical node in the readout, represented by the white squares numbered 1 to 4. You could click on any one of these and drag the node vertically to change its amplitude, or horizontally to move the frequency band.

Finally, the Channel One Insert window shows that a Compressor (see Jargon buster page 67) has been activated on the Insert to audio Channel one. The graph shows the curve of the compression in decibels between the input and output. The gate and limiter (see Effects and Processors, page 162) options are not active.

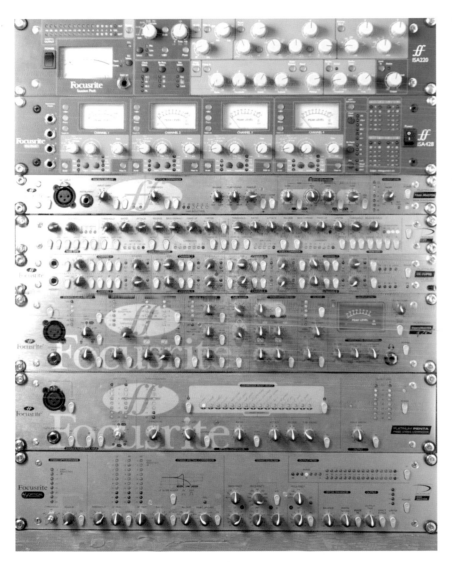

Above: Resist the urge to overuse effects and EQ when you first start mixing, but do not be afraid to get creative! That, after all, is what your gear is for.

TIPS FOR A GOOD MIX

INPUT

When recording an analog audio source, such as a human voice, record it with no alterations to EQ (switch EQ off, or turn the controls to center). Remember: any changes in a signal's EQ at this stage will be recorded along with the audio. Equalize the recorded track on playback.

If the person who is speaking or singing is unhappy with the way their voice sounds through their headphones, fix the sound for them in the monitor channel, not in the audio channel you are recording to. Consider adding a little reverb to the foldback or monitor channels (which will not be recorded). In a piece of music, this will give your performer a virtual space to sing into—singers respond to the acoustic properties of a space.

Remember: how you mix the sound in their headphones will affect the way they perform, if the backing track is too loud, they will strain to hear themselves, too quiet and they may underperform.

Without EQ, the voice may sound flat or dull on initial playback, but you will fix this in the mix by "digging out" the frequencies to bring the voice back to life. The secret is: don't panic—if you have a good mike, the information will be there.

When equalizing the signal (or applying EQ, depending on which school of thought you prefer), remember that you are dealing with complex waveforms, frequencies, harmonics, and phase relationships. Accentuating one band of frequencies will bring to light different aspects of a voice. For example, stressing a band of 8 kHz or so will make it brighter and hissier; focusing on the bass 120–200 Hz range will bring out a richer, rounder aspect. Combine the two and you have a voice with edge and depth. But every voice is different, and every mix is different. The best advice is: experiment, not just with getting the right vocal sound in isolation, but also with "sitting it in" with the rest of your audio.

STEREO IMAGING

If you are going for a "widescreen," cinematic type of sound, try thinking of your mix as the audio equivalent of looking at characters in a landscape, such as in the view you might have from a hilltop. Why do this? Because it encourages you to consider perspective.

When you look out over a landscape, distant objects appear small and near objects vast. Apply this to your mix. In other words, you don't achieve an expansive sound by turning everything up and positioning it dead center—quite the reverse: you create it by positioning some objects at a distance.

If you are going for realism when recording a voice or musical instrument in a specific space, such as a medium-size, wooden-floored room (see page 165), try to preserve the ambience of the space when you add audio from digital sources. Don't throw effects, EQ, or reverb times into the mix that contradict or ignore the acoustic signature of the room.

Try to record as much of the room sound as possible using additional stereo mikes, listen to the ambience they capture, and program your signal processors accordingly. Alternately, try feeding the digital signal back into the room and re-recording it by analog means.

OUTPUT

Once you've gathered all the audio for your finished piece, be bold. Save off a backup of your work, then take all the faders down, switch off any EQ, and take every effect out of the chain. Save again if you're working virtually. Then walk away.

For your final mixdown, leave perhaps a day or a week (if time allows) before returning to your work. Then build up your mix from scratch, listening to each track in isolation, and in relation to other tracks or groups of tracks. Prepare different mixes and save them off, some extreme and impulsive, others conservative and more predictable. From time to time, compare the results with your original saved backup.

The right mix is the one that makes you sit up and listen, or feel you've exceeded your inspiration. If a mix fails to move you or involve you as you're doing it, walk away from it and return when you're feeling more inspired. Or take a leaf out of Eno's *Oblique Strategies* (page 42) and try a change of tack.

MIXING AND SAVING IN A WAVE EDITOR

Once you've completed your mix and saved off your work as a WAV or an AIF, for example, you can apply further edits to it in a wave-editing program, such as SoundForge, Wavelab, or BIAS Peak. This is particularly useful when you are saving your work for different types of output, such as CD, DVD, the Web, and so on, or synchronizing it with a video source.

For example, you could program fades in and out, and edit out whole sections of your piece, joining the ends invisibly. You could even strip out a section, then perhaps drop it in backward.

■ Remember: audio is your raw material; be as constructive or as destructive as you like. Don't set limits on your imagination. As engineer Marco Migliari says, "There is no right and wrong when you record audio. Only different people, and different studios."

A WORD ABOUT EQ

It is tempting to go for "extreme EQ" when you first get into mixing. Professionals rarely do this, as EQ is really designed to compensate for the problems of capturing and reproducing sounds accurately. As long as your input from the analog world is good enough, you will not greatly improve the sound of a human voice, or a bass guitar, by radically altering its EQ—unless you are aiming for a specific effect.

It may be better to leave the EQ neutral, and take out frequencies within a similar band from "around" the instrument instead. Remember: EQ can achieve the same effects by subtracting information from other elements as it can by adding information to the subject.

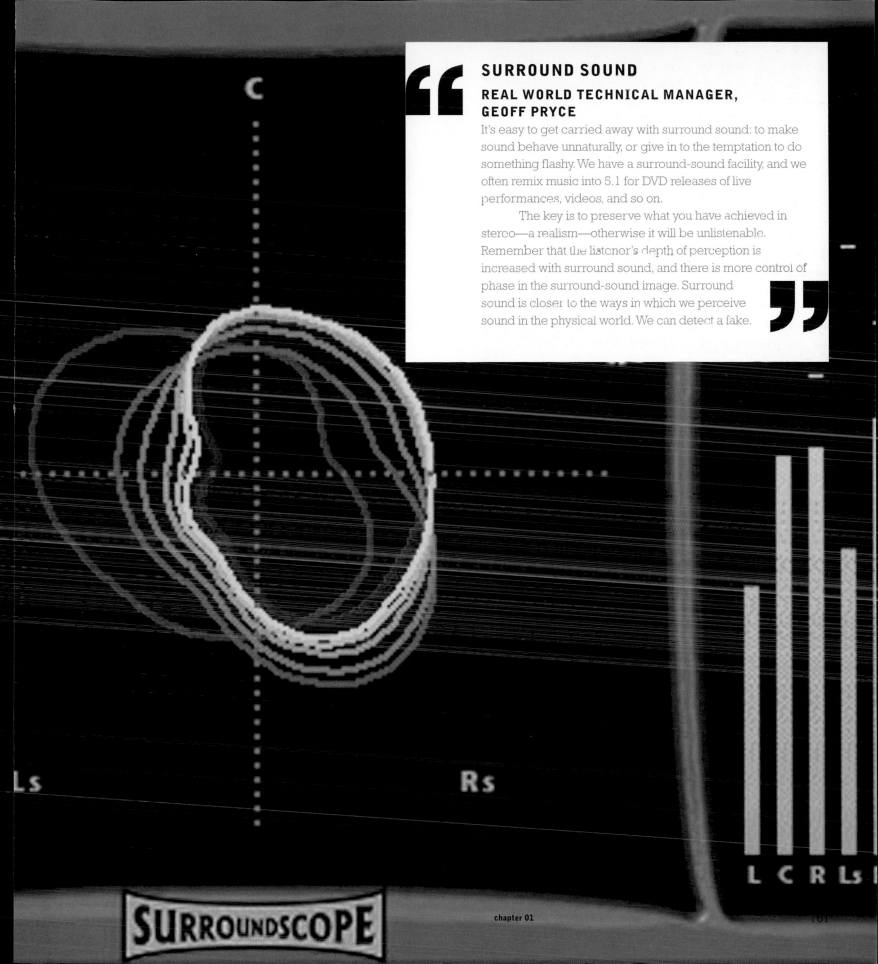

SURROUND SOUND
REAL WORLD TECHNICAL MANAGER, GEOFF PRYCE

It's easy to get carried away with surround sound: to make sound behave unnaturally, or give in to the temptation to do something flashy. We have a surround-sound facility, and we often remix music into 5.1 for DVD releases of live performances, videos, and so on.

The key is to preserve what you have achieved in stereo—a realism—otherwise it will be unlistenable. Remember that the listener's depth of perception is increased with surround sound, and there is more control of phase in the surround-sound image. Surround sound is closer to the ways in which we perceive sound in the physical world. We can detect a fake.

Once your audio has crossed over into the digital realm, signal processing is the group of technologies that plays with the dimensional aspects of your audio signal: its dynamic range, its dimension in virtual space, and its relationship with time.

Often called simply "effects," signal processing is all about creating virtual environments in time and space—some of which bear no relation to the real world. On your computer, you can explore them via suites of plug-ins; in the hardware world, you can find them within multieffect rack units, or pedals (stomp boxes).

Some effects, such as reverb (reverberation), emulate the acoustic signatures of physical spaces, and the ways in which a signal is reflected off surfaces, such as walls, floors, and so on. Others apply spatial movement to a signal, either across the stereo image, or in three dimensions. Yet more apply the dimension of time to a signal in any number of idiosyncratic ways.

PART 03. IN THE STUDIO

CHAPTER TWO

EFFECTS AND PROCESSORS

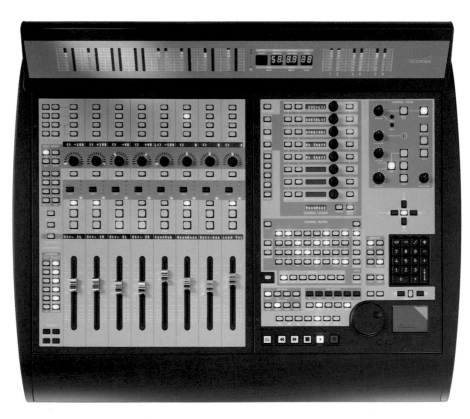

Right: **Many portable integrated studios, control surfaces, and digital mixers contain built-in digital effects boards.**

Left: **Effects and signal processors range from the very basic to the extraordinary. The more, the merrier—but beware of flashy mixes.**

USING EFFECTS Exploring and creating virtual spaces is one of the most exciting aspects of creative digital audio, but it is easy to get carried away by applying reverb to anything that moves.

If you listen closely to professional recordings, you will hear that there is rarely much audible reverb there.
That said, the use of effects changes with fashion: in the 1970s it was all about distortion, flanging, and the application of echo; in the 1980s, expansive reverbs on voices and drums, plus chorusing and delay on instruments; in the 1990s and up to the present day, an increasing focus on compression, tightness, and clarity.

Here are some of the hundreds of effects and effect types available, both hardware- and software-based.

DYNAMIC EFFECTS
■ **Compressors: manage the dynamic volume changes of a signal within editable parameters**
■ **Limiters: set a dynamic threshold above or below which a signal cannot move**
■ **Expanders: create the inverse of compression, increasing a signal's dynamic range under editable parameters**
■ **(Noise) gates: let signals above an assignable threshold pass, but attenuate signals that fall beneath that threshold. Used subtly, they can omit background noise from a vocal**
■ **Distortion, overdrive, fuzz, etc: increase signals' amplitudes by controllable amounts to create harmonic distortion**

TIME-BASED EFFECTS
Reverbs and echoes mimic the acoustic signature of real spaces by creating echoes of the original signal. In the case of reverb, these echoes are subtle, complex, and minutely spaced. By editing timing parameters along with a signal's EQ, reverb effects can build virtual spaces in the listener's mind by imitating the ways in which sound behaves in real environments.

DELAYS
These delay echoes of the input signal by assignable amounts, and with varying degrees of feedback and repetition. Programable "tap" delays create rhythmic patterns of delays—you could, for example, create a delay in $^3/_4$ time, or imitate the footfalls of a galloping horse.

PHASERS
These delay an echo of the input signal by fractional amounts so the two signals are out of phase. "Flangers" is a similar process using variable short delays.

CHORUSES
This is a mix of a minutely delayed signal with a subtle change in pitch between the two signals.

PITCHSHIFTERS AND HARMONIZERS
These are a group of dozens of effects that address the frequencies of signals, adding or multiplying related harmonics, or transposing the original signal through harmonic intervals.

So, are you on the road to delay, man?

REAL SPACES IN VIRTUAL SPACE

ARENA

Reverb time: 2–3 seconds
Reverb predelay: 50ms
EQ: (High) 8 kHz to -2 dB; (Mid)
2 kHz to 0 dB; (Low) 200 Hz to
+2 dB High frequency reverb
damping at 3.2 kHz to -6 dB
Early reflection predelay: 10ms
Reverb level: 80%
Direct signal level: 70%

CATHEDRAL

Reverb time: 5 seconds approx
Reverb predelay: 30ms
EQ: (High) 8 kHz to -6 dB; (Mid)
4 kHz to –4 dB; (Low) 200 Hz to
+3 dB High frequency reverb
damping at 3.2 kHz to -9 dB
Early reflection predelay: 50ms
Reverb level: 60%
Direct signal level: 80%

MEDIUM-SIZE ROOM

Reverb time: 0.7–0.8 seconds
Reverb predelay: 5ms
EQ: (High) 8 kHz to -1 dB; (Mid)
2 kHz to 0 dB; (Low) 200 Hz to
+6 dB High frequency reverb
damping at 10 kHz to -1 dB
Early reflection predelay: 15ms
Reverb level: 90%
Direct signal level: 100%

WOODEN FLOOR

Reverb time: 0.6 sec
Reverb predelay: 0ms
EQ: (High) 8 kHz to +4 dB;
(Mid) 1.6 kHz to –3 dB; (Low) 200
Hz to +9 dB Reverb high-frequency
damping at 2 kHz to -9 dB
Early reflection predelay: 15ms
Reverb level: 75%
Signal direct level: 100%

For metallic room reverbs,
increase the delay time to one
second or more; boost High to
+8 dB, take Mid down to -6 dB,
and boost Low to +6 dB; increase
reverb predelay to 10ms, and
damp at 2.5 kHz to -9 dB.]

■ Did you know that...? When
dealing with echoes of up to 35
ms, the volume of the echo has to
be 10 dB higher than the original
signal to be discernible as an
echo (F. Alton Everest, *Master
Handbook of Acoustics*, 2001).
This is the secret of reverb.

Above: When adjusting reverb settings,
remember that in professional
recordings there is usually not much
audible reverb in current production
techniques, although it can be useful for
specific effects.

One aspect of sound is often forgotten: there is no "correct" environment in which to hear it. Every sound that you hear is not only the product of whatever makes it, but also of the space in which it is made and heard. When the sound has been recorded, it will be reproduced in an infinite variety of physical and atmospheric environments, by any number of different devices—cheap radios, expensive hi-fis, tiny laptop speakers, and so on.

Of all the creative digital arts, audio is by far the most subjective, and the least predictable. This is why the single most important factors are confidence, imagination, the ability to listen (*truly* listen), and a good set of monitors. Think only this: there is a small corner of a foreign sound field that remains forever analog.

As we said in Channel One, the problem for the creative audiophile is that you have no control over how your listener will hear your work, on what device, and in what environment. So when monitoring audio, it is clear that you need a known reference source, plus a physical environment to work in that "colors" the sound as little as possible.

WHAT ARE MONITORS?

Monitors are not "special" in any way; they are distinct from other loudpseakers only in that they are designed and calibrated to be "reference" sources. In other words, they are intended to reveal as much of what is there as possible, but to add little to it.

If you're a music fan, you might choose hi-fi speakers that add a "kick" to the music you like for home listening. But when choosing monitors, you want speakers that reveal all the details that motivate you—those bass sounds, that vocal edge—but which don't enhance them artificially.

If your speakers add too much detail to your work, that extra kick will be missing when you play your recording back on lesser systems. Similarly, if your speakers are tinny and unresponsive, you will overcompensate in your work in an effort to make them "sing."

PART 03. IN THE STUDIO

CHAPTER THREE

MONITORS, MONITORING, AND MASTERING

Left: **Monitor speakers should offer very good fidelity without artificially enhancing any elements of the sound.**

NEAR AND FAR

Broadly speaking, there are two types of monitor: far-field, and near-field. (Monitors can be active or passive as well, but these are best compared in situ at your retailer.) Far-field monitors are large speaker systems that are designed to sit some distance back from (or above) the mixing desk, and be driven at relatively high volume. If you have floor-standing hi-fi speakers, consider deploying them in this way.

Near-field monitors are similar to "bookshelf" hi-fi speakers. They should sit about six feet apart on either side of the mixing desk or workspace, pointing toward you. In this way, you are at the center of the stereo image (in the "sweet spot"). They are best deployed at low to middling volume. Obviously, you can also monitor via a surround-sound system, adding center, surround left, surround right, and effects monitors. But for audio that is intended primarily for stereo consumption, resist the temptation to mix and monitor in surround sound.

Below: **Your near-field monitors are important because you will probably do a large portion of your work on them, to begin with at least, and many models approximate what you will hear on a hi-fi.**

part 03. in the studio, present and future

Left: **Pop stars like Kylie have to consider the fact that their songs will often be heard on mono radios or personal stereos, so their songs are mixed accordingly.**

MONITORING

REAL WORLD TECHNICAL MANAGER, GEOFF PRYCE

The producer Bob Clearmountain spearheaded the success of Yamaha NS10s [ubiquitous near-field monitors] as they approximate what most audio will sound like on a hi-fi. But monitoring is not an exact science, it's just good sense. Kylie comes in to record vocals and she rehearses here. When she's finished, she sometimes plugs a ghetto blaster into the mixing desk and listens to the mix on that. That's because most of the time her stuff will be heard on the radio, or in clubs—an environment we can imitate on far-field monitors.

■ **Choose a reference CD: a favorite commercial recording, perhaps, whose production values appeal. Listen to that on your monitors. How does your work compare in terms of overall EQ? Examine your reference CD in a spectrum analyzer, in your hi-fi's graphic equalizer, or in the equalizer within Apple's iTunes, for example. In which frequency bands is the reference CD superior? Can you match this in your work without spoiling the mix?**

■ **Remember to listen to your work at a range of volumes. The high and low frequencies that really "sing" at high volume will not do so when you turn the volume down. Conversely, frequencies that sound dynamic at low volume will sound exaggerated when you push the volume higher.**

MONITORING TIPS

■ **If you can't afford a pair of dedicated monitors, you need to establish your reference points (you must do this anyway!). Listen to your work repeatedly on your chosen speakers, then also on as many different devices as possible: hi-fis, car stereos, personal stereos, mono radios, a stereo TV via a DVD player, and so on. Mono is vital: your listener may not be using a stereo.**

■ **What are the differences when hearing your work on each device? Is there a consensus that you need to roll off some bass, or add some brightness? Once you have established these reference points, you can predict your monitors' behavior, and perhaps compensate in your work, or via a dedicated monitor EQ channel in your mixer. Again, it's all about checks and balances.**

■ **When recording voices or musical instruments with a microphone, ensure that your performer wears headphones, preferably "sealed" ones that prevent the sound from being picked up by the microphone. Using monitor speakers in the same room as the performer risks creating feedback. This happens when a microphone picks up the sound it is sending to the speakers and creates a feedback loop, that all-too-familiar whistling sound. (Also set up a cheap PC mike so you can talk to your performer.)**

Monitoring is not a discipline that you can pick up in a day. It's a lifelong learning process. It's also part of the fun.

MASTERING You could be forgiven for imagining that once you've invested all your time and energy in getting the perfect mix, that would be all there is to it—just burn it onto CD, and wait for the phone to start ringing. You'd be wrong. Mastering is an art itself. It's also a two-part process:

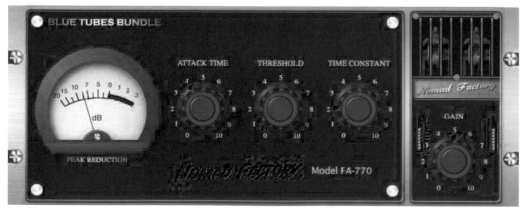

First, listening to a completed mix and deciding what else needs to be done to it as a whole, rather than to each of its component parts and the balance between them. Can it be made more punchy, more spacious, harder, warmer, tighter, more bassy, harder and brighter for radio (and so on)? Does it sit with the visuals in a video? Could it be richer, less invasive?

Second, considering its output—all of those multitudinous access points that we have discussed throughout the book, Web, DVD, video, online video, CD, radio, and so on. What did you lose in the transfer to 16-bit CD from 24-bit in your original work? Does your work sound thinner as an MP3 aimed at Web consumption? Can you fix it in a wave editor?

Most software applications offer you some basic mastering tools. Logic Audio, in particular, offers a superb range of tools that take your finished mix, whether it is a WAV or an AIF, and apply a range of editable preset mastering parameters, from gentle to "brick wall" (massive compression and limiting).

Left: You might want to add subtle effects to your master mix, like a bit of vintage tube sound to give it some retro-style warmth.

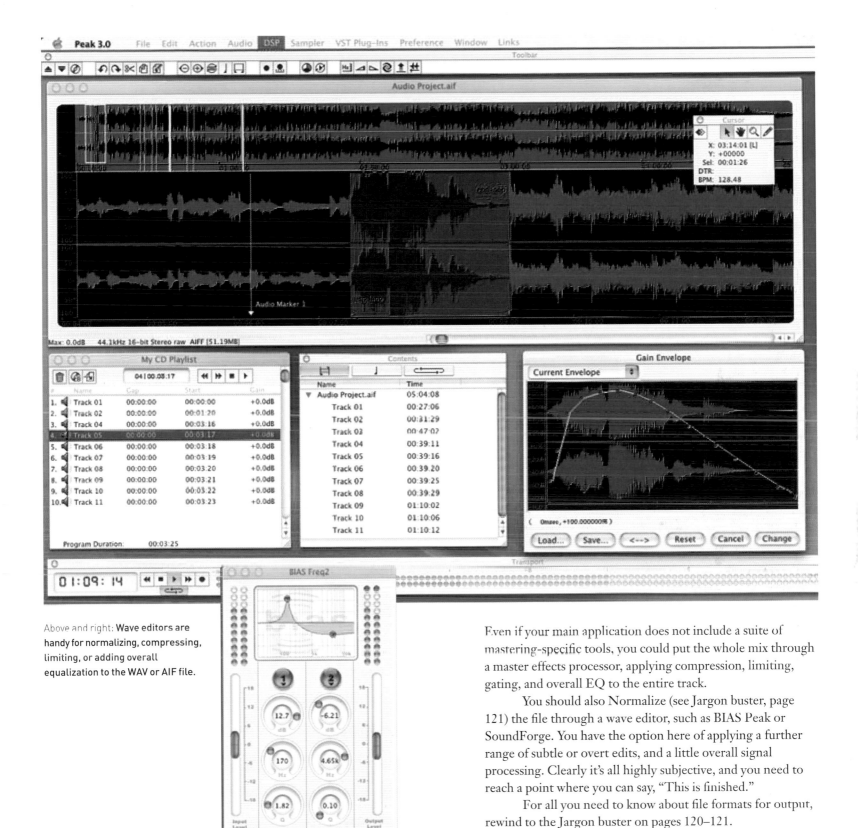

Above and right: Wave editors are handy for normalizing, compressing, limiting, or adding overall equalization to the WAV or AIF file.

Even if your main application does not include a suite of mastering-specific tools, you could put the whole mix through a master effects processor, applying compression, limiting, gating, and overall EQ to the entire track.

You should also Normalize (see Jargon buster, page 121) the file through a wave editor, such as BIAS Peak or SoundForge. You have the option here of applying a further range of subtle or overt edits, and a little overall signal processing. Clearly it's all highly subjective, and you need to reach a point where you can say, "This is finished."

For all you need to know about file formats for output, rewind to the Jargon buster on pages 120–121.

CHANNEL FOUR

FUTURE VIEWS Q&A GLOSSARY INDEX

04

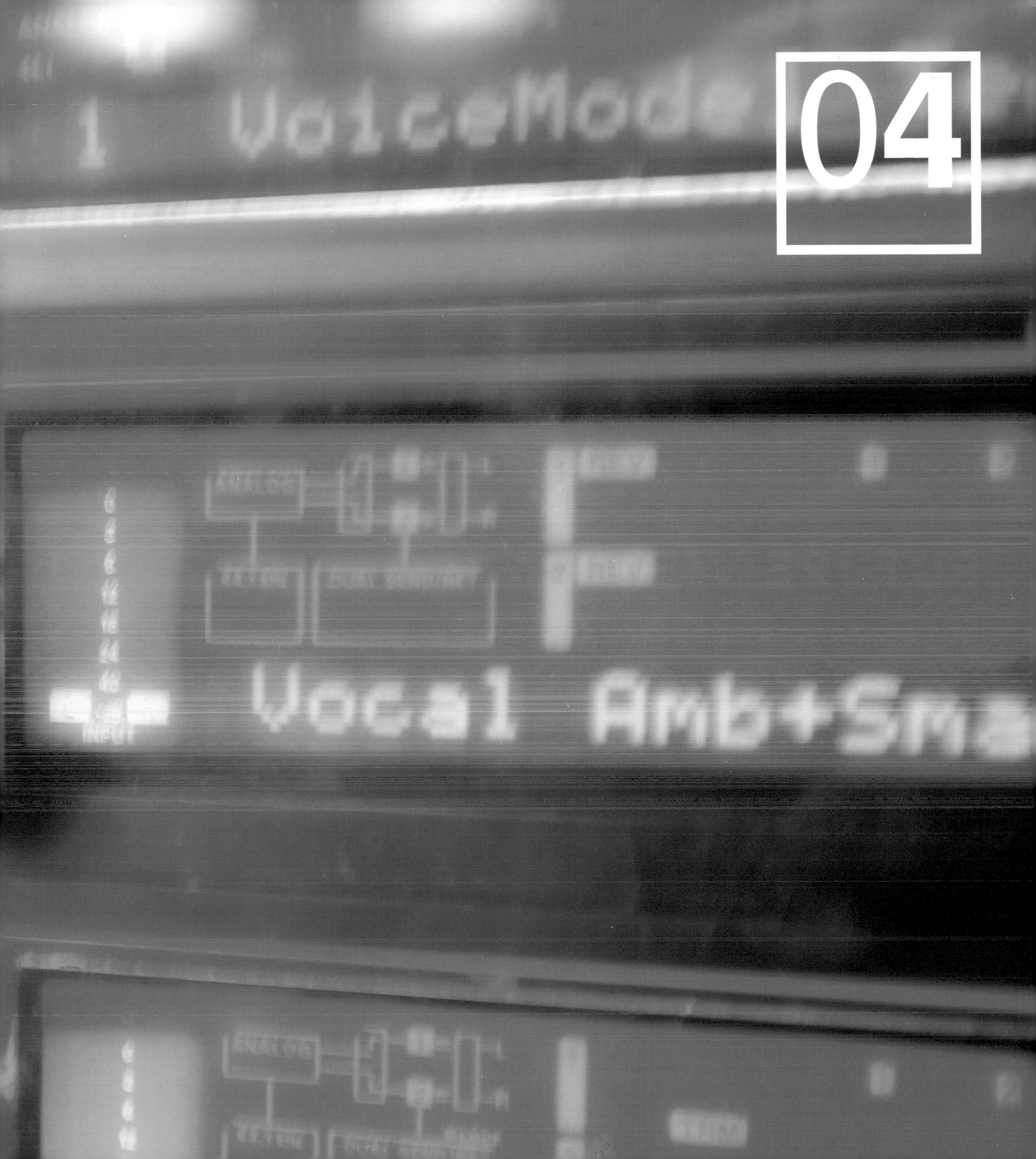

It's been a long journey, but your *Complete Guide* hopes it has also been a challenging, fun, and provocative one—that's what any creative digital art should be. Now, let's get back to the future we were discussing at the start of our journey: that on/off romance with technology. In reality, of course, we live in an eternal present. There are an infinite number of possible futures, and as any futurist knows, it is usually the unpredictable ones that happen.

That said, even the ground we've covered so far has given us many clues about the likely shape of the next five years of technology development and how they will affect audio- and music-making, sharing, and consumption.

LINUX

The freeware, open-source operating system will challenge the audio software industry as a whole, and thereby the hardware manufacturers too, by driving down the cost of audio software for Linux machines. High-end organizations that run Unix will be well placed to make a jump, and developers who have made the move to supporting Apple's OS X will be in an advantageous position.

But the economic repercussions of this for some companies will be damaging—if Linux distributors can present a united face and begin operating like the corporations many in that community affect to despise. This means trouble in the ranks internally if a Linux distie decides to be the next Microsoft. Certainly one to watch.

FUTURE VIEWS AND VIEWS FROM THE TOP

DIGITAL RADIO MEETS INTERNET RADIO, GOES MOBILE

Otherwise known as radio with pictures, but the real key lies in technology convergence around mobile devices. At present, digital radio is seen as a euphemism for "expensive radio," despite bolting the broadcast model onto the digital advantage—and digital sound quality, of course. But it won't take long for the penny to drop: that's *broadcast* and *digital*.

Consider the implications. We know that digital data consists of those precious streams of ones and zeros, and that it doesn't matter whether the digital words describe audio, video, text, images, animation, and so on. That means broadcast video, digital audio and, most significantly perhaps, broadcast software and upgrades.

The whole impetus of digital technology in recent years has been toward establishing and maintaining one-to-one relationships, and toward location-specific services. There is no reason to assume that this will not apply to digital radio as well.

Above: There are many possible futures, and anyone can shape the one that actually occurs. It may not look like this, unless you enjoy dressing up.

Left: There are now many Web broadcasts offering features on new and cutting-edge music of any genre.

WHAT ARE THE IMPLICATIONS?
SOME OF THE PREDICTABLE ONES MIGHT BE:

■ a selective or predictive direct relationship with preferred artists, groups of artists, or music type

■ access to the whole world of Internet radio, offering an idiosyncratic program of content, and balancing the selective, "pull" nature of the Net with the broadcast principles of radio and TV

■ new forms of pirate radio, bringing new content (just as they did in the 1960s, forcing national broadcasters to change their programing)

■ subscription-based access to preferred audio and music services

■ software upgrades on the fly for your main audio application

■ interactive radio, bringing all the pulling power of pushing that red button

■ location-specific audio and video

■ access to visual data with your selected radio content

You can already download Internet radio software off the Web, and turn your Mac or PC into an online radio station broadcasting to a potentially global audience. As ever, legislation may take the hammer-blow approach to kill off potential licensing obstacles and piracy, but there is nothing preventing you from broadcasting your own audio to the world, and perhaps selling it commercially off the back of any interest.

Given the ability to embed one type of content in another thanks to metadata formats, such as XML and XMF, any broadcast digital content could trigger any other type of digital content. One repercussion might be an intelligent radio version of the TiVO personal video recorder, which seeks out audio content of a certain type.

GAMES, GAMING PLATFORMS: NEW FORMS OF AUDIO CREATION AND CONSUMPTION

These developments are already happening. Given that the next installment of *Tomb Raider* has an orchestral score recorded at Abbey Road, we know that audio is seen as an emerging area in which games developers can differentiate their products. *The Complete Guide*'s contact at Sony has outlined a new strategy for the diversified giant.

Sony has long been seeking a new demographic outside of gamers for its PlayStation hardware. Sony is now developing a range of lifestyle music and audio games (some of which may be in the shops as you read this). Using these games, players can create and remix licensed content read directly off the hard disk, and also rip original material to their hard disk. What is new is that Sony could give away the software on a CD of licensed content that you buy in the shops like any other album. In this way, audio software becomes an impulse, lifestyle purchase.

GENERATIVE AND VECTOR AUDIO

It's inevitable that digital technology will maintain its contingent relationship with audio and with music, with each pushing the other to new places, and the creation of new sounds and possibilities. One recent evolution has been the emergence of generative audio and music engines, a technology that uses computers' number-crunching potential and speed to generate music, rather than simply process sound.

The most successful example of this is Koan, software developed by British, BAFTA-award-winning company Sseyo, now part of the Tao Group. Using Koan, composers plant the "seeds" of an idea in the software, and the audio and music environments "grow" organically within the system. (Game software such as *The Sims* uses generative principles, where you create characters and environments and then leave them to interact).

CAN YOU MAKE IT IN THE SOUND INDUSTRY?

REAL WORLD STUDIO MANAGER OWEN LEECH, CHIEF ENGINEER MARCO MIGLIARI

OL: We take on work-experience people, and we always remember the good ones and try to keep them. But it's all about communication. A good doctor is the one who communicates best with the patients. It's crucial to be good with people. IT knowledge is useless if you can't get on with people!

The "tape op" who goes on to become an engineer or a producer doesn't exist any more in most studios—technology has stifled that route. Now you need a knowledge of IT to assist at that kind of level, and be qualified to do it. The best producers are artists; the best engineers are technicians, and there are fewer places to study. Nowadays it's harder to break out than to break in. The problem is that if someone leaves one of the big studios, where do they go? Set up their own local studio?

MM: Whoever starts now needs a good knowledge of computers; it's inevitable. Setting up a home studio is valuable experience, as long as you learn how to relate to people and experience the demands of working with real musicians. The vibe is more important. Sometimes PCs detract from "real performance." I did an HND in music technology. That helped me with MIDI, it was a grounding, a foundation. But with engineering it's better to learn on the job. It's 50% human relations, real life, real people.

Koan files are tiny set of direction sets, sometimes as small as 1 kb. This means that Koan files are not just about creating music that is never the same each time you listen to it. Koan is ideal for the Web environment, as complex audio environments can be created within your soundcard from tiny Koan instructions on a website. There is negligible download time, and no audio streaming. The Koan engine can also drive Flash animations online, creating generative animation, as well as audio.

WI-FI

Intel's Centrino wi-fi (wide-fidelity) processor and chipset will undoubtedly open up new ways of working, networking, and collaborating on the move. Intel is betting its business on Centrino, so its future is assured.

Q&A Sseyo co-founder Tim Cole answers *The Complete Guide*'s questions about generative music and the emerging field of vector audio. Tim's views are not those of Sseyo, nor of the Tao Group. Tim Cole is now Audio Products Manager at Tao Group.

What you do, Tim?

Help determine the audio capabilities that should be in Tao's "intent" multimedia platform. intent® is a binary portable, language-independent multimedia platform that is used in client products for home and mobile networks.

Tell us about a possible future for generative audio

I think the greatest potential for generative audio is when it is used in a truly networked sense—one where GME (generative music engines) are interlinked and interdependent. This should lead to emergent behaviors. In this sense it has been my vision for years. The possibilities for this to happen, such as mobile phones with GMEs, are nearly here.

I think GMEs, to be really effective, need to connect to existing music and audio tool chains. At their core they are event and control generators, like MIDI, and they should be able to drive any renderer (from MIDI synth to soft synth, sampler, and so on). They are also getting more exciting as they can accommodate musical structure and exhibit more intelligence.

Explain vector audio

Basically, vector audio is MIDI in text form, plus the ability to include parameters for configuring software synths and music engines. It is like "interactive MIDI" and a simple form of structured audio. Ultimately it can drive any kind of MIDI gear. Vector audio does not contain any audio samples—it is pure text. We have plans to greatly extend and refine it, but I can't talk about this for the moment! The reason it is in text form is that not being binary data makes it easy to embed in web pages. MIDI does not define how to drive GMEs or how to connect up modular synth chains. Vector audio does.

What does it have in common with vector graphics?

It uses parameters to control how the sound is rendered through synthesis techniques. So it's parameters rather than recordings, vector graphics rather than pixelated images.

Which environments do you see it having the greatest impact in over the next few years?

Mobile music-making, mobile and networked devices, the Internet, and on the desktop of course! You will be "aware" of it in that you will need to have tools to create it, but we hope conventional tool chains can easily support it.

As for the future generally, recorded audio formats will always be important. Interactive formats are much more tricky to second-guess. Synth (rendering) modules that ship with the music are one possibility. Much more shared music-making and consumption on mobiles and PDAs. More and more devices will become networked. More realtime use of GMEs in music-making.

What excites you most about what you do today?

Everything!

GENERATIVE MUSIC 1

BRIAN ENO

Q & A

AUDIO IN COMPUTER GAMES

Is audio one way in which leading games brands can differentiate themselves from the competition, given that, in smaller developers, audio and music elements are cut back when budgets overrun?

I guess the company that stands out in terms of money poured into audio production is my old employer, Electronic Arts. The building of (recording) studios within its Chertsey, U.K. complex ran to several hundreds of thousands of pounds, and the same can be seen at its other offices worldwide.

EA can afford to have several people within the audio department who each have their own skill set. EA is also leading the pack when it comes to outsourcing music. In the industry now you have *Medal of Honour*, or the *Harry Potter* games, where a leading VG (video game) or film composer, with the help of an orchestral arranger, is scoring award-winning music, performed by full orchestras. It's a well-known fact that if a budget is small or decreasing, the first thing to be cut back is audio. It's sad. People relate to audio far more easily than they do to visuals. You can achieve a real-world quality with audio in games far more easily than you can with graphics. Audio can put you in a certain mood, give you the tiniest of clues, instantly.

How important is audio and music now to the gaming environment, and in creating a truly immersive experience for the player? Do players even care?

It depends on the style of game. For an arcade game, or a racing game, yes, tire screeches can tell you that you are losing control of a vehicle, and the engine note can tell you when to change gear. But it's not vital. In adventure and first-person games, however, audio is a required sense, not only for the player to play the game well, but for the designer to incorporate events that are about to happen "around the corner," as it were.

Do you see leading games franchises moving much closer to creating the experience of cinema?

The companies that like to play it safe will move closer to it, as it's a proven medium. But hopefully, there will always be companies that are unique in what they design. It won't be too long before voice recognition, and realistic voice synthesis, work their way into games—full time, and in real time.

Given that the sound and music for the next *Tomb Raider* is being originated and recorded at Abbey Road, will all games audio soon be mixed in surround sound?

From an audio point of view, there are already many games using surround-sound technologies. Most games by the larger companies certainly are. In fact, as far as I am aware, if a company owns Dolby's license, it states that 5.1 has to be used on every title produced by said company. But—theoretically, of course—you could get around this by mixing the front-end FMV (full-motion video) in 5.1, and nothing else.

How is audio and music tied in at the development stage to the main characters in a game? Are the audio and music tracks now an essential part of character development?

Again, it depends on how important audio is to the developer. The Audio Lead [member of staff] should be sitting down with the designers from day one, getting a feel for the project. Once a musical style has been decided upon, you'll soon see whether music is going to play an important role for a character. If the game is going to have techno-based music, then it may not be that important to individual characters.

Do developers tie in audio to intuitive game play? Or is it just "part of the scenery"?

Yes they do. You hear it in *Harry Potter* for example. To hear a monster in the background, before you walk around that corner. You know it's there, somewhere, and it's going to try to kill you, but you can't see it. As more companies use 3D routines such as Creative Labs' EAX, you'll hear more usage of sound reflection and occlusion algorithms, which all help submerge the player (in a realistic acoustic environment).

Are there any standard technologies for recording the audio and the music tracks, for example Pro Tools, Cubase, Logic, and so on, or is the audio created and tied into the visuals by other means?

On PC, the main sound-design weapon is SoundForge, and to a lesser extent Wavelab. I've also used Reaktor many times in engine creation. Steinberg Nuendo is getting more popular on the PC for multitrack laying, while on the Mac, Pro Tools is still the (expensive) boss. Spark and BIAS Peak are Mac alternatives.

For sound effects, the route would be to source the material, be it from real-world recordings, CD libraries, or creating folex. This can then be manipulated in your sound-design package, before being mixed.

Music tends to be at least mocked up in a sequencer like Cubase, Logic or SONAR, using both hardware and software instruments. It'll then be recorded back into the sequencer, or Pro Tools, to be mixed. Most "normal" editing is done within these editors, ready to be loaded into whatever proprietary tools the developer has, to utilize their own technologies.

So, how is the audio tied in with onscreen action—doors opening, and so on. How is this achieved? And using what packages?

Some companies will hard-code an audio trigger, which will tell their sound player to trigger a sound. Other companies have "level editors." Once a designer has created a level, the audio designer then adds his or her contribution within the same editor.

In the same way, some developers put triggers into object editors. The artist would draw a clock, for example, and they'd embed an audio trigger into the actual graphics file. Most companies will use their own tools here, while a few might use the likes of 3D Studio Max, and so on.

Are audio and music outsourced by developers, or do most developers now have this facility in-house?

Big developers have the facility in-house, but from a musical point of view, it tends to get sourced out of house (at least at the composition stage). There are many talented composers who can produce a quality soundtrack in their bedrooms now, while film and TV composers are also coming across, when the money is good enough. The trouble with an in-house composer is, he will be good at a particular style or two, but not at everything. However, an in-house composer is always available, and has access to the designers at any time. An in-house music director/arranger/lead would be a big advantage, to bridge the gap between the designers and the composer.

How do you go about sourcing music for a game?

I have a number of talented composers with whom I have worked in the past. Again, each is good at a couple of particular styles, so I will match the game to the composer. I would normally get maybe six composers to create a number of short demos, and choose from there. If it were in a style that I felt I could achieve myself (my background was as a VG composer), then I would give myself a chance.

Do licensing problems within multinationals prevent existing music being used more frequently in games?

No, not at all. It's generally very easy to license from these people. They have specific departments to deal with this. There are also "middleman" companies that will deal with it for you, from sourcing the "correct" track, all the way through to the licensing itself.

The hardest thing is finding the correct music that will fit into the budget! A chart or well-known track can be expensive, especially if the record company doesn't understand how they can benefit from placing the music within a game. Some games companies take licensing very seriously. Take EA Sports. It tends to get what it wants. In fact, EA Sports now has an ex-music-industry executive working for it now, whose job it is to work and liaise with the music industry.

I have to say, though, that I'm in the anti-license camp, but I agree that for a limited number of games, it works.

Do you foresee closer ties with the music, film, and gaming worlds—for example, products that are music driven, but are designed for a gaming platform and available as albums?

I think there will be closer ties with the film industry. Films and games are very closely linked anyway, and the film industry does notice games companies turning over a billion dollars a year. As for the music industry, I'm not sure how this would work, to be honest.

How would you like to see audio and music being used more creatively in games in the future?

To be honest, there is one thing I personally miss. And that is "game music." Nintendo still seems to be able to produce it, as it has the titles in which it works stylistically.

There are many games out there where I feel people are trying too hard to be clever, follow the crowd, or do it on the cheap. I'd like to see audio and music matched properly to titles for better reasons than, "It's got great marketing potential."

For me, licensed music doesn't work unless the title is based on a brand. *Snowboarding* for example has a Hip Hop style associated with it, and licensed music works very well there—check out *SSX Snowboarding*. But then you get the racing sims with in-game music, normally licensed dross, which does nothing for gameplay at all.

ADULT.

Renowned and respected for their signature ultrasynthetic electro style, which predated and outlived the Electroclash boom, Detroit's ADULT. continue to influence all styles of dance and electronica.

Please identify yourselves and tell us what you do.
Adam Lee Miller: One half of the band ADULT. and founder and co-owner of the label Ersatz Audio. Both are based in downtown Detroit.
Nicola Kuperus: One half of the band ADULT. and co-owner of the label Ersatz Audio.

What excites you most about what you do?
ALM: The most exciting part for me is when we're writing a song, and it is that moment when all the rudimentary lines and sounds and ideas come together, and you know you have the beginnings of a song!
NMK: The options are unlimited! How far can you push the boundaries? How are you going to react to what is expected of you?

Does technology attract you in itself, or by what it can do for you?
ALM: Computers and programs are tools, so, just like a carpenter might be excited to get a new tool belt, that fades, and the utilitarianism becomes prominent. I am a manual reader. Any new software or hardware I get, I read the manual cover to cover. I have even bought some programs that I had hacks of just for the manual. I don't *love* reading manuals, but I want to know what my tool (my technology) can do, and then use it as efficiently as possible.

NMK: I am very attracted to it, but sometimes I do not have the patience to learn everything the way Adam does (as a manual reader). I just want to start. To use it , but not study it, which is bad sometimes.

What unique opportunities does digital technology open up?
ADULT.: Ah, that question is huge! Too huge to answer.

How important is performance, spontaneity, and play?
ALM: Performance is very important. There is nothing like seeing a band you like live. Spontaneity: 50/50. I'm more interested in arbitration than spontaneity. Play is harder the more you know, that is why I like arbitration.
NMK: Performance is very important. Does spontaneity exist any more? Play? Do you mean "To occupy oneself in amusement?"

If you were 16 years old, would you buy a laptop or a guitar?
ALM: When I was 16, I bought a guitar. Now that I'm 32 (but if I was 16), I would buy a computer, because with shareware/freeware and cheap CD-Rs, you can actually have a finished product for very little investment.

NMK: I think I would buy a car, but if those are my only options, a laptop.

When does music and audio history begin for you?
ALM: Early '70s
NMK: '70s.

Who first inspired you?
ALM: My first big inspiration came from Gary Numan/ Tubeway Army. That was the day I was hooked on synthesizers. There are so many bands we could never equal, like Throbbing Gristle or Cabaret Voltaire to name just a few.
NMK: PiL, Dead Kennedys, the Clash. I agree with Adam's TG and Cabaret Voltaire answers.

What types of experience do you see developing in the next few years now that technology is "coming out of the bedroom"?
ADULT.: I don't think much will change. I don't think it is too much different from Depeche Mode having a reel-to-reel on stage in '81. People like to go to a venue where they can get a drink, listen to music, and talk with friends (and those fundamentals will never change). Relating to this idea, my father asked me just last week if we were looking into alternate ways of marketing ADULT., and if there were any new "ways" of doing this. My answer was, "Sure, there are a lot of PR tricks and new packaging methods, but at the end of the day, people want a good album with good songs—that to me is what sells (and yes, that idea is old-fashioned, but we have been running Ersatz Audio for eight years that way, and we're still here)." The message is the same—just the medium evolves.

Mac, PC, or Linux? Do you care?
ALM: Mac.
NMK: …And yes, we care.

DAT POLITICS
Lille, France trio DAT Politics has been causing a stir in international electronic music circles with what could be described as bizarre video game tunes. Answers provided jointly by Claude and Gaëtan.

Please identify yourselves and tell us what you do
Mixing audio research and entertainment, DAT Politics propose a music based on middle-class technology, a fizzy electronic acid pop composed of digital raw signals and old-fashioned acoustic sounds. We have created and designed our own label Skipp, our website www.ski-pp.com, and all of DAT Politics' and Skipp's album covers. Just as some low-tech entrepreneurs, we have extolled the myriad possibilities of home production. Starting from a totally unfixed geographic point, we live, eat, and communicate through our own network!

What excites you most about what you do?
To know that our home production turns into a global diffusion. And to be able to meet people everywhere through this.

Does technology attract you in itself?
We've never been the victims of technological Utopias! It's just a tool.

What unique possibilities does digital technology open up?
The quality of this tool is amazing! It has multiple uses, it's portable, and it's easy! It's like bringing your studio everywhere.

How important is performance and play?
The performance is more about gesture. It's not really important for us. The spontaneity is not simulated. We don't try to behave spectacularly because the audience demands it. As we're three people in DAT Politics, we always have to think about each other. It's a real exchange: three unconnected laptops—it's all about trust.

You're 16. Guitar, or laptop?
16 in 2003, I would buy a computer for sure!

When does music history begin for you?
When was the first noise?

The Complete Guide **says: now the future is up to you. Enjoy it.**

ADAT (Alesis Digital Audio Tape) See *Digital Storage Formats*, p. 55.

ADR (Automated Dialog Replacement) See *Jargon Buster*, p. 120.

ADT (Automatic Double-Tracking) This refers to an analog studio technique whereby a sound—for example, a bass line—is copied to another track and played back almost simultaneously to "fatten up" the result. This effect can now be achieved more easily by using digital delay, but more accurate digital reproduction of this effect is also possible with some plug-in effects.

AIF/AIFF (Audio Interchange File Format) See *Jargon Buster*, p. 120.

ASiO (Audio Streaming Input/Output) See *Jargon Buster*, p. 90.

AVI (Audio Video Interleave file format) See *Jargon Buster*, p. 120.

AVoption See *Jargon Buster*, p. 90.

acoustic While the actual definition of this word refers to sound in general, it is often used to define an instrument that can be played without the aid of electric amplification, such as an acoustic guitar.

aliasing See *Jargon Buster*, p. 67.

ambience In the recording process, this often refers to the reverberations produced by an analog instrument or a vocalist that are shaped by the room or environment in which they are sounded. Some engineers will place microphones in various parts of a room to capture some of the ambient sound while an instrument is being recorded, and will then incorporate these sounds into the mix to achieve a more natural and powerful result. Most of these effects are also possible to emulate digitally, but it can be difficult to reproduce more complex environments.

amplification The process by which sounds are made audible or louder by using speakers, for example.

amplitude In a graphical illustration of a waveform, the amplitude generally refers to the distance by which the highest peak (positive amplitude) and the lowest peak (negative amplitude) deviate from the center of the sound wave; however, amplitude can be measured at any point along the waveform. Put more simply, the amplitude represents the level of the signal, or the amount of pressure exerted by the sound source on surrounding air molecules. An increase in volume increases the amplitude of the signal.

analog Sound that is not produced or recorded using digital means is usually referred to as analog, as are the processes by which that sound is produced or recorded; for example, recording to traditional reel-to-reel tape is considered an analog process. However, strictly speaking, all sound that is played or heard is analog sound. "Digital sound" can only be audio that is stored or produced digitally, but even this must be converted to analog sound by a set of loudspeakers or headphones to be heard by humans.

arpeggio In music, this means the individual notes making up a chord are played in rapid succession instead of simultaneously.

attenuation This usually refers to equalizer settings, when certain frequencies are manually or automatically attenuated or "cut back" in an effort to alter the sound or draw attention to other frequencies.

BPM (Beats Per Minute) This is a measure that can be applied to all music but is most often associated with electronic rhythms and drumbeats. Most rhythm-based software or hardware offers a BPM setting to control the speed of the rhythms produced—more beats per minute means a "faster" song. Knowing the BPM of songs also helps DJs to match beats when they are mixing tracks; this can be read on most electronic music using special hardware or software devices.

bandwidth In digital data transfer, bandwidth refers to the amount of data that can pass through a given channel at once; wider bandwidth means a faster rate of data transfer. Similarly, the bandwidth of a set of loudspeakers is the range of frequencies across which it can reproduce sound; so, a wider bandwidth allows for a greater range of sounds, and thus, more accurate sound reproduction—this is related to *dynamic range*.

beat-mapping or **beat-matching** See *Jargon Buster*, p. 120.

binary All digital data, no matter how complex, is stored on hard drives or in memory as a series of ones and zeros—this is binary information. In a digital recording, an analog-to-digital convertor transforms audio information into a series of binary digits—or bits—that the computer can save, read, and process.

bit-depth Bit-depth refers to the word length, or number of bits, used to describe each sample in a piece of digital audio. The higher the bit-depth capability of a digital audio device, the greater the detail with which it will transfer, record, produce or reproduce sound. 16-bit is the standard for CD-quality audio and is considered to be sufficient for consumer devices. The recording industry standard is 24-bit, which can be saved and reproduced by DATs (Digital Audio Tapes) or computers with 24-bit soundcards and analog-to-digital convertors.

Blu-Ray or **blue laser disks** See *Digital Storage Formats*, p. 55.

Broadcast Wave (B-Wave, BWF file format) See *Digital Storage Formats*, p. 55.

bus See *Jargon Buster*, p. 120.

byte A unit of storage equivalent to 8 bits. For example, the memory capacity of a RAM module is usually measured in megabytes (MB) while the storage capacity on a hard drive is usually measured in gigabytes (GB). Typically, one minute of CD-quality audio (16-bit, 44.1 kHz) will require about 10 MB of space.

CD (compact disc; also CD-R, CD-RW) See *Digital Storage Formats*, p. 54.

CEL (Cool Edit Loop file format) See *Jargon Buster*, p. 120.

COSM (Composite Object Sound Modeling) Roland Corporation's technology for digitally reproducing the sounds from analog equipment, such as instruments, amplifiers, guitar pickups, effects, and even room reverberation.

CV (Control Voltage) MIDI's analog predecessor, which was used to control or direct communications between analog synthesizer modules using small bursts of voltage.

Cakewalk DXi (DirectX instrument) See *Jargon Buster*, p. 90.

cardioid The heart-shaped pattern which applies to the way a cardioid microphone picks up sound: most from the front, less from the sides, and very little from the rear. In other words, it is a directional pattern. Hypercardioid mikes also pick up sound from behind in a similar pattern.

click or **click track** See *Jargon Buster*, p. 120.

clipping Unlike recording to magnetic tape, where a small amount of overdrive can produce a desirable fuzzy effect, any digital audio signal over 0 dB is in danger

GLOSSARY

audio signal over 0 dB is in danger of clipping. This creates awful-sounding digital distortion and should be avoided by making sure the highest peak of your audio file does not exceed 0 dB.

compression See *Jargon Buster*, p. 67.

compression wave A compression wave is a graphical representation of how sound travels through the air. On a continuous waveform, the individual "waves" are closer together at the point of origin, and this area of higher "pressure" moves along the wave. This is similar to how sound creates higher areas of atmospheric pressure that ripple through the air, except that in reality sounds move in all directions at once, even if they are somewhat directional.

condenser microphone Ideal for percussive elements as they capture nuance better than dynamic microphones through the use of two charged plates of metal. They require a battery or other power source to operate.

continuous tone In digital audio, this refers to a tone that repeats the same cycle (high peak, then low peak) continuously until the source is switched off.

cycle See *frequency*.

DAC (Digital-to-Analog Convertor) See *Jargon Buster*, p. 67.

DAT (digital audio tape) See *Digital Storage Formats*, p. 55.

DAW (Digital Audio Workstation) This refers to a digital recording device that can be used alone to record, mix, and master tracks of audio, often with various built-in effects available.

DLS (DownLoadable Sample file format) See *Jargon Buster*, p. 120.

DSP (Digital Signal Processing) See *Jargon Buster*, p. 120.

DVD (digital versatile disk or **digital video disk; also DVD-A,**

DVD-R, DVD-RW) See *Digital Storage Formats*, p. 54.

DWD (DiamondWare Sound Toolkit file format) See *Jargon Buster*, p. 120.

DXi (DirectX instrument) See *Jargon Buster*, p. 90.

decibel (dB) A measurement used to describe the sound pressure level or intensity of sound. One decibel is the smallest change in sound level that the human ear can detect. It is based on a logarithmic scale—a 10 dB increase at any point indicates a doubling in sound pressure level.

delay A delay effect gives the illusion of one or multiple distinct echoes, which can be adjusted to achieve a variety of effects. It also refers to the amount of delay carefully applied to sound emerging from the rear speaker in surround-sound systems, which gives it a slight separation from a corresponding front-end sound, creating the illusion of space.

degradation This occurs in analog recording, where some detail and quality is lost with each step of the recording process; in other words, every modification of the audio piece requires a new generation of tape, each of which introduces distortion and other noise.

destructive editing This refers to editing (effects or other processing) that is applied directly to the data of an original digital audio file, the result of which may then be saved, overwriting the original file. Non-destructive editing takes place when effects are applied to one or more audio files within a software program (such as a virtual mixer), the result of which may be rendered to a new file while keeping the original files unchanged.

digital As in digital audio, refers to information that is broken down into binary language and

understood by computers and other devices with digital capability.

directional microphone See *microphone*.

DirectSound See *Jargon Buster*, p. 90.

DirectX See *Jargon Buster*, p. 90.

distortion Whenever the output of audio sound does not exactly match the input, distortion has been introduced into the signal whether it is audible or not—and this usually happens, even when a digital audio file is converted to a magnetic impulse and then played through a pair of loudspeakers. This also refers to a desirable effect brought about by applying an extreme amount of overdrive to a sound, but it cannot be done "naturally" on a computer as it can on a guitar amplifier. As such, many digital filters are available to digitally emulate a wide variety of distortion effects.

dithering See *Jargon Buster*, p. 67.

dongle A software security device that plugs into a port (usually USB) on a computer.

Doppler effect When the source of a sound is moving towards the listener, the pitch of the sound will seem higher, and when it is moving away the pitch will seem lower. This is the result of shifts in frequency brought about by a compression of the sound waves on approach, and a stretching of the sound waves on moving away, as can be observed by standing near a passing train. Measuring the rate at which the pitch changes would allow you to estimate the speed of the train.

dry signal This refers to an audio signal with no effects applied to it. See also *wet signal*.

dynamic microphone As opposed to a condenser microphone, this type of mike uses a vibrating diaphragm and a magnetic field to convert sound into electrical impulses.

dynamic range This is the range of volume, measured in decibels, at which an audio system can perform without introducing noise (at low levels) or distortion (at high levels)—this is related to *bandwidth*.

echo A secondary sound that is heard by the listener after the original sound that produced it. This can happen naturally, if the sound bounces off a surface, or it can be introduced into an audio recording through the use of effects. For example, "slap-back" echo was an effect often used on Elvis' vocals.

effect This refers to artificial enhancement or modification of an audio signal.

envelope The envelope of a sound refers to its attack (the initial stab of sound), its sustain (the main body of the sound), its decay (the gradual lowering of volume, if any), and its release (the final point at which the sound dies). Many software programs introduce various other elements into an artificial envelope control function, but in most cases, adjusting the envelope of a sound makes it seem much less natural to the human ear.

equalization (EQ) This refers to a process whereby the amplitude of certain frequencies is adjusted either to make a sound more "realistic," or to make it stand out in, or fit into, a mix. Also, it is common for various frequencies to be enhanced when playing back songs, particularly in a club environment, so as to achieve a bass boost, for example. A graphic equalizer allows adjustment of a limited number of frequencies, while a parametric equalizer allows adjustment of any frequencies in the sound as well as its bandwidth.

fader A slider or knob control on a mixer which adjusts the sound level of a given track, or the entire mix. A "flying fader" on a hardware mixer is a motorized slider control whose levels can be recalled later on, and will reset itself. This is a standard feature on all virtual mixer software.

FireWire (IEEE 1394) A standard for digital data transfer developed by Apple, which, like USB, is also capable of providing power to external computer components.

flange Flanging is an extreme phasing effect that was originally done by using the same track on two reel-to-reel tapes, and then slowing one of them down. It can be emulated digitally and all of the parameters can be set to change at predetermined intervals.

frame rate Usually measured in frames-per-second (fps), this is the rate or resolution at which video or animation plays.

FreeMIDI See *Jargon Buster*, p. 90.

frequency Measured in Hz or kHz, it refers to the number of complete sound waves—or cycles—that pass a certain point during one second; the higher the frequency, the higher the pitch. The frequency spectrum refers to all possible sounds, and the audible frequency spectrum is from about 20 Hz to about 20 kHz (20,000 Hz), although this can vary somewhat from person to person.

GUI (graphical user interface) The means by which input and adjustments are made, and information is read by the user of any software program or any hardware component which has a screen as its main interface element.

gain Simply, the level of a signal; a volume control, for example, adjusts the output gain of your audio system.

generative music A computerized system of producing music or interesting sounds whereby a software program uses a

soundcard to randomly generate sound, restricted only by some previously set musical parameters and probabilities.

graphic equalizer See *equalization*.

HTDM (Host Time Division Multiplexing) See *Jargon Buster*, p. 91.

hard limiting See *limiting.*

harmonic No two instruments produce exactly the same waveforms (or middle A would sound identical on all instruments) because they produce additional frequencies called partials. When the frequency of a partial is a complete multiple of the original pitch, it is called a harmonic.

hertz (Hz) See *frequency*.

high-fidelity (hi-fi) This refers to the quality of sound; in other words, how closely an audio system reproduces—or is *faithful* to—the original sound.

hypercardioid See *cardioid*.

insert An insert jack on a mixer is a port that sends sound to be processed through an external effects unit, which then sends the processed sound back through the same port.

limiting Inhibiting certain frequencies or setting amplitude parameters during recording, mastering, or playback. A hard limiter effect will allow a signal level to increase, but will attenuate any portions of a sample that are going past the defined limit (often 0 dB in digital audio) so that clipping does not occur. This is related to *compression*.

loop In electronic music, a loop is a piece of rhythm or percussion that loops seamlessly to a specific tempo.

loudspeaker A device that converts electrical impulses to acoustic energy, turning signals to sounds.

MAS (MOTU Audio System) See

Jargon Buster, p. 90.

MID (MIDI file format) See *Jargon Buster*, p. 120.

MIDI (Musical Instrument Digital Interface) See *Jargon Buster*, p. 90.

MME (MultiMedia Extensions) See *Jargon Buster*, p. 91.

MOV (Apple Quicktime file format) See *Jargon Buster*, p. 120.

MP3 (Motion Picture Experts Group Level Three file format) See *Digital Storage Formats*, p. 54.

MPEG (Motion Picture Expert Group file format) See *Jargon Buster*, p. 120.

magnetic induction A process by which electrical impulses cause the magnets in a loudspeaker to vibrate, thus transmitting sound.

marquee selection A typical means of selecting multiple elements on screen, usually by holding down the mouse button and dragging the resulting marquee over these elements, releasing the mouse button to complete the selection.

master/slave See *Jargon Buster*, p. 120.

MediaManager See *Jargon Buster*, p. 90.

metadata See *Jargon Buster*, p. 120.

microphone A device that picks up sounds and converts them to electrical impulses that can be recorded, or converted to digital information. They may be directional, in that they pick up sound primarily from one direction, or omnidirectional, in that they pick up sounds equally from all directions.

middle A 440 Hz, otherwise known as the "concert pitch" to which orchestra musicians tune their instruments.

MiniDisc (MD) See *Digital Storage Formats*, p. 54/

mix This refers to adjusting the

levels and EQ of various recorded and/or live tracks to achieve a desired overall sound.

modulate To alter a sound in some way, as with a musical instrument or a human voice.

monophonic (mono) Describing sound that is stored and played back using only one channel, as opposed to stereo sound which uses a left and right channel, or surround sound which uses multiple channels.

multitracking Using more than one channel—or track—to record separate sounds which can later be mixed.

noise reduction Procedure meant to reduce the amount of noise produced by audio components and systems; this can be done digitally using a variety of software methods.

normalization See *Jargon Buster*, p. 121.

Nyquist Theorem In digital audio, the sampling rate must be twice as high as the highest frequency in the sound to be represented digitally.

OMF (Open Media Framework) See *Jargon Buster*, p. 121.

Oblique Strategies Brian Eno's series of "over 100 worthwhile dilemmas" is actually a list of phrases intended to help creative people to think of new ways of solving problems or approaching situations in their work. These are published on cards but many different versions are also available online.

omnidirectional microphone See *microphone*.

oscillator Often associated with synthesizers, this is a device that can be made to generate a tone at any frequency.

overdub Sound added to an existing recording to enhance or correct it. This can refer to plain sounds or music.

GLOSSARY

PCM (Pulse Code Modulation and file format) See *Jargon Buster,* pp. 67, 120.

pan To create an apparent location for a signal within the stereo spectrum. For example, in a musical recording some sounds are panned a little bit to the right or left to represent the actual physical area at which that instrument might appear. It is also commonly used for special effects.

parametric equalizer See *equalization.*

partial See *harmonic.*

peak See *amplitude.*

percussion Sound made by the impact of an object when striking a resonant surface; drums are percussion instruments.

phase When two waveforms match each other and are playing simultaneously, they are *in phase,* and as such they reinforce each other. If one of these waveforms is playing back at a slightly different speed, they are *out of phase,* and this causes them to weaken each other. If one waveform is exactly 180 degrees out of phase (say, if the polarity is reversed on one stereo speaker), the waveforms will cancel each other out. A phasing effect involves playing a copy of a sound simultaneously while varying the delay by anywhere from about 1 to 10 milliseconds.

polyphony This refers to music or a synthesized sound that is made up of a combination of more than one melodic sequence simultaneously to produce intertwining harmonies.

proximity effect Many condenser microphones emphasize the bass frequencies of a particular sound when it is close to the mike itself. This is known as the proximity effect, and it has influenced the singing style—or at least the recording style—of many vocalists since the 1930s, but it can also reduce intelligibility.

quadrophonic Obsolete standard which was meant to replace stereophonic sound in 1970s homes, but was too expensive to implement. However, surround sound is a similar concept.

quantize See *Jargon Buster,* p.121

Quicktime See *Jargon Buster,* p. 93, 122

RAM (random access memory) A type of computer memory that can be accessed randomly, which means that any byte of memory can be used by any program without having to access any of the preceding bytes. RAM modules are often used in various audio devices, such as MP3 players or DAWs. As opposed to ROM, RAM can be written to and read while ROM can only be read.

REX (Propellerhead loop file format) See *Jargon Buster,* p. 122

RIFF (Resource Interchange File Format) See *Jargon Buster,* p. 122

ROM (read-only memory) This is memory which often contains important programs such as the ones that boot a computer or device. Unlike RAM, it is not erased when the computer is switched off.

RealAudio or **RealMedia (RA, RM or RAM file format)** See *Jargon Buster,* p. 122

remix This refers to a process in which the entire mixing phase of song production is redone either by the original artists or by another artist or DJ. While the same sounds and tracks are generally reused in a remix, it usually involves a fairly drastic restructuring of a song to bring out certain interesting elements at the expense of others. Many modern remixes leave a song barely recognizable. In the 1980s remixes were often used to create "extended versions" of Top 40 songs for playing in a club, but now they are often used simply as alternate versions to add value to a 12" single release.

S/PDIF (Sony/Phillips Digital InterFace) A high-quality, audio-specific file transfer format which can be used with a variety of digital audio equipment, through an RCA-style connection or an optical cable. It can also be used with specialized speakers.

S-VHS (Super VHS) While VHS is an acronym for Video Home System, and these are indeed videotapes, they offer 20-bit audio and are also used in ADAT machines.

SACD (Super Audio Compact Disc) See *Digital Storage Formats,* p. 56

SKD (Sseyo Koan Design file format) See *Jargon Buster,* p. 122

SMF (Standard MIDI File format) See *Jargon Buster,* p. 122

SMPTE timecode (Society of Motion Picture and Television Engineers) See *Jargon Buster,* p. 123

SND (Apple sound file format) See *Jargon Buster,* p. 122

SPL (sound pressure level) Put simply, this is the volume of a sound measured in decibels.

sample Broadly speaking, this is a unit or piece of audio. See also *sampling rate.*

sampling rate This refers to the number of samples taken of a piece of audio in one second during a digital recording. For example, the standard for CD audio is 44,100 samples per second, or 44.1 kHz. According to the Nyquist Theorem the sampling rate must be twice the amount of the highest frequency to be reproduced.

sequencing A process first developed with analog synthesizers whereby timed electronic pulses were used to trigger sounds in a rhythmic fashion. Sequencing now covers a range of digital audio functions, as it is now used to trigger MIDI, percussive elements, prerecorded audio clips, and even effects.

signal processor An electronic effects component, or a virtual effects plug-in.

signal to noise ratio (S/N) See *Jargon Buster,* p. 69

sine wave A perfect sound wave in which the positive and negative peaks are equal. Test tone generators can produce these pure waveforms, and they are often used for testing purposes.

soundcard A component which adds higher audio functions to a computer system. High-end audio work usually requires an external soundcard which sits outside of the desktop tower or notebook case, so as to minimize the noise inherent in any computer system.

sound wave A sound or a graphical representation of a sound. See *sine wave.*

SoundManager See *Jargon Buster,* p. 93

spot effect See *effect.*

stereophonic (stereo) Describing sound that is stored and played back using two channels, a left and a right, to more closely resemble sound as we hear it in nature. Surround sound takes this a step further by incorporating more than two speakers to add artificial depth.

streaming Streaming audio can be listened to at the same time as it is downloaded over the Web. Due to the limitations of bandwidth, it is usually compressed to a very low quality so that there is less data to download (or "buffer"), and fewer interruptions required in the broadcast to catch up with the download.

surround sound See *Jargon Buster,* p. 123

synthesis This refers to the process of creating or developing sounds. There are many types of synthesis, including additive (constructs sounds by combining various simple waves), subtractive (filters a complex waveform to achieve a desired result), granular (putting a variety of short sound samples together to form a longer, more complex sound), amplitude modulation (source signal multiplied by a simple positive signal), ring modulation (like AM but multiplied with a more complex bipolar modulation signal), frequency modulation (oscillating the frequency of the source signal), wavetable (similar to sampling but in this case a sustain portion of the sound that can be held), and physical modeling (very complex but closer to the actual creation of the sound that is being synthesized).

synthesizer Synthesizers began as analog instruments that used oscillators to generate tones and a variety of other components to modify or filter those tones, but partly due to a recent resurgence in the popularity of these instruments, most of these sounds can now be reproduced fairly accurately using digital emulators. In fact, most virtual synthesizers or even the standalone electronic synths use the same analog-style parameters to create and modify sounds. The basis of synthesis was not to be limited by traditional instruments, so the challenge was to create new sounds and also to be able to reproduce existing sounds with a certain degree of accuracy, but truly original and high-quality sounds could only be generated with a complex series of modular synth components. Sounds of comparable and often superior quality can now be achieved through several much simpler digital means.

TDM (Time Division Multiplexing) See *Jargon Buster,* p. 93

tempo The rate or pace of a piece of music. In digital audio this is usually measured in BPM (beats per minute).

time-stretching See *Jargon Buster,* p. 123

timeline Refers to the time reference meter along which audio elements are arranged in most music software.

total harmonic distortion (THD) See *Jargon Buster,* p. 69

transduction The process by which electronic signals are converted to acoustic signals, as with a loudspeaker; it also applies to when the process is reversed, as with a microphone.

USB (Universal Serial Bus) A digital data transfer technology which first boasted daisy-chaining (connecting one peripheral through another) and hot-swapping (plugging or unplugging without having to reboot) abilities. The standard was upgraded in 2000 to include higher bandwidth capabilities as well.

VST or **VSTi (Virtual Studio Technology instrument)** See *Jargon Buster,* p. 93

vector audio A concept developed by Koan which is similar to that used with graphics and also similar to MIDI, vector audio uses the minimum possible information to describe musical parameters to a browser plug-in, thus generating music on the fly.

velocity Under normal atmospheric conditions, the speed of sound is 344 meters/1,128 feet per second, but this also refers to the speed at which MIDI instructs a note to be played.

vinyl Short for the analog vinyl record format, still the medium of choice for club tracks and punk music releases.

WAV (Wave file format) See *Jargon Buster,* p. 122

WAVE PFH Acronym for Wavelength, Amplitude, Velocity, Envelope, Phasing, Harmonics, and Frequency, which are the basic components of a waveform.

WMV (Windows Media video file format) See *Jargon Buster,* p. 122

waveform See *sine wave.*

word In digital terms, a word is a string of binary information. Word length refers to the amount of bits used to describe a sample of digital audio. Se also *binary* and *bit-depth.*

wet signal This refers to an audio signal with effects applied to it; the more effects that are applied, the "wetter" it is. See also *dry signal.*

XMF (eXtensible Music file format) See *Jargon Buster,* p. 122

INDEX

INDEX

part 04. future views

INDEX

ACKNOWLEDGMENTS

Big thanks to my editor Allen Zuk, for his patience, enthusiasm, and extra signals; to Tull for his digital inputs and PC knowledge; to Ben Tudor for the iBook and OS X assist; and to Adam Elliot for some extremely helpful software and hardware. Thanks to all of you.

Thanks also to: Owen Leech, Geoff Pryce, and Marco Migliari at Real World Studios in Box; Tim Cole at Sseyo and Tao Group for our ongoing digital conversation; Liz Cox at Digidesign for patience and assistance; Chris Clark, late of Abbey Road (with best wishes for the future); Peter Gabriel and Charles Grimsdale at OD2; David Amor at Computer Artworks; all at The Guitar, Amp, and Keyboard Centre in Brighton, and everyone at Turnkey in London. I still have a storecard; all at Native Instruments, Yamaha, Apple, Korg, Syntrillium, Steinberg, Digidesign/Avid/Pinewood Studios, Emagic, Ableton, Propellerhead Software, and BIAS; and to Mark Knight, ADULT. and DAT Politics for the Q&As.

Personal thanks to Paren (Muh), Hiren (thanks for modeling!), Rimel, and to Uncle and Aunty C; Andy Cruse, my co-conspirator and friend; Emily Swift-Jones and John Steels; Joanna and Tavina for our big day out to Box; and to Nathan for taking me on, along with this gooseberry.

Ilex thanks to Steve Luck, Sophie Collins, Alastair Campbell, Rolo, Tony Seddon, Rebecca Saraceno, Jonathan Raimes, Rob Turner for photography, and to Calvey Taylor-Haw also for photography and a useful tip-off. Finally, belated thanks to Andy Mold, Chris Mk 2, and Danny Moss; and to Robin Guthrie, late of the Cocteau Twins, for an earlier conversation recycled here. God bless you and your reverb unit.

...r and out.

Picture credits:

Apple Computers Inc: pp.15, 24BL, 132

Bayer Corporation: p. 24TM

Blue Man Group: p. 27BR

Benedict Campbell/www.debutart.com: p. 175

Cameron Collection: pp. 22T, 22BR, 24BR

Compaq Computer Corp/Pocketscript: p. 27BL

Carl Desouza: pp. 12, 143

CORBIS: pp. 16L, 16R Bettmann, 17T Araldo de Luca, 17M Hulton-Deutsch, 17B, 19B Nubar Alexanian, 18T Bettmann, 21 Bettmann, 24TL Bettmann, 29 Fotomorgana, 42T S.I.N./Sygma, 58 Louis K Meisel Gallery, 61 Catherine Karnow, 65 Jacques Langevin, 131 Kraft Books/Sygma, 150 Shelley Gazin, 152M Lynn Goldsmith, 152B David Lees

GETTY IMAGES: pp. 59 Eric Dreyer/Stone, 62 Marcus Lyon/Taxi, 63 Michael Tcherevkoff Ltd/Image Bank, 157 Paul Arthur/Stone

Kenwood USA Corp/Microsoft: p. 26TR

Nokia: p. 26M

Real World pictures: Chris Middleton

Sony Electronics Inc.: pp. 24TR, 25R, 26BL, 27BM

Universal Electronics Inc: p. 60

Zenith Electronics Corp.: p. 26TL